Making It Big

Making It Big

Sex Stars, Porn Films, and Me

by Chi Chi LaRue
with John Erich

alyson
books
LOS ANGELES • NEW YORK

Manufactured in the United States of America.
Printed on acid-free paper.

This trade paperback original is published by Alyson Publications Inc.,
P.O. Box 4371, Los Angeles, California 90078-4371.
Distribution in the United Kingdom by Turnaround Publisher Services Ltd.,
Unit 3 Olympia Trading Estate, Coburg Road, Wood Green,
London N22 6TZ, England.

First edition: September 1997

01 00 99 98 97   10 9 8 7 6 5 4 3 2 1

ISBN 1-55583-392-6

Library of Congress Cataloging-in-Publication Data
LaRue, Chi Chi, 1959–
Making it big : sex stars, porn films, and me / by Chi Chi LaRue with John Erich. — 1st ed.
ISBN 1-55583-392-6
1. LaRue, Chi Chi, 1959–   . 2. Motion picture producers and directors — United States — Biography. 3. Female impersonators — United States — Biography. 4. Gay men — United States — Biography. 5. Erotic films — Production and direction. I. Erich, John. II. Title.
PN1998.3.l39A3 1997
791.43'0233'092—dc21   97-23969 CIP
[B]

Photo Credits
Author as young boy: courtesy the author
Author as a drag queen: courtesy the author
Weather Gals flier: courtesy the author
Alex Stone: Johnathan Black
Hal Rockland: Johnathan Black
Hank Hightower: Olivier
Jordan Young: Greg Lenzman
Ryan Idol: D/X Co.
Zak Spears: Chuck
Joey Stefano: A+ Studios
Author with Sharon Kane (from the production *The Hills Have Bi's*):
    courtesy Catalina Video
John Rutherford: courtesy Falcon Studios

Cover design by Christopher Harrity.

Making It Big

IN HIBBING COLOR
OR

WHERE I CAME FROM
BEFORE I GOT TO BE WHERE I AM

THE SCENE: PARIS, MAY 1993. I am in the dark, cramped, foul-smelling men's room of a well-known gay nightclub. I am wearing a dress. In fact, I am in full drag, complete with frilly women's underwear, a face full of makeup, and a big blond wig. I am on my knees looking up at a semicircle of three hot and horny Frenchmen. Their uncut penises are hanging out of their opened pants in various stages of erection, awaiting the loving attention of my talented American drag queen mouth. I am only too happy to oblige.

I begin to suck. I move from one to the other, back and forth, up and down, rapidly bringing them all to full erection. I know I can suck cock, and these guys are discovering just how good I am at it. Time flies. In just a few short minutes, they are all near orgasm. I sit back for a moment to admire my handiwork, three erect penises drooling pre-come and bobbing in my face, and then I choose the lucky one to bring over the top first.

I descend on him, and in just a few more strokes, he's ready to blow. He pulls out of my mouth and steps back, about to explode into ecstasy, and then, then...

...his bladder fails him. What comes spraying out of his engorged cock is not pearly white semen but steaming, boozy urine. Stunned, I jump back, but I cannot escape entirely; it douses me from the waist down, drenching the insides of my legs, leaving me with the embarrassing stain and rank smell of piss for the rest of the evening. The French guy is embarrassed, he's sorry, but he didn't do it on purpose. It was an accident, just a failure of self-control.

"Okay, that's it," I say, climbing to my feet and patting down my dripping legs with a handful of paper towels. "Let's get back to the bar."

This is a success story. Not the incident above, which wasn't very successful at all. This is *my* success story. A sordid and depraved one, perhaps, depending on your point of view, but a certifiable Cinderella rags-to-riches fairy tale nonetheless.

This is the story of a boy from a small town in Minnesota who made it to the big time in a field he loved with all his heart. A boy who endured the cruel taunts and relentless scorn of his classmates and survived to achieve wild success in the big-business world of video. A homosexual lad, effeminate of manner and portly in girth, who, through hard work and dedication and a bit of good fortune, rose to the pinnacle of the buffed, gym-perfect world of gay pornographic filmmaking.

And is still somehow able, through it all, to get pissed on in dirty French bathrooms.

If you think this all sounds a bit incongruous, you're right. This is a tale of irony and paradox. That is to say, imagine the baby-faced bodybuilding giants of the porn world — men viewed and adored by millions of masturbatory Middle Americans, the perfect achievements of physical beauty — at the beck and call and self-indulgent whim of a 300-pound drag queen directing a film. An unusual picture, no doubt. But then, how this drag queen came to wield this power is an unusual story.

———————

If you have purchased this book, you are probably gay. Additionally, if you have purchased this book, you are probably a consumer of gay pornography. If that is the case, then you have probably seen my movies. I have directed more than 100 full-length XXX-rated films for nearly a dozen different companies. I have worked with (and known and loved) the most beautiful young men of my generation, literally thousands of *models*, which is the polite term for porn stars. I have won awards too numerous to mention here and been credited with helping change the face of gay adult video.

There are those in our society who will regard me as a villain. As a gay man who dresses in drag and turns out smut for the hungry masses, I will be viewed by some as a heinous, depraved example of everything that's gone wrong with American morality. But let's face it. Those people aren't going to be reading this book. People like that may make my life more interesting, but this is not for them. This is for sex-crazed little porn hounds like you.

You are probably reading this book expecting a behind-the-scenes glimpse into the world of gay pornography. And if a few titillating tales of beautiful boys in sin and debauchery are thrown in, well, all the better, right? So that's what I will try to provide in the coming pages. I want to share with you the entire spectrum of my fabulous drag-queen/porn-director existence: the highs and the lows, the triumphs and the defeats, the perks and the pricks. You are about to get a crash course in the wonderful world of gay porn — Chi Chi's guide to life.

I'll cover breaking into the business, giving an intimate firsthand account of how I did so; the science of making a porn flick, examining some of my own best and what I think made them good; revealing personal glances into the lives of the hottest boys in the business, some of whom I discovered, some of whom I merely had the lucky opportunity to work with; the fine art of drag, including creating and maintaining a look that will dazzle your fans; the timeless art of performing, working a crowd and projecting an authentic "star" aura; the upsides and downsides of fame, including the uninhibited sex, the unchecked drug use, and the exotic flights of fancy to glamorous locations around the world; and, finally, a few thoughts on where we're headed and what's next for the industry I love. Fasten your seat belt, sweetie, it's going to be a wild ride.

——————

Chi Chi LaRue was born a man (just in case any of you were laboring under the misconception that I sprang from the womb in full makeup and garish drag — that didn't happen until at least the first grade). I was born Larry Paciotti in Hibbing, Minnesota, in 1959. Hibbing is a town of about 18,000 people located in the northeastern horn of the state, near Duluth and Lake Superior. It is roughly seventy miles from the Canadian border and is most notable for being the hometown of Bob Dylan. Northern Minnesota is a land of glacial lakes and thick pine forests and soft-spoken, hardworking citizens. Life is uncomplicated, blue-collar, and largely industrial and agrarian. The nearest metropolis of any significant size is the Twin Cities area of Minneapolis and St. Paul, some three hours due south at those times of year when the roads are passable.

Though still small now, Hibbing has grown since the 1960s. When I was a child, the population was a bit smaller, around 14,000 to 15,000. Hunting was big in Hibbing, as was fishing. The major industries in town were mining, specifically iron ore, and the railroad.

There was exactly one demographic group in Hibbing: Caucasian, of European descent. Most of us were of Scandinavian or Italian extraction. How there got to be so many Italians in northern Minnesota, I'm not so sure, but there were enough that the section of Hibbing where they were congregated was known as Brooklyn. This was my part of town.

Other minorities, such as blacks and Latinos, were virtually nonexistent. It wasn't that they wouldn't have been allowed or accepted; it wasn't a racist town by any means. It was simply that there were none there. It was a hard, cold place to live, and we didn't attract many outsiders. Those who were there stayed there, but those who weren't there didn't come.

As a result, Hibbing was spared much of the social turbulence the rest of the nation endured in the 1960s. There were no great racial confrontations and relatively few generational hippie-square conflicts. *Everyone* was square. It was a sedate and sedentary place where the issue of the greatest civic importance was more likely to be the addition of a new police car to the city fleet, taking it from two to three, than some protesters' sit-in at the local lunch counter.

Making It Big: Sex Stars, Porn Films, and Me

The biggest employers in town were the iron mines operated by National Steel and U.S. Steel. They were the lifeblood of Hibbing, our economic sustenance and a source of civic pride. Everyone wanted to work at the mines. Not that it was glamorous or even especially safe (in the '60s it was neither), but the mine-workers union was powerful, and the wages they earned were good. The going rate ran about $15 an hour, more on holidays, and that was more than a quarter of a century ago! The mine was the place to be; even my older sister, Carlene, worked there for a while. I had some pretty awful jobs as a teenager, but I always resisted everyone's constant urging to work in the mine. It was where my nelly fag persona kicked in and I drew the line: I was not butch enough, I was not a 9-to-5 day-labor type, and I was not, no way, under any circumstances ever going to do it.

Hibbing was insular. If I wanted to torment my father, I'd tell him, "Dad, I'm going to run away and marry a black girl." He wasn't a prejudiced man, but that did rattle his cage; it was still a pretty radical concept for that place and time. I wonder how he would have reacted if I had told him instead, "I'm going to run off and marry a big black man!"?

My father, Lawrence Paciotti, was an engineer who piloted trains for U.S. Steel. My mother, the former Eileen Rien, sold clothes at Feldman's, a local department store. Their dual incomes provided us with a lifestyle that was comfortable, if not spectacular: a two-bedroom house in a middle-class neighborhood and a lakefront cabin a few minutes out of town for getaways every weekend. We were well-fed and well-dressed and got most of what we ever wanted. And as the youngest child, I was especially pampered. With my brother and sister, who were much older, grown up and gone from the house, I had the space and freedom to do pretty much as I pleased. I did that, but I kept to my own devices. I had my friends, but I was a solitary child at times as well. We had a furnished basement rec room that became my private refuge, the place I would go to listen to records or do homework or furtively jerk off to *Playgirl*.

My parents were kind and attentive, and I had all the necessities and many of the luxuries of life. Dad was away a lot early on, guiding his trains around the country, but he was always there when the family needed him. He retired when I was still young and took a job driving the Hibbing library's bookmobile around to outlying communities that were literarily challenged.

I was the only child of my parents' marriage. Each, however, had been married once before, providing me with a half brother and a half sister. Richard was my father's son, and Carlene was my mother's daughter. Both are about a decade and a half older than me, and both were on their own by the time I came of age. I never actually lived very much with either one.

I've always been very close to Carlene, though, despite the sixteen years of difference in our ages. For fifteen years of my childhood, she was my best friend and confidante. She's a gorgeous woman with striking features and a petite build. How she was the only one in our family to get that, I don't know. Maybe she was switched at birth, because the rest of us have fought a lifelong battle with big. She was kind and sympathetic to the problems I confided in her while growing up.

So beautiful was Carlene, in fact, that at one point she was close to pursuing a modeling career. I remember taking snapshots of her to school with me and having my little heterosexual classmates trying to buy them from me. These were just plain old snapshots, not even cheesecake! Even today, in her fifties, the woman is striking. And we have remained close despite our various moves around the country (at present she's in Minneapolis). My sister is everything in the world to me, and every time I sit down to put on my drag ensemble, I hope to turn out as beautiful as she is. Unfortunately, there's not that much makeup in the world.

I was never quite so close to Richard, unfortunately. He was in the Air Force by the time I came of age, and he spent several years stationed in Turkey. He later married and created a life of his own, and I don't think he was ever very comfortable with my homosexuality. We've never talked about it, and we don't have much contact now. Nor has he remained a part of the rest of the family. When my father died on Christmas Eve of 1996, Richard attended the memorial but snubbed us by not sitting with us. I don't know why, but it was a real slap in the face. The whole uneasy relationship really saddens me because you get only one family, and it's one of the most important things in the world.

My heritage is half Italian (Paciotti) and half Norwegian (Rien, pronounced "rain"). This created, to put it mildly, an *interesting* blend of influences in our household, influences that sometimes stopped just short of triggering an intra-European World War III. We were passionate people, unafraid to express our own opinions, challenge each other's, and demonstrate our reasonable differences by reasonably hurling food at each other across the dinner table.

Both my father's family and my mother's family were large, and most of them lived in the same general vicinity, so we all kept in close touch. But we in the Paciotti household were not exactly the Cosbys. There were times — like, I'm sure, in most of your own childhood homes — where we fought like caged animals. My father brought the passionate Italian temperament to everything he did, so he was always very emotional and very demonstrative. When he got angry he wouldn't hold anything back. Conversely, he was never afraid to express a tender side or show his love for his children. I think it's from him that I get what temper I have. I've tried to avoid it, but you know how it is; you inevitably turn into your parents as you get older whether you like it or not. I find myself now flying off the handle sometimes when things don't go smoothly — just like Dad used to.

Dad lost his hair at age thirteen in a fit of fever, and it never grew back, so he was hardened by a childhood of being a little bald-headed boy teased by his schoolmates. But I think it made him a stronger and better person (as I hope the teasing I endured did to me). He was hot-blooded, hot-tempered, and demanding, but he was kind, fair, and loving as a father and a wonderful provider for our family.

My mother was also true to her ethnic background and had an abundance of the calm and composure peculiar to Scandinavians. She was a rock, and nothing could shake her. But she was also a lot of fun. She had a great sense of humor, and she knew how to enjoy life. Not only did I get a lot of my physical features from my mother (I'm told the resemblance between us is uncanny, which probably should flatter me more than it should Mom), but I like to think I got a lot of my personality from her too. We're alike in so many ways, even down to the things we eat. There aren't a lot of people who will snack on anchovies at midnight right from the tin, but that's where you'll find my mother and me, bumping elbows at the refrigerator.

I was close only to one grandparent, my mother's mother. She lived in Hibbing and would take me to the movies when I was very young. My father's mother, who had come here from Italy, lived in Brooklyn and also saw us occasionally, but I never had quite the same relationship with her (she spoke very little English), and both of my grandfathers died before I was old enough to know them.

Both of my grandmothers could cook like nobody's business, and my mom's mom passed many of her secrets down to my mom for our benefit. My mother, in all modesty, may have been the best cook in Hibbing. If her spaghetti sauce had ever been canned and sold nationally, Paul Newman would be just another old, forgotten movie star today. To this day I've never been able to find Italian food half as good as what my mother could make.

For some reason, as generally happy as we were, my most vivid childhood memories are of the fights. Shouting, screaming, and slamming doors were all part of the routine. In my youngest days, Dad and Carlene were always going at it. She was in her late teens or early twenties then, and it was my parents' only experience at raising a young woman. (Although they had already seen Richard through his teen years, boys aren't as difficult at that time. They can't get pregnant.) My parents were always accusing Carlene of sneaking boyfriends in through the basement window — something that's pretty funny in retrospect, since I was the one more likely to try that — or something else that she hadn't done. She could do no right in my father's eyes; he simply didn't like her, and as good as he was to me, he was very mean to her for a very long time, and my mother let him set the tone. Dad mellowed only as he got older and Carlene moved away and lived her own life.

Strife in our family usually centered around the dinner table. That was where we gathered each night for the family meal, and that was where we would discuss the happenings of the day and the events of our lives. If confrontation was going to happen, it usually happened at the dinner table. It wasn't uncommon for our family suppers to degenerate into screaming free-for-alls. This, I think, may be one reason why I've always struggled with my weight: Eating was a way of quieting the stressful situations of my childhood. You can't scream at each other with your mouths full.

My mealtime memories range from the traumatic to the absurd. I remember Carlene flinging a hot dog at my father and leaving a skunk-stripe trail of mustard across the top of his bald head. I remember coffee splashed on white Sunday dress clothes and whole bowls of spaghetti thrown on the floor and pieces of toast hurled like square buttered Frisbees. Dinners could be ordeals at the Paciottis, and that, combined with our family's love of food, explains to my complete satisfaction why so many of us became rather large. I'm big, Mom's big (actually, most of Mom's whole family are a bunch of heavyweights), and Dad, if it weren't for his amazing high-speed metabolism, would surely have been big too.

Eating was simply a major part of life in Hibbing. Not only would we clean our plates, but we would slurp up the juices afterward. Mom would bake bread every Friday, and

I would rush home from school to get at it while it was still hot. She combined our Scandinavian and Italian heritages in her tuna spaghetti, which may sound disgusting, but, believe me, to us it was wonderful. We'd have it regularly for dinner on Friday, and I'd wake up early Saturday morning and head straight for the refrigerator to shovel down more of it cold.

Having so much family nearby kept our household hopping. At the right time of year aunts and uncles and cousins just came out of the woodwork. The right time of year was on weekends during the summer, when we'd visit our home on Perch Lake. We had a cabin there, a small, unassuming getaway place that my parents worked hard to keep up and enjoy. Our extended family, invited or not, tended to enjoy it as well. I always loved getting out of Hibbing and retreating to the woods for the weekend, even if an assortment of freeloading relatives did tag along and cramp our style. My father had four siblings, and my mother had four siblings, so by the time you factor in their spouses and children and in-laws and assorted hangers-on, we'd have as many as a couple dozen people descending on us every weekend. We'd never hear from them during the week or at other times, and it's occurred to me since that they were simply using us for our vacation property. I don't think that a lot of them really cared about us at all. For this reason I'm not very close to a lot of these people now.

But Perch Lake represented the best of times for me growing up. It was only twenty miles or so out of Hibbing, so we were able to get there every weekend, except in the dead of winter. In April, though, as soon as the lake turned from solid to liquid again, we'd be at the lake and in the water; late-season Arctic cold fronts be damned.

In Hibbing Color

I also loved — and be prepared because this is way out of character for me — fishing. Yes, fishing. Squirmy worms on the ends of hooks and slimy, scaly fish on the ends of lines. I don't know why, and I don't know how it happened. I can just explain to you the allure I find in fishing: It's very relaxing, very soothing, almost comforting. If you can get past the boredom and the icky bait, fishing is almost like therapy — and for a lot less money.

It could almost soothe even the feared Paciotti temper. Almost. I remember being very young and catching a small perch from a pier on Perch Lake. Only this fish had swallowed its bait, and the hook, instead of catching in its mouth, was embedded deep in the fish's stomach. So no matter how hard I tried, I couldn't get the fish off the hook. I became angrier and angrier, and I finally lost it and ended up beating this fish against the dock, trying to dislodge the hook and get it off my line. This odd contrast of rage and relaxation summarizes my childhood in a way that's pretty apt. Even at the most peaceful of times, there was the possibility of explosion boiling under the surface. I don't remember if we ate that particular fish, but I'm fairly certain that it was in no condition to be returned to the lake.

Once I got into my late teens, I began taking friends out to the cabin during the summer. We'd go in the middle of the week, when my parents were home or at work. This freed me from having to go there on the weekends, so instead of dealing with the swarm of half-familiar mooching relatives, I could stay at home in Hibbing and drink beer and listen to my idols, Joan Jett and the Runaways. More than just asserting my typical teenage independence, I got to totally resent the way my parents and their generosity were exploited by these people who otherwise wouldn't have had anything to do with us. They weren't all bad, of course; I grew close with one cousin, Chrissy, and we did a lot together — swimming, playing, riding horses on her folks' farm — until she caught religion and, with no explanation, suddenly refused to have anything to do with me. That hurt me a lot, but it was typical of the behavior of my extended family. They were negative, gossipy, backbiting users. My parents greeted all of these people with open arms, and they'd tromp right in, arms conspicuously free of food and other supplies, and act like they owned the place. I, for one, got tired of being walked all over.

My parents finally sold the cabin about ten years ago, when the upkeep became too much for their advancing age. One of my big regrets is that I couldn't afford to buy it myself and keep it in the family. If I could have, I'd still be getting up there a few times a year. I miss that place a lot.

All in all, my immediate family is pretty wonderful. They all know what I am and what I do, and they have come to accept it. I may be closer to them now, in fact, than I ever have been. You may be surprised to hear this, but I haven't missed a holiday season with them in years. That's right, the drag queen porn director flies home to spend each Christmas with his loving middle-American family.

I figure that the importance of family can't be overstated. If you have a loving, supportive family, well, any battles you might have to fight are already half won.

In my coming out as gay, my doing drag, and my involvement in pornography, my parents have always given me their unqualified support. They were practicing Catholics (as I was until I got out of high school), so of course they probably had some inner religious conflicts with it. But if they did, they never discussed them with me. Whether they approved of it or not, their support of me, their son, never once wavered.

I knew I was gay...well, virtually from the beginning. I can't remember just when I realized it, but I know it was early, and there was never any question about liking girls. I just didn't.

But I didn't come out to my parents until after I had left Hibbing for Minneapolis in my early twenties. It was Christmas of 1982, my second year away, and I had gone home for the holidays. By that time I was doing drag at the gay bars in Minneapolis and St. Paul (though I had not yet broken into the world of gay smut). Mom had called me into the kitchen to help her prepare dinner, everything pleasant and seemingly normal. And it was *she* who dropped it on *me:*

"Larry, would you pass me the antipasto and check on the raviolis, and, oh, are you gay?"

Well, I was floored. I passed her the antipasto and checked on the raviolis (they were fine) while I carefully formulated my answer to the last, tricky part of the question. But since there was no use in denying it — obviously Mom was already wise — well, why lie? So I said yes, and Mom gave me a big hug and said, "Oh, honey, are you sure you're not just insecure because you're fat?"

Okay, so she wasn't real knowledgeable then. What mattered was that she supported me.

Really, Mom was very accepting, more so than a proper Catholic Midwestern girl has any right to be. She was tremendous. I was lucky in that; given our religious and social background, my coming out could have been much, much worse. And even my dad, while he wasn't happy about it and we never once spoke about it, didn't reject me or love me any less. I guess he felt that if it made me happy, then whatever. There simply wasn't a whole lot of trauma in coming out to my family. Shortly thereafter, I told them about doing drag, and they even took that well. This is just one of the many reasons why I consider my mom and dad such remarkable people.

Carlene also dealt well with my being gay. I don't think it was any surprise to her; she had watched me grow up and baby-sat me when I was too young to stay home alone, so she had probably drawn some conclusions long before I made it official. I wasn't exactly the most masculine kid on the block, you know? I preferred dolls and dress-up games to baseball and cars, so the clues were there if you knew how to look for them.

In fact, the only one who didn't take my coming out well was Richard, my brother. Richard hated it and hated fags, and he wasn't shy about expressing it. I never understood his fear and loathing of it, of me — except in light of one thing: My dear half brother showed some tendencies himself in our childhood years, so maybe it strikes a little too close to home for his comfort. I remember Richard as a teenager stepping out of the shower and waving his prick at me, taunting me with "Look at this!" We'd wrestle, and he'd challenge me, "Wanna touch it?" Maybe it was typical teenage testosterone overflow, just a "boy" thing to do, but it's something I remember to this day. I was very young, certainly too young to interpret such actions sexually or respond in any sexual way, but I remember being really embarrassed by them at the time.

Being gay did pose some conflict with my religious upbringing. Anyone who was raised Catholic and turns out gay can tell you that the guilt is a gift that lasts a lifetime. And we weren't passive Christians or occasional churchgoers; we were regulars, and I was even an altar boy. I loved being an altar boy because I got to get up in front of the whole congregation and perform — the natural ham in me, I guess. That ham has taken over now, and we'll talk more about her later, but this was maybe her earliest appearance.

I loved performing from my youngest days, and I could not be shamed or embarrassed. Any attention was good attention. Once, during services, I stood to hand the priest something and accidentally kicked his little bell all the way across the altar. The whole congregation broke up, and far from being embarrassed, I remember getting a little charge from making so many people laugh. I just knew, somehow, that I had brought them a little bit of pleasure that day. (Given our priest's usual dry sermons, it was the only pleasure they'd likely get.) It was the first real time that I had been such a center of attention, but it was nice, and I knew then that it wouldn't be the last.

Still, being Catholic and gay caused me some inner turmoil in my adolescent years. I collected several years' worth of *Playgirl* and *Foxy Lady* magazines — the only masturbation material I could really get in Hibbing. But even as I enjoyed them, over time the religious guilt would build up inside of me, getting bigger and stronger and harder to ignore, and I would finally give in and resolve to get rid of the magazines and be a better person. So I would take my magazines down to the railroad tracks and discard them there. I'd go home, feeling all clean and redeemed, and then...I'd get horny again. I'd resist for a day or two, but inevitably I'd head back down to the railroad yard and retrieve my magazines from among the trash littering the tracks. They'd be torn, stained, waterlogged, generally worse for the wear, but I'd take them back home and beg their forgiveness and promise never to treat them so badly again. And they always forgave me.

I still believe in God today, and that Catholic background still won't quite let me rest easy. In 1996, when I was in Paris to perform for the first time, I visited one of the ancient cathedrals with my friend Bradley Picklesimer. Bradley was mesmerized by the beautiful giant stained-glass windows and was moved to say, quite articulately, "Jeez, look at these fucking windows!" Well, I lit a candle for that one. This is one homosexual transvestite pornographer you won't catch cursing in church.

I guess it's odd to some people to reconcile a faith in God with what I do for a living and everything else about my life. After all, directing all-male fuck flicks hardly seems a career for a pious man. The reason I don't have a problem doing it is, I guess, because I believe something like this: If God made me gay, it's because he wanted me to be gay. To deny it or to try not to be gay would be a slap in his face. God made me what I am, and I'm not going to argue with him.

Moreover, the human body and human sexuality are gifts to be cherished. Sex is a wonderful and natural thing, and it's beautiful, not dirty or sinful or wrong. Most Christians are way off base about that. The human body is a wonderful, miraculous creation. And what I provide with my movies is an outlet for that wonderful, miraculous creation. If people can stay at home and jerk off to one of my films (that's a natural need, and fulfilling it can't be bad) rather than going out to the clubs or the baths and having unsafe sex with some stranger of uncertain morals and dubious hygiene, then I'm helping to keep them healthy and safe and alive. It's an alternative to unsafe sex. If you look at it that way, what I do is almost a public service.

That it's gay — that I'm gay — is nothing to apologize for. *Why* doesn't really matter. As far back as I can remember, there was never any question in my mind that I was gay. No doubt, no struggle, no internal turmoil — that's the way it was, so plain and simple that it couldn't be wrong. I suppose I tend to agree with the theory that homosexuality is a matter of genetics. My parents certainly never did anything to push me in that direction. I wasn't sexually abused, and they didn't dress me in girl's clothes as a child. I had good relationships with both of them. As early as I can recall, I just knew it. Long before I even reached puberty, my friends around the neighborhood were all girls, and our favorite pastimes were girlish things like playing house. I had no desire to ever play sports. And I always thought that Cher, even when she was married to that dweeb Sonny, was simply the most fabulous person on the planet.

I'm no scientist, and I won't speculate about what makes people gay. Maybe it can be environmental for some people. A woman who's beaten throughout her life by abusive men might come to mistrust all men and turn to other women for comfort, becoming a lesbian that way. Who knows? The best scientists of our day haven't figured it out, so I'm not going to wonder about it. I don't have any profound answers.

I will suggest that most people are to some degree bisexual and can, if they let themselves, swing whichever way they want to. Socialization merely prevents it.

But if that's true, if we're all on a scale from basically breeder to full-on faggot, then I'm one of the 1 percent on the far gay end. A lot of sociologists believe in that model and suggest that most people are on the straight half, spread out between the far end (completely straight) and the midpoint (bisexual). Well, I'm planted firmly on that other end, thank you very much. I have never fucked a woman, and I've never so much as had the desire to try. Okay, I once experimented a little with Sharon Kane, the straight-porn veteran who's become a sort of gay icon, but as far as penetration — that is, actual intercourse — I've never gone there. You should see how just writing about it here makes me shrivel.

It's always been about men for me. Men in films, men in bathrooms, men on street corners and in public parks. Big men, little men, fat men, skinny men. All kinds of men are great. Nothing gets my juices flowing faster than a big old drippy dick primed for action. I've had my share of action, but it's never been as much as I'd have liked. There have been orgies with gangs of beautiful porn folk and quickie bathroom blow jobs to unknown men in nightclubs (some of them, as I've mentioned, having untrustworthy bladders). In fact, if you see me on the street and are in need of some quick relief, well, stop on by and say hi!

I'm a big ol' bottom who never gets tired of sex. You might think that when sex is your life and you have to direct it every day on the job, it would become tiresome after a while. Well, maybe for some folks, but not for me. The sight of two (or three or four or fifteen) perfectly sculpted men worshiping each other's bodies never, ever loses its charm for me. I could watch it every day for the rest of my life and die a happy man. There are too many variations, too many possibilities, too many damn men for it to ever get old.

I will say, though, that being a porn director has broadened my horizons sexually. Old-fashioned vanilla sucking and fucking just doesn't cut it for me now. This business has turned me on to things I never knew existed (some — but not all — of which you've seen in my films), and regular sex just bores me today. Fisting, felching, water sports, double penetration — it's all fair game now. If you have a new variation, let me know. Maybe I can make you a star.

Which is all very good, I guess, considering what I do for a living. Me and the porn biz have been a perfect match, a marriage made in heaven and consummated on television screens around the world. And how that happened is a story in itself...

Ooey, Gooey, Rich, and Chewy
OR
How This Chi Chi Creature Came to Be

SOME PEOPLE ARE BORN EXTROVERTS. Other people have extroversion thrust upon them. And some of us become extroverted out of necessity, as a way of just making it through another day.

I was one of those who developed personality as a survival technique. Let's face it, when you're overweight and feminine, school is about as much fun as an eight-hour root canal every day of your life. Nobody's crueler than kids. Any gay child will tell you, locker-room fantasies aside, school is mildly unpleasant at the best of times and downright unbearable at the worst.

By the time I was in high school, I was being teased a lot. I was big, but I was not physically imposing. I was a boy, but I was noticeably effeminate. In junior high and high school, that makes you a lightning rod for abuse. Hurt? Of course it hurt. You can develop a thick skin toward a lot of things, but all that does is deny your tormentors the pleasure of seeing your pain. You can deny it, you can hide it, you can put a brave face on it, but you'd have to be Superman for all the meanness I endured to roll off your back.

So you do what you have to do to survive, and for me, that was humor. Laughter is the great defuser, and I could make people laugh. People may have no other redeeming values, but if they're funny, they can get by. This is especially true in school — your class cutups are always the most popular kids around.

I was naturally funny, and I made my personality work for me. I was always ready with a quick quip, an impression, a comical dance step, a funny story, a bit of slapstick — stuff you can't really learn; maybe you just have to be born with it. I could laugh at myself, and a lot of my humor came at my own expense. But that was okay because it took the heat off. People weren't threatened. They saw the Larry underneath the girth and the girlish mannerisms, and they liked him. Because I could make people laugh, with me or at me, I achieved a measure of popularity.

And it was a popularity that transcended the usually impenetrable borders of high-school cliques and castes. Hibbing had the standard assortment of types: the jocks, the brains, the stoners, the geeks, the popular kids. They all kept to their own little groups, and never did they mingle. But I mingled. I mingled with them all. I mingled with the somebodies and the nobodies, the wanna-bes and the already-ares. I was an equal-opportunity offender, and so I established a wide-ranging circle of friends, one which included many types and tastes.

I did the social scene too: the dances, the parties, even sporting events. Football has always been big in the small-town North, and in Hibbing Friday night's games were *the* places to be seen. Who cared what was going on on the field? It was a social function, and it wasn't school spirit that took me there. I don't even remember if our team was any good or not.

Like a lot of young gay men, my closest friendships were formed with girls, not boys. Funny or not, I was still too much of a fag for some of the guys to want to associate with, and though I managed to get by, a few of them still weren't very nice to me. That was true of the girls too, but for the most part they accepted me more easily. So most of my best friends were girls: Sandy Kiddo, Michelle Chez, Robin Lindstrom. Not girlfriends but friends who were girls, though I guess this deflected a lot of people's suspicions as well.

At that point it was the athletes who got young Larry all hot and bothered. I had schoolgirl crushes on football and basketball players, always the BMs on any C. I admired them only from afar, of course; we could talk and joke at school, but it never went beyond that, and nothing romantic ever came of it.

My favorite was Michael Sander, and he was a two-sport star in football and basketball. Michael looked like a young version of macho video star Al Parker; that is to say, he was hairy. Hairy arms, hairy legs, and, even by the ninth grade, a hairy chest and a full mustache. I've always loved hair on a man, and Michael Sander had it in abundance. He was a man among boys long before some other kids' voices even changed. Too bad he was hopelessly straight.

Fifteen years after I graduated, Hibbing High had an all-class reunion, and that night I finally told Michael's wife how much of a crush I had always had on him. His wife, who had seen me on Joan Rivers's TV talk show, thought that was simply hysterical and asked me to send her tapes of some of my movies. No word on what Michael thought of them.

I also had it bad in those years for two other football players, John Engarro and Randy Southgate. Engarro, sadly, barely recognized my existence, and Southgate...well, he acknowledged it all too well.

It was during the ninth grade that I had a party at my house one weekend when my parents were away. Teenagers love a good party, of course, and with little else to do in Hibbing, turnout was excellent, the house just teeming with people. Beer flowed, pot burned, and carelessly handled cigarettes left little holes in my parents' furniture.

Now, let me tell you about Randy. Randy was tall and blond with really striking Nordic good looks. Square jaw, perfect features, great profile — to die for. He kind of resembled a young version of video star Rex Chandler. So anyway, Randy was at my party along with two of his jock friends, and they kept telling me of the impending arrival of a guest they really wanted me to meet. Their friend "Big Sid" was en route, they told me, and they couldn't wait to introduce me to him.

Well, as the evening wore on, the party got bigger and rowdier, and as damage began to be done to my parents' house, I began to want everyone to just clear out. I finally declared the party over and chased my friends away. But by the time I finally got them all dispersed, Randy Southgate and his buddies included, Big Sid never had made his much-anticipated appearance.

I pretty much forgot about it until a week later, when Randy and one of those same friends called for me to join them in a dark corner of the school locker room. In what I can best describe now as a scene straight out of one of my movies, Randy had his jockstrap pushed down in front and his dick hanging out. "This," they told me, to no end of amusement, "is Big Sid." Fucking hysterical, right? To a teenager, I guess. I was humiliated. Sure, deep inside I wanted to drop to my knees right then and there and suck him till his toes curled, but all I could do then was play along and laugh it off. As I look back now, however, the whole episode seems very homoerotic, though as far as I know, Randy was not and is not gay.

Another big shot around the Hibbing High campus was Kevin McHale, who not only was the star of our basketball team but also went on to a long and successful career playing professionally with the Boston Celtics. I know you didn't buy this book to hear about sports, so suffice it to say that McHale was part of some great Celtics teams that won several championships in the 1980s. He is now a front-office executive for his home-state professional team, the Minnesota Timberwolves.

I had never been that hot for McHale in high school (too tall and gangly; he eventually topped out at six foot ten), but he was also at that fifteen-year reunion catching up with his old jock buddies. Whether he remembered Larry, who knows, but somehow he knew who Chi Chi was. (Maybe he'd been talking to Dennis Rodman?) He even said to me, "I guess we're the two most famous people here," the Hall of Fame forward and the drag queen porn director. I'm sure he was just thrilled.

I encountered him outside later, and he asked me (jokingly? Who knows?) if he could be in a porn movie. "Well," I told him, "I'd have to see your cock, and I'd have to see it hard." Much laughter, but alas, no Celtic penises were shown that night. Still, we chatted at length about the industry, and he seemed genuinely interested. Read into that what you will. And it left me with something to think about as well: How big do you think a six-foot-ten guy's dick might be, anyway? Call me, Kevin, sweetie, let's talk.

I kept a diary throughout those years, daily documentation of my defeats and triumphs and trials and tribulations. It was a little red book that I called, in a fit of creative inspiration, my Little Red Book. It contained my innermost thoughts, my hopes and dreams, my most secret desires, my perverted fantasies about the unknowing boys in my classes. This book, were you to get your dirty little hands on it now, would provide an intimate tell-all glimpse into Larry, the teenage years. That's why it's safely locked away under tighter security than most of this country's nuclear weapons. You don't think I'm going to volunteer *all* of my information, do you?

Anyway, at one point I gave my LRB to my good friend Peggy Maley. I don't remember why she wanted it or why I would've parted with it, but I trusted her and gave her the book. Now, Peggy eventually turned out to be a fine adult and an upstanding citizen, and she flinches in embarrassment when reminded of this now. But at this point in our youth, she inexplicably succumbed to coldhearted adolescent cruelty. She thought it would be funny to fake some salacious entries in my diary about certain boys (yeah, as if I didn't have enough salacious entries of my own). Well, of course it got around, and it caused a lot of trouble for me that year in high school. There was factual documentation of what everyone had long suspected: The big kid's a fag. It then became common knowledge around Hibbing High that Larry Paciotti liked boys.

———

Making It Big: Sex Stars, Porn Films, and Me

This was not a surprise to many people. As far back as I can remember, it was men, not women, who turned my crank, and that was before I even really had a crank (or at least a big one with hair around it) to turn. I think I was gay from the day of my birth when the doctor slapped my ass. Unconfirmed reports have me saying, "That's good, but drop your elbow a little so we can all see it." Great directors are born, not made, you know.

To anyone watching, it would have been painfully obvious that this little boy would grow up to be a great big fag. Still, Hibbing was pretty clueless. When you talk about white-bread, well, Hibbing wasn't even as sophisticated as that. There were no gay bars and no adult bookstores. It was the kind of town where you could leave your door not only unlocked at night but standing wide open, and some kindly neighbor who happened by was more likely to close it for you than to take your television. With a background this protected, the fact that my friends and community have now accepted me for everything that I am is an immense credit to all of them. There was nothing in our background that could possibly have prepared them for this.

By the time I was six or seven and had seen naked men swimming, on cable TV, whatever, I knew where my interests lay. Of course I hadn't had a conscious realization by that time; sexuality is not a concept to be grasped by someone that young, especially nontraditional sexuality. In fact, even though I knew deep down that I was gay, it took me until I was well into my twenties to admit it to myself and come to peace with it.

Since there was no porn in Hibbing, I got through my teenage years with the aid of magazines. One of my favorites, *Foxy Lady*, which was kind of similar to *Playgirl*, had pictures of naked guys in various stages of lovemaking with beautiful, impossibly big-breasted women. That's what was under my mattress in the 1970s. There were fantasies too, dreams of such teen hunks as David Cassidy, Elton John, Paul Stanley of KISS, John Travolta in his *Welcome Back, Kotter* days, and, toward the end of the decade, the Village People. Don't laugh. You preferred girly men like Shaun Cassidy and Leif Garrett, perhaps? Well, my tastes ran more toward the manly men, the Colt types, the Michael Sanders. Facial hair was good, and body hair was better. Leave the boys for *Teen Beat*; I wanted a man.

All teenage boys are furtive about exploring sex, and I was craftier than most. One year in junior high we were given an assignment that required us to write about our favorite singer or band. Well, this gave me a good excuse to send Dad out to buy me a copy of *Playgirl*. *Playgirl* printed profiles of recording artists, you understand, so whatever recording artist was featured in the *Playgirl* that Dad brought back, well, that was who my "favorite" was going to be, and that was who I would write my report on. Okay, it was a pretty transparent ploy to get some masturbation material, but Dad, white-bread and clueless, didn't see through it. So, bless his heart, he went out and bought me a *Playgirl*. (I'm surprised *he* didn't get a reputation around Hibbing after that.) And my "favorite" recording artist whom I wrote about for that assignment was...Paul Williams.

I happened upon masturbation, like a lot of guys do, by happy accident. You know, you play with yourself because it feels good, but unless you've been instructed early — and I wasn't — you probably don't know what the end result is supposed to be. So the first time that my playing with myself resulted in ejaculation, I simply freaked out. I thought I had broken something, and how would I ever tell my parents and explain it at the emergency room? It felt too good, it couldn't be right. Imagine my young Catholic terror. You've probably been there yourself.

I went to school the next day desperate for some morsel of information — extracted with a maximum of subtlety, of course — that might put my troubled mind at ease. "Oh," I would say, "I was talking to this guy who said he was playing with himself, and..." Well, classmates more knowledgeable than I eased my fears that day, and Larry the scared little innocent became Larry the rampantly sexual being. Larry has never looked back.

––––––––––

Masturbation was fine for a while — four to six times a day every day, more on weekends or when Mom and Dad were out of the house — but as we all know, jerking off can't cut it forever. For me, going solo eventually gave way to an ever-increasing curiosity about boys and the treasures that lurked in their trousers.

I had one special friend — let's just call him Tony. He still lives in the area and doesn't want to be recognized, so we won't use his real name. It was with Tony that I finally discovered all the carnal pleasures that men have to offer each other. From about the sixth grade on, Tony and I began experimenting, just fooling around in our awkward teenage way, determining what felt good, what felt bad, and what we could get away with doing to each other. This continued all through high school, by which time I was getting pretty good at these things.

Basically, Tony and I refined our cocksucking techniques on each other. It was all strictly oral at that point; he wanted to fuck me once, but his dick was just too big, and I didn't want any part of it. (Pretty fucking ironic now, huh?) After practicing for years on Tony's cock — and it was a nice one, let me tell you — by the time I graduated, I could suck a bowling ball through twenty feet of garden hose.

Still, the learning process wasn't always easy or painless. The first time Tony came in my mouth (we were in maybe the tenth grade), I almost threw up. Another time I was blowing him in the basement, and we had just started to experiment with finger fucking. Only this time, when I put my finger up his ass, I decided to lubricate it with Brut shampoo. I didn't warn him in advance, but you can imagine how this felt, the sting of the cologne meeting his tender insides. Picture him hopping madly about, hands on his ass, screeching in agony at his burning butt. It was pretty damn funny if you ask me, although he might remember it differently.

Besides being a good friend and a coconspirator and a fellow explorer of hot man sex, Tony was a vehicle of great convenience. He saved my ass more than once. One Christmas when I was about sixteen, I had left one of my beat-off mags in the bathroom, where my mother found it. I had simply forgotten it, but now I had some quick explaining to do.

"What is this?" Mom demanded, highly upset.

"Oh, it's Tony's," I replied, fast on my feet. So Tony was outed to my parents; I don't recall their ever holding it against him.

So that's the development of Larry the fag. Larry the performer evolved in much the same way. I had always wanted to act, to perform, to be the center of attention. In our old home movies, it was always me shoving my way to center stage. I craved the spotlight and the adulation of the crowd. From elementary school on, I knew I was destined for the stage.

One performance more than all the others really hooked me. It was at a grade-school pageant, and my act was based on a popular commercial of the time. Remember the Fig Newtons commercial with the giant dancing cookie? The cookie was actually a guy in a giant Fig Newton costume, and he performed a catchy little jingle: "Ooey, gooey, rich, and chewy inside; tender, flaky, golden cakey outside..." Ring a bell? The ad was very popular in the '70s. Anyway, I found that commercial extremely funny, and I would perform the jingle and the little dance step that accompanied it for the amusement of anyone who would watch.

In about the sixth grade I performed my Big Fig Newton act onstage in front of all my classmates. It could have been a recipe for catastrophe in the wrong hands, but somehow I pulled it off. They loved it. They laughed, they cheered, and I became a celebrity. I became popular and was associated from then on with that song. I *was* the Big Fig Newton. No doubt, that was one of the major turning points of my entire youth. From that day on, I knew I was destined to perform.

I brought my fig act back for an encore in high school, this time at my ninth-grade homecoming pageant and wearing a more elaborate fig costume. Again, success. People thought it was hilarious, and I got a standing ovation. By this time the performing bug had sunk its teeth so far into me that there was no escaping it. It was only a question of how I would make my name.

I began jumping at any and all chances to play to a crowd. Homecoming pageants, student assemblies, skits, plays — no opportunities passed me by. And after a while what I wanted to do with my life started to come more clearly into focus. I had tried a couple of plays with the drama club and found that boring. I found it too restricting, too confining. You learn your lines, you rehearse until they're running around in your head under their own power, you deliver them by rote — *b-o-o-oring!* I knew that that was not where my talents lay. I wanted to be funny for people — but my *own* brand of funny and on my own terms. Screw the script, I wanted to improvise. Improvisation gave you freedom, creativity, the liberty to decide what was funny and the ability to take the show where you wanted it to go. Don't like this routine? Change it. Crowd not reacting to this bit? Try something else. Tired of doing the same old act every night? Shake it up, move it around, be original. Dare to be different.

Even today that's what I try to do onstage. If you're freewheeling and spontaneous, audiences will pick up on that. If you're having fun, they'll have fun. I have the utmost respect for those acting professionals who can do long runs on Broadway, churning out the same lines night after night, but that's not me. Chi Chi does her own thing.

———

By the time I escaped Hibbing High School (class of '78), I was well ensconced in my public role as a performer and my private role as a basement cocksucker. However, the different aspects of Chi Chi LaRue hadn't yet begun to all come together. It would be another four years before all the pieces fit properly in one place.

Graduation from school did nothing to diminish my love for pornography. In fact, the older I got, the more I liked it. From the very beginning I was enamored of the idea of fucking on film. Men and women, men and men, women and women, it didn't matter. It was all good, and I savored every tortured grimace of ecstasy and every splash of bodily fluids.

But Hibbing was a porn-free zone, if not by governmental edict then by civic pressure and conspiracy of local retailers. To get my needed dosage of porn, I had to travel to Duluth, some seventy miles distant. There I would go to the local XXX movie house, the Strand Theater, for my fixes of fornication.

Still not quite comfortable with being gay then, I directed my interests instead toward the superwomen of '70s straight porn: Seka, Marilyn Chambers, and their peers. After seeing my first fuck flick at age sixteen — *Pretty Peaches*, the blue-movie debut of Sharon Kane — I became obsessed, going all the time. I was these women's biggest fan. I followed their careers film by film, fuck by fuck, blow job by blow job. Through devoted reading of an industry publication called *Cinema X*, I even knew when their hairstyles changed. Everyone needs a hobby, and this was mine. Porn. It's always been the love of my life.

I loved all these women, but despite my own denials, it was the men I looked at for pleasure. I'd sneak into Duluth's various adult bookstores to get my surreptitious fix of man-to-man sex. I enjoyed it, I got hard, but I always felt guilty about it afterward. Don't get me wrong, there was no internal confusion or conflict; I was just having a hard time dealing publicly with who I was.

This went on for a couple of years. During that time I bounced around from job to job, working in a pizza joint (where I gained thirty pounds in a year), a movie theater, a shoe store. Nothing clicked. I was young and aimless, still looking for my niche. Ultimately, it would take leaving Hibbing to find it.

When I was twenty-two I finally made my break. It was at the urging of my friend Scott, whom I had known for about two years. We had been ushers together at a local movie theater, and though neither of us would admit it to the other then, he was a big fag too.

Scott was the one who convinced me to leave Hibbing. "Whatever it is you want in life," he told me, "you're not going to get it in Hibbing." I wasn't exactly breaking down doors to get out of town, but there was no denying the truth of his argument. And so I gathered up my courage, and the two of us set off into the setting sun, bound for the big city, to that land of dreams and cheese: Minneapolis. Los Angeles wasn't even a trace of an idea in my mind at the time. You have to take these things in small steps.

So there we were, two unsophisticated small-town closet cases, all alone and ready to take on the world in the big, cold city. The quality of our lives didn't improve immediately, but we were at least in a position now to be exposed to bigger things. What we would do about them would be up to us. So we got an apartment together, landed some menial jobs, and set about making lives for ourselves in the grand metropolis.

My first job in Minneapolis was at Green Mill Pizza, a job I kept for six years. Believe me when I tell you, I loved working at Green Mill. I was the queen of to-go, and life was deep-dish good.

Of course, it didn't help my weight any more than my previous stint in the pizza business did. I used to sneak into the cooler and eat the toppings when no one was looking. I am not known for my willpower. Green Mill had a crab pizza creation, and that crab was my favorite thing to snack on. They eventually took it off the menu, I guess because it seemed like they weren't making any money, but in reality that was only because I was eating up all the crab.

Other times I'd write out an order for four or five deep-dish pizzas — all totally fake, of course — and have them made up. Green Mill's policy was that any pizzas left over at the end of the night were to be given to the employees, so when these pizzas were never claimed, I got to take them all home. It was a system that was easy to abuse, and you can see that it wasn't exactly profitable to have me as your employee.

While I was at Green Mill, I also became obsessed with The Artist Known Then as Prince. TAKTAP, as you probably know, is from Minneapolis, and he frequented a local club called First Avenue, where he would occasionally perform surprise shows with his band, the Revolution. These concerts were never announced in advance, so you couldn't plan to be off work to attend, but I always managed to get there anyway. I'd have one friend or another, usually Debbie Wickland, hear of the impending show via the grapevine, and they'd know to call me at work to alert me. I'd tell whichever friend called, "Call me back in five minutes," and when he or she did, I'd claim some emergency that required me to leave work immediately. "What's that you say? The water main in my house broke, and my basement is flooded? I'll be home right away!" And then I'd go off to the concert.

This happened more often than I'd like to admit. But since Green Mill paid me by the hour, it hurt me more than it hurt them. Sometimes I'd take home paychecks of $35 for two weeks' work. I wasn't getting rich, but it was a homey place, and my fellow employees were like a family to me. It was a good time.

Scott and I never really came out to each other per se, but our blossoming sexuality could not much longer be ignored. For two young men in their early twenties, the hormones were becoming more and more difficult to suppress. For my part, I'd go to straight clubs like First Avenue with a bunch of female friends, and once I got a few drinks under my belt, I'd make some lame excuse to leave. Then I'd walk down the street to one of the nearby gay clubs and watch the men and the drag queens there. In this way I could keep my gay urges secret and separate from my friends and social life. Even I couldn't handle them without the artificial courage of a half-dozen drinks.

I discovered that Scott was gay quite by accident. We were both taking classes at Horst Hair College with the eventual goal of becoming hairdressers. Yeah, two straight male hairdressers. Who were we fooling? Styling hair wasn't exactly a dream for us, but it was a decent way to make a living and something we thought we could do. Over time Scott became friends with one of our instructors, whose name was David. Well, one night I came home from the clubs and caught Scott and David in Scott's room together. I wasn't surprised, and I didn't give him any grief about it, but even that didn't give me the courage to meet him halfway. It took a little while longer for me to come out to him.

Once I finally did, Scott and I embraced all the gay life had to offer with a vengeance. Minneapolis's premier gay bar at that time was called — prepare to bust a gut at the cleverness of this name — the Gay '90s. And we would be there or at some other club every night, drinking, tricking, partying, and making up for the lost time of our youth.

The first time I was exposed to drag had been on a weekend trip from Hibbing to Minneapolis sometime before. I had accompanied my friend Tammy Peterson to a club where her brother Paul worked as a deejay, and for the first time I saw men in dresses strutting around in faux feminine elegance to the drunken adoration of throngs of shrieking fans. And they were lip-synching to the songs of Cher, Dolly Parton, and Melissa Manchester. That was fabulous enough. Then, when I realized that some club patrons would actually demonstrate their appreciation by *coming up onstage and sticking wads of money down your fake bosoms*, the proverbial lightbulb went on over my head. Drag: what a concept. That, I knew, was a vocation I was made for.

The idea of doing drag had been percolating in my head for years, and my first opportunity to actually try it came soon after our move to Minneapolis. First Avenue, Prince's hangout, was to have a lip-synch contest. Patrons were invited to gather their bravest buddies, summon their courage, and get up onstage and pantomime to a favorite record. Those who looked the least foolish got to split some moderately insulting cash prize, like $50. That probably wouldn't even cover your costumes, but it was promised to be fun, so you were supposed to do it anyway.

Well, that sounded like something we wanted to do. So Scott and I joined forces with two of our Minneapolis friends, Bob and Greg, and dreamed up what would become a major part of my life: the Weather Gals.

We were based on the 1980s group Weather Girls, and we were to perform their gay-bar standard of the day, "It's Raining Men." We conceived drag identities for each of us: Scott became "June," Greg became "Flo," Bob became "Alice," and I became "Chi Chi." That's right, this was the first public in-drag appearance of Chi Chi LaRue, although she was known briefly at that time as Chi Chi Box.

The name, by way of explanation, came from Tony, my basement blow buddy from Hibbing. Years back, my mother had a set of boxes in which she would pack food for our family's weekend excursions to Perch Lake. She called these, cleverly, her lake boxes. Well, Tony had come into possession of one of these during one of his many moves, and he hadn't returned it. I was under heavy pressure from my mother, so I nagged him repeatedly to give it back: "Do you have my mother's lake box? Where's the lake box? My mother wants her lake box back!" After hearing enough of this, Tony dubbed me "Larry Lake Box," later shortened to just "Lake Box" and finally just to "Box." Today I call my video-production company Lakebox Productions. Tony was also responsible for "Chi Chi," simply pulling it out of thin air one day. Scott later came up with "LaRue," which I liked much better than "Box," and so I changed my name to that just before our first public appearance.

Once we signed up for the contest, we set about creating our drag personas. The first thing we needed was costumes. I knew I'd never find women's clothes that would fit me off the rack, so I had to adapt other outfits into something I could use. (We'll talk more about the art of drag later in the book.)

The look we adopted was basic "hag drag," more intentionally funny than glamorous. In all honesty, we probably were quite hideous. I even still had a mustache at that point. As for my frock, I wore a long peach-colored skirt cut from a formal evening gown and tied with a drawstring, and a long army coat transformed into a peplum jacket. I borrowed earrings and other jewelry from my mother, then completed the outfit with sneakers and a ratty wig.

My band mates were no more elegant: Alice (Bob) combined a cheerleader skirt with ripped panty hose and white sneakers; Flo (Greg) wore a low-cut dress that revealed his unshaven chest. In fact, of all of us, June (Scott, always the most effeminate) was the only one who at all resembled a woman.

Then we rehearsed. We all knew the song already, so that was the easy part. Finally, on show night, the Weather Gals at last made their long-anticipated debut.

And we killed. They loved us. Not only did we win the contest (on our first attempt at drag and lip synch, mind you), but the Weather Gals were invited to return for future engagements at First Avenue on a regular basis.

So back we went, again and again, playing to an ever-increasing fan base. As we refined our act and got better, mastering the subtleties and nuances of live performing, our popularity grew. We developed a reputation. First

Avenue began building entire shows around us. We head-lined performances on Halloween, New Year's Eve, and other special occasions throughout the year. In a town where drag queens covet regular gigs — that being where the prestige and, most certainly, the money was; you could do guest spots at other bars, but your regular gig was what brought in the best tips — we had that regular gig.

For Scott and Bob and Greg, it was an interesting and profitable diversion; they stuck with it, and we had a lot of fun. But for me, more or less the ringleader, our cross-dressing success was clarifying everything I had ever wondered about in my life and my future. I came to the real-ization that this was it, this was my niche, this was what I wanted to do and was good at. Whether I could make a living at it, well, we'd just have to wait and see, but by the time we had a few shows under our belts, I was absolute on one point: I was going to do drag.

Chi Chi LaRue was born.

Curiously, I never had any real reservations about becoming a drag queen. After all of the horrible difficulties I had with coming out and accepting my homosexuality, the transition from man to man-in-a-dress was a strangely smooth one. In retrospect I look at this as proof positive that I made the right decision. Surely, if this wasn't a good choice for me, I would have experienced doubts and fears and second-guessed myself endlessly. But I did none of that. It was a perfect fit: Larry, Chi Chi. The Twin Cities would never be the same.

As the Weather Gals' reputation grew, we were asked to perform at other clubs. Now, in Minneapolis and St. Paul, there was a clear boundary of territory between the two cities. Minneapolis queens didn't venture into St. Paul, and

St. Paul queens didn't venture into Minneapolis. There may as well have been the Berlin Wall dividing the two.

But the Weather Gals were big enough to breach that barrier. Our fame became so great that we were invited to perform at a club called the Townhouse in St. Paul. This was a landmark event, and it didn't pass without backlash in the St. Paul drag community.

You need to know this about drag queens: They are, to a one, the cattiest of the catty. Drag queens combine the worst of men and the worst of women. They're vicious, territorial, backbiting bitches, and that's if they like you. They can be even worse if they don't.

(I don't want to totally disparage my own kind here. For all of their cruelty, drag queens can also be wonderful and fabulous and fun. Why, some of the nicest people I've ever known have been drag queens. You just don't want to cross them.)

So you can imagine that a lot of established DQs resented our success, and the St. Paul queens were really up in arms about our intrusion. And when we wowed them at the Townhouse, were invited back, and became regulars there, it created a lot of serious tension within the DQ community.

No one was rude to our faces, because we were by that time powerful enough to call the shots at the clubs we were playing. You had to be nice to us, at least outwardly, if you wanted to be a part of the show. And everyone wanted to be part of our shows because we packed in the fans and made a fortune in tips. But behind our backs there was a lot of hatefulness spread. Our hag drag, while a lot of fun and hugely popular with our fans, made us an easy target for ridicule.

Ooey, Gooey, Rich, and Chewy

Behind our backs they would call us names like the Weather Pigs and the Weather Heiffers. They mocked our slovenly shtick. We came out of nowhere and became so popular so fast that a lot of them were simply jealous.

It wasn't that we were attitude queens or lorded our popularity over anyone either. In fact, we were quite open to sharing the spotlight. We were always willing to let new girls perform, but sometimes that generosity simply wasn't enough. There was just no way to answer the animosity some of these people had toward us.

Take Cleo, for instance. Cleo was an established performer who, for some reason that was never fully explained, felt personally threatened by the Weather Gals' success. And of all of us, she hated my guts the most. I had nothing against her, and we had sort of an uneasy politeness when we were face-to-face, but the truth was, she despised me, and she wasn't afraid to tell anyone else who'd listen.

So one year Cleo had loaned me a wig for a performance at a country club on New Year's Eve. By the time we got to the Gay '90s afterward, we were all already drunk. (By this time the Weather Gals had evolved into a trio. Flo and June had left the group, and Alice and I replaced them with my friend Kevin, who took the drag name of Rose.) I was wearing Cleo's wig when we got to the club, and I encountered a very drunken and belligerent Cleo in the dressing room backstage. We argued, and she reached up and snatched her wig right off of my head. Now, of all the things you can do to a drag queen, the very worst is to pull her wig off. This is the ultimate slap in the face to any female impersonator. But Cleo did it to me. (Sure, it was her wig, but she had said I could borrow it.)

So Rose (Kevin) stepped in to my defense and grabbed the wig back from Cleo. And, to the horror of everyone in the room, Cleo pulled back and decked him. Knocked him out cold, right there in the dressing room, with a single punch. This is one of the reasons I say, you don't mess with a drag queen.

(I myself accidentally snatched my friend Gender bald years later in Paris. It was over a man, of course; I wanted him, and she got him. We faced off, and I tried to grab her shoulder but got her wig instead, and it came off in my hand. I got off easier than Kevin did, though — all Gender did was fling a drink in my face, not knock me out. I will tell you, though, that even with your eyes full of whiskey, Gender without a wig is a scary sight to behold.)

Some years after that hideous Gay '90s scene, I was in L.A. when another old-time Minneapolis DQ, Stevie, called me to tell me that Cleo had died of AIDS complications. I cried all day. We had become closer after she got sick, and it was like losing an old friend. For all of our petulance and infighting, there is still a certain camaraderie among drag queens. We may argue and fight, but we do respect each other. After all, we all really are in this together, aren't we?

———

There just wasn't a lot of togetherness apparent all the time in Minneapolis and St. Paul. Things were so tense in the DQ community there that the Weather Gals eventually decided to do something to bridge the gap. We wanted to extend the olive branch of peace. What we came up with was our very own awards show, the Weather Gal Awards, wherein we would honor members of the drag community for their sometimes-dubious achievements: Best Dressed, Biggest Cocktail Queen, Biggest Bitch, Biggest Slut, Best Performer, Best Lip Synch...I can't name you all of them here, but they became our own little Academy Awards. It was a gesture of recognition for the hard work all the queens put into their acts. Hey, we had to give something back. If anyone else were running the show, we'd have cleaned up in every category!

The Weather Gal Awards were met with a mixture of interest and disdain. A lot of our fellow queens pretended they didn't care, but they were always secretly very interested in knowing who was up for what, and none of them were ever known to turn down an award if they won. And so the WGAs became an annual highlight. It was something we really enjoyed doing too; I've always been an award queen (that's why I helped come up with the Gay Video Guide Awards). But to me, winning is not as much fun as presenting. Nothing beats seeing the look on the face of someone who's just come up onstage to be rewarded publicly for a job they've done well. To me, that's the most worthwhile thing I can do. I've won plenty of awards, and at this point in my career, I couldn't care less if I ever get another Best Director. I'd rather see the actors or editors or camerapeople I work with get a little bit of the glory.

While other members of Weather Gals came and went, I remained constant. Each time up onstage left me hungrier for more. Each laugh my routine got, every kiss and compliment and balled-up dollar from the crowd just whetted my appetite and sharpened my focus. If I wasn't the biggest, bawdiest, best-known drag queen in the Twin Cities, then I don't know who was. But I wanted more. My desire was soon to become the biggest, bawdiest, best-known drag queen in the country. Boy George and Culture Club were atop the charts, exposing a whole new audience to drag, and Divine had amassed a huge cult following by her appearances in John Waters's bizarre films. So why couldn't I do the same? Drag was in! Drag was cool! Drag could become an actual paying career!

I performed tirelessly, and my reputation grew. I was known in all the bars; everyone had met me or at least seen me perform. I schmoozed relentlessly, meeting people, charming them, leaving an impression. You don't become famous by accident. In my case it took a lot of hard work. I marketed myself furiously. My plan for self-promotion couldn't have been more intricately devised if it had been drawn up by a boardroom full of trained PR professionals. Chi Chi was going places, and you could either jump on the bandwagon or get out of the way before it ran your tired ass over.

Through devotedly working the club circuit, I eventually became acquainted with the man I had so long idolized, Prince. This was the mid '80s, and Prince was at the peak of his popularity. *Purple Rain* was a box-office bonanza, and he had a harem of beautiful, glamorous, coattail-riding starlets: Vanity, Apollonia, Sheila E. At that time Prince was *it*, and — at least socially — I was a friend of Prince's. We wouldn't call each other up or go over to each other's houses, but we'd hang together at the clubs or eat together at restaurants when a group of us were there. I think he liked that I respected his privacy and didn't hang all over him the way other, more starstruck people did.

I even was given a bit role in *Purple Rain*. I was in full drag, sitting in the front row of the theater where Apollonia was performing "Sex Shooter." In my scene a comedian and a juggler were doing their preliminary act, and I was asked what I thought. My single line, which I rehearsed for days, was "Oh, that's so stupid!"

The final mix didn't quite work out like I'd hoped, though. A few weeks after shooting was completed, I ran into some members of the Revolution, who told me what a great close-up I had. But then I went to a special screening of the movie and found out...my scene had been cut out. I was heartbroken. Prince, my beloved Prince, had decided that there was too much Morris Day in the film and had rearranged things to feature himself more prominently. It was nothing personal, I suppose, but I was still very disappointed.

So time passed, and as big as the Weather Gals were in the Twin Cities, the potential for stardom anywhere in Minnesota was only so great. I knew that I would eventually have to leave even Minneapolis, which had been so good to me, to reach my real goals. If you want to achieve *true* fame, big-time notoriety, there are two places in this country you can go: New York and Los Angeles. And given my interest in pornography, which had abated not at all during this time, the sunny shores of Southern California seemed the natural choice for my next destination.

Again, though, I needed some prodding to actually get off my ass and make the move. This time it was with my friend Kevin — the Weather Gals' Rose, who had been knocked out by the drag queen — that I finally made the great move West. "You're not going to get famous in Minneapolis," he had told me. "The only thing you're going to get in Minneapolis is fatter." And like Scott had been back in Hibbing, he was right.

Kevin was a perfect match for me and someone with whom I felt very comfortable striking out across the country. We'd originally met at a bar in Minneapolis, and we'd gone home together and had sex that night. We never had sex again, but we did go on to become close, close friends. He and I basically sustained the Weather Gals for a long time as other members came and went. Kevin was my straight man, my foil, the Ricky to my Lucy, the Abbott to my Costello. He's wise and protective while I can sometimes be trusting and too impulsive. And he had a lot of self-confidence and was always encouraging me to do things I wouldn't normally do (like moving to California). Kevin is responsible for a lot of my growth as a person, and I owe him big-time for that.

The proposed move cross-country would require a little more planning than our previous move, which took us just a little ways downstate. Mostly the difference would be financial. We scrimped and saved from our menial little jobs, we pawned most of our possessions, and we borrowed from our parents. Finally, we had accumulated a bankroll and were ready to make the jump.

Basically the whole journey was done on a shoestring: We packed up our little green Chevy with everything we could fit in it, sucked up our courage, and off we went. The trip took us across the heart of farm-belt Middle America, all very *To Wong Foo* long before Patrick Swayze and Wesley Snipes ever donned dresses. We nearly died in Denver when we almost drove off a mountain.

Ooey, Gooey, Rich, and Chewy

We were always seemingly just one step ahead of any trouble. We weren't in drag, of course, but with two loud, flamboyant fags crossing the country, looks and stares and mumbled comments followed us the whole way. Finally, two days before Halloween of 1987, we arrived at last in the City of Angels.

Like so many newcomers to California, we arrived virtually penniless and with no one to turn to for help. We settled into a tiny rattrap apartment in Hollywood (located for us by Scott, who had come out some time before) with the following inventory of worldly possessions: one pan to cook with, a dining-room table given to us as a gift, a miniature black-and-white television set, and a hideous green velvet easy chair we had been given by Kevin's sister, a chair Kevin and I would fight for possession of at the end of each long day.

We slept on sheets laid out on the floor and subsisted on ramen noodles and meat byproducts, stuff scraped off the slaughterhouse floor and sold for pennies a pound. There wasn't a lot of money for frivolities like club hopping or, often, electricity and running water. But that didn't matter, none of that mattered. All that mattered was that we were finally, excitingly, unbelievably there in Los Angeles, where any Midwestern rube with a dream of fame and fortune can sleep his way to the top and make it come true. I was eager to start sleeping, and so we started immediately looking for employment.

It took two weeks, give or take a day. Kevin was hired by a department store, where he worked in their restaurant. I, meanwhile, concentrated on the porn industry. I wasn't overly hopeful about actually landing right away in the field I loved so dearly, but I wasn't going to write it off without at least taking a stab at it. *Who knows what might happen!* I thought. *They have to hire people from somewhere. Maybe I'll get lucky.*

I got lucky. It was at Catalina Video, where I applied for a sales job. And it really was a case, when it came right down to it, of my life's devotion to pornography actually paying off. (All of you teenage boys out there, take heart.) The folks at Catalina — specifically its president, Chris Mann — were so astounded by my knowledge of the industry, names and faces and films and cock sizes down to the last millimeter, that they hired me on the spot to do sales. I could not believe my good fortune. Who would have conceived it? The Minnesota farmboy packed up for L.A. and promptly became the porn-video sales representative. I started the next day with great anticipation.

For the first few weeks, it was like living a dream. I walked around with my feet three feet off the floor, and at my size, that's some accomplishment. I got to rub elbows with the biggest stars of the day: Leo Ford, Mike Henson, the giants of '80s smut. When I actually met Jeff Stryker for the first time, to me it was like meeting Barbra Streisand; I was as giddy as a schoolgirl.

But it wasn't all wonderful for long. What I discovered in my first days on the job is that there's a business side to the porn industry just like there is to any industry, and it's no more enjoyable trying to push porn on people than trying to push encyclopedias on people. A desk job is a desk job, and a sales job is a sales job. And might I just say, *yawn!*

Maybe I was good with people, but sales was not a field

that interested me a whole lot. "Hello, is this the Orgasm Chasm Adult Bookstore? Hi, this is Larry with Catalina Video. I'm calling to talk about our hot new release, *Fat Fanny Fist Fuck*. Would you be interested in meeting me for lunch sometime this week?" It quickly became apparent that I wasn't going to spend my whole life doing this.

Once the novelty of being in the business wore off, I began to grow restless. The reality was, I didn't like sales, it wasn't where my talents lay, and it wasn't what I wanted to do. It was porn, but it wasn't porn, you know? The situation begged for success; Catalina had just released the Jeff Stryker classic *Powertool*, which practically sold itself, so it would have been an easy job to succeed in. But I simply hated having to call people up and solicit them like a common...salesman.

However, since I had been there for only a few months, I couldn't just up and ask Catalina for a promotion. So I took matters into my own hands and began to spread out a little bit, trying to learn more on my own time about other aspects of the business. I didn't shirk my sales job, but I was always off in the art department or in the editing room, poking my nose into what was going on, asking questions, soliciting the wisdom of others. I wanted to learn, and I wanted to take on more responsibilities. I hoped that if Catalina saw me able to handle more, they would give me more. I wanted to make myself indispensable.

While Larry was quietly carrying out his master plan for success, Chi Chi hadn't exactly retired. I was still doing drag on weekends at a bar called the Four Star. It was there that the famous director William Higgins, Catalina's founder, saw me perform, and we became acquainted. We had known each other from work, of course, but we never really got to bond and become friends until we got together outside of the office, in a social environment. What Bill Higgins saw in my live performances, I don't know, but he liked them, and it led to a great friendship. And Bill would later prove instrumental in my ascent through the industry.

My efforts at Catalina were eventually noticed, and as time went on I began to be given the additional duties I was seeking. I was moved from sales into promotions, which was closer to the glamour side of the business I fantasized about. My new job involved directing still photo shoots, mostly for box covers and chromes (chromes are the slides from films that are sent to magazines and others for publicity purposes). I got my own office, and I got to oversee photo shoots every day. Yes, you imagine it correctly: naked men with erections prancing about and doing my bidding. "Over here, baby, like this. Spread them wider. No, wider. That's it. Oh, this needs adjusting. Let me just reach in here..." If this wasn't my Xanadu, at least I was getting closer.

It also fell to me to screen prospective new models during that time. Michael Brawn and Alex Stone are just two who came through my door and eventually made it big. Still, I wasn't satisfied. I was rising quickly in the industry, much more so than I had ever dared hope, but instead of satisfying me, it made me think bigger still. What I really wanted by that time was to direct. Surely I had watched enough pornography to know what was good and what was bad, and now I had hands-on experience in the business. I watched some of the other hacks who were allowed to make movies, and the realization was inevitable: *Not only can I do that, but I can do it better.* I reached the same conclusion I'd reached back in hair college: *I want to be the one in the chair giving the orders.* All I needed was the chance.

Knowing I needed to learn on my feet, I started going on other people's movie sets. Since the straight-porn industry had been around longer and had more resources and sophistication than its gay counterpart, I began going onto their sets. What better place to learn? I made myself useful as a production assistant, a boom man, whatever kind of gofer they needed at the time.

The very first straight set I worked on was a film called *Tracy and the Bandit*, a loose adaptation of Burt Reynolds's *Smokey and the Bandit*. I was supposed to be the boom man, and let me tell you, I was scared to *death*. Right there in front of me, in front of everybody and their mothers, these people were actually having sex! My stomach was in an uproar by my first day on the job.

The first scene we were to do was a lesbian scene between Tracy Adams and Jeanna Fine. They were eating each other out on a bed, and I was standing in a closet holding the boom. Once the pussy eating got started, though, I kind of freaked out. My knees got wobbly, I started to sweat, my stomach was churning, and I was afraid I was going to throw up. I turned away for a moment to collect myself, and in the process I inadvertently lowered the boom almost into these nice women's faces. Okay, it was an inauspicious debut.

Tracy and Jeanna were professionals all the way, and they put all of themselves into their roles. You might laugh at the concept of professionalism among adult-film stars, but from my perspective, nothing is more important. Tracy and Jeanna were the best, and they really, *really* had a chemistry together. When the cameras stopped rolling and the crew broke for lunch that first day, they were still there on the bed going at it. And I, still in the closet with my boom, was not very much more at ease. *This is weird, this is bad, I shouldn't be here* was all I was thinking. My palms were sweating, and my head was aching. Any second, I feared, the police were going to knock down the door and haul us all away.

Needless to say, that never happened. We completed *Tracy and the Bandit,* and I went on a couple more straight sets after that. And the experience I gained on those sets, in everything from boom manipulation to coffee making, would prove helpful later on.

As I was getting my feet wet on actual porn sets, I also continued to schmooze the right people. I worked my way into the party circuit, where my drag persona helped me be remembered. One way or another, I was going to get people to know me. These parties presented great opportunities for that. And for other things as well.

One of the first porno parties I ever attended was at a house in the Valley shared by Catalina president Chris Mann and Paul Norman, director of the bisexual classic *The Big Switch.* Kevin accompanied me, and we both went in full drag: Chi Chi and Rose, the Bobbsey Drag Twins, out and looking for trouble.

I found it in the person of an aspiring young porn star who was also in attendance. The was a sexual spark when we first met, and I ended up taking him out into the backyard to give him a blow job. I sucked his dick, and he fucked me against a tree right there as the party went on all around us. Kevin eventually wandered out and discovered us and, declaring "Now I want some!" moved in to get a piece of the action.

So I went inside to freshen up, and when Kevin was done with Catalina's young model, we got in my car to go to the Four Star, hoping to continue our night of debauchery. On the way there I was telling Kevin about my encounter, and when I got to the part where the guy fucked me, he interrupted me with a look of horror on his face. "He fucked you?" Kevin shrieked. "I just sucked his dick!"

Now, what we didn't know at the party was that the backyard was where Chris and Paul, our hosts, walked their dogs. And somewhere along the line while I was sucking this guy's dick and he was fucking me, I had stepped in dog shit. The bottom of my shoe was covered with it. And now, with Kevin imagining this guy's dick being up my ass just before it had been in his mouth, we both suddenly noticed the smell of shit.

"Oh, my God!" Kevin exclaimed, frantically sniffing the air of the car. "It smells like shit in here! *Is it my breath?*"

I discovered the shit on my shoe and set him straight, but I should have let him think that for the rest of the night just for moving in on my trick!

As much fun as we had on our own time, my career continued to consume most of my efforts. It was at a staff lunch with Bill Higgins and the other big shots of Catalina that I finally scrunched up my courage and told them that

I wanted to try my hand at directing. At that time Catalina was putting out a series called *Hard Men.* These were stripper videos, nothing hard-core, and so I figured it would be a feasible place for a novice to make his directorial debut. I asked if I could direct a segment of one of the *Hard Men* videos, and to my surprise, Higgins, my friend from the Four Star, said yes. I could barely contain my excitement.

You may be thinking by this point that this meteoric rise through the porn world was happening awfully fast, with awfully little resistance. And you'd be right. It had occurred to me as well that at some point things weren't going to go as perfectly as I'd like. Somewhere there was bound to be the old fly in the ointment, the pubic hair in the teeth. Well, once Higgins promised me the *Hard Men* segment, that fly landed.

His name was Scott Masters, and he was a producer at Catalina. Now, what I ever did to Scott Masters, I cannot tell you. But for some reason, maybe none better than plain jealousy or insecurity, he seemed to feel threatened by me. I can only guess that I was climbing the ladder too fast for his comfort, and maybe he felt that he himself wasn't on the most solid ground. Whatever the reason, Masters decided to make things hard for me. He began to throw up little roadblocks in my path, minor impediments, things he could do to slow me down without appearing vengeful or childish or drawing anyone's wrath down on himself. At one point he even told me that I had to lose a hundred pounds before I would be allowed to direct. Now, you tell me, what on earth could the weight of the director possibly have to do with the quality of a finished film? And this was coming from a man who was overweight himself and not by just a little.

But I'll tell you what: As big of a pain in my ass as Scott Masters was, the man also helped me a lot. In his own spiteful way, he made me a better director than I would have been without all of his bullshit. He made me do a complete storyboard from start to finish. He made me put together my own sets. He made me do it all, expecting me to fail, but I did not fail, I got it all done, and I was the better for it and more knowledgeable and more prepared afterward. And my segment turned out to be the best one in the video.

After that Catalina dispatched director John Travis — known for discovering Jeff Stryker and directing the classic *Powertool* — to watch over me and guide my future progress. John had advised me in my *Hard Men* debut segment, and he knew the business inside and out. I thought it was a positive sign that Catalina wanted him to tutor me. But when time passed and I wasn't offered another directing gig, I jumped ship for InHand Video with a deal to be in charge of promotions and direct two movies a month.

It was late in 1989 when I was hired by Bob Leone and moved to InHand. By that time I was living with Kevin and another friend from Minneapolis, a model named Carolyn, in a house in the nation's porn heartland, the San Fernando Valley. I went to InHand and dove right in, and immediately I found myself...over my head. But InHand, to its credit, gave me the opportunity to learn by doing.

The thing about learning by doing is that you're inevitably going to make mistakes. And not just little mistakes but whoppers, doozies, colossal fuckups. And in a business like pornography, your fuckups are going to be on film, distributed nationally for all to see and preserved for eternity with your name attached. There's no ducking the blame or passing the buck in porn; if it says in the credits, "Directed by Chi Chi LaRue," you alone are responsible for the quality.

My first two movies for InHand were called *Flexx* and *All Night Long*, and they really spanned the spectrum of quality. Anyone who reviewed both of these movies would have been quite confused about my potential as a director.

Flexx showed some promise. I had some definite ideas, I knew what I wanted to see, and I was able to approximate it with some degree of skill and panache. Considering that I was such a rank beginner, *Flexx*, which starred Alex Stone, was not a bad flick.

All Night Long, on the other hand, was dreadful. It was heinous, simply a hideous mishmash of images and themes and non sequitur cuts with no cohesion or sense of unity or progression. Even worse, *All Night Long* was filled with a cameraman's cutaways of lamps and plants and ceramic dogs and other miscellaneous household items that bore no relevance to the film. Why these were used in the final cut, I have no idea. Don't get me wrong, I'll take responsibility for the way this one turned out. But it turned out the way it did because I had no freaking idea what I was doing. I wasn't clear about what I wanted to see, and I didn't know how to control what was happening on the set. It was a valuable experience, to be sure, but it was a painful illustration of someone learning by doing. To this day I am mortified to have my name attached to such a piece of crap.

Ooey, Gooey, Rich, and Chewy

I directed a handful of films for InHand before moving on again, this time to Vivid Man, the gay arm of straight-porn giant Vivid Video. It was nothing really against InHand; all in all they were pretty good to me. But things were always such a drama there, nothing could ever be easy or simple, and when Vivid Man started wooing me, I had to listen.

At that time Vivid Man knew me better as a drag queen than as a director. But there was some bad blood between Vivid Man and InHand in those years, and the opportunity to steal me from InHand was too appealing for Vivid Man to resist. Officially, they hired me to do promotions with a chance to direct as well.

Shortly before leaving InHand, I had happened upon one of my first true "discoveries," Ryan Yeager. (There were other "discoveries," some with bigger names, and we'll talk more about them later.) Ryan had sent a friend of mine a tiny little photo in the mail, asking about breaking into the business. That friend brought him to my attention. When I made the move to Vivid Man, I stole Ryan and took him with me, and one of the very first scripts I cowrote for Vivid Man — a military flick called *Buddy System* — was designed with Ryan Yeager in mind. He went on to become a major star.

While the opportunities to direct were coming more regularly now, I felt like I still had some improving to do. I continued my habit of devouring all things pornographic just to see what everybody else was doing and maybe draw (it's called "adapting," not "stealing") some good ideas from them. I watched Steven Scarborough's stuff for Falcon, Jim Steel's stuff for Vivid Man, anything I could get my hands on. And by this time I was beginning to really get a feel for what was good and what was not.

Making It Big: Sex Stars, Porn Films, and Me

At that time there was a reviewer for the *Adult Video News* named Stan Ward (he wrote under the name Sid Mitchell). Stan was one of the first people to really offer me encouragement, to really believe in what I was doing. He had given good reviews to some of my earliest efforts, I guess seeing the potential in them more than any great merit of their own. For whatever reason, Stan Ward kind of took me under his wing. We would talk on the phone daily, with him offering constructive criticism or, less frequently, actual praise. Stan was very intense for a reviewer, very temperamental, and if something stunk, he wasn't afraid to say so. I later found out that Stan, like so many porn reviewers, was a frustrated director himself. By 1996 Stan had finally achieved his dream and was directing for All Worlds. (My good friend Jerry Douglas has promised me the chance to someday review one of Stan's finished products in Jerry's magazine, *Manshots*. I plan to be absolutely fair and open-minded despite any past criticisms Stan may have had of my work. Heh-heh-heh...)

In addition to watching and learning, I bettered myself through direct tutelage from the masters. In directing films, I always tried to surround myself with people who were the very best at what they did. I wanted the best camera operators, the best production staff — any weak link could have undermined everyone's efforts. And I sought the wisdom of the most respected members of the industry. Jerry Douglas, also an established director, and camera whiz Bruce Cam were both been invaluable to me in this regard, as was John Rutherford.

Jerry Douglas, a graduate of Yale drama school, is, in my opinion, the absolute best in the business at directing dialogue, and John Rutherford and Bruce Cam are, in my opinion, the best in the business at camerawork. Rutherford, now the top director for Falcon Studios, has told me that he thinks I'm the best around at directing the actual sex, and that means a lot to me. Dialogue, though, is something that has always posed a problem for me. It's not that I can't talk, God knows, but you and I both know that dialogue is rarely essential to any porn movie. And more than that, porn performers don't get their roles because they're gifted thespians who can act their parts convincingly. They get their parts because they're buffed and well-hung, and if they can speak clearly and in more than a monotone, well, all the better.

My problem with dialogue is that I want to do it too quickly. Say the line, get it over with, get on to the fucking. That doesn't always work, though, because if the spoken parts are too laughable, they will detract from the overall enjoyability of the movie. But I do recognize this weakness and am trying to correct it.

At any rate, I made a concerted attempt to learn from the best, and I think it paid off. After my stint at Vivid Man — during which time I was the first to cast Joey Stefano (more on him later) — I returned to Catalina for another go. They hired me back in their promotions department for a short while, but my time away hadn't changed the fact that I was simply not cut out for a 9-to-5 job. More than ever, I needed to direct, and I needed to don my dresses and go out at night and perform as Chi Chi LaRue. My reputation was such by that point that I could almost do that.

Also by this time, my films were getting pretty darned good. It was shortly after beginning my second tour at Catalina that I finished what I felt was my first top-notch,

A-1 quality film: *Billboard*, starring Joey Stefano. It may not have brought me quite into league with the big boys, the Matt Sterlings and John Travises of the business (and, to be honest, I may never get there), but *Billboard* was a good film, and I think it established me as a good director.

———————

I suppose, with all due humility, that the rest of the industry thinks so too. The intervening years have been very, very good to me. I was eventually able to leave Catalina again and start working independently, which is a rare and wonderful position to be in. I've worked with some of the brightest and most beautiful people in the business, and my movies have sold well and been appreciated by fans and reviewers alike. I have a nice home and great friends, and I want for very little.

Additionally, I get to travel, meet a wide assortment of fabulous, famous people, and indulge most if not all of my fantasies. I've appeared on national television, I've done Cannes during the film festival, I've been treated like royalty from Los Angeles to New York. Fame has its downside, which we'll also discuss later, but given the perks and my love for what I do, I have to consider myself one of the luckiest people of dubious gender in the world.

GREAT LENGTHS
OR
WHAT GOES INTO A GOOD PORNO FLICK

YOU MAY BE WONDERING by this point what it is that makes a good porno movie. There may be as many different answers as there are people who watch the stuff. Everybody has different tastes in bed, and so everybody is going to be looking for different things in his or her pornography. The truth of the matter is if you want to please everybody, you're just not going to do it. It's not possible. The conventional wisdom is very true in this case: If you try to please everyone, you're going to end up pleasing no one.

On the other hand, there are some standard factors that go into every good porn flick, and these don't really change. No film can succeed without them, and any film that has them can't really be a total failure. Most of all, the bottom line boils down to one thing:

Hot sex.

I know what you're thinking: *That sounds pretty obvious, and I didn't need to shell out money for this book to learn that.* But let's face it, I know you've seen flicks where the guys may have been knockout gorgeous, but they just weren't into it, they just weren't into each other, and the sex was mechanical and boring. And it reduced your enjoyment of the movie, am I right? Of course I am. On the other hand, you've probably also seen flicks where the guys maybe weren't that attractive, maybe they weren't what you personally were into, but they were so totally into *each other* that the sex between them was just incredible. So maybe it wasn't your cup of tea, but it was hot, and you could derive some enjoyment just from that. And that's the key I'm talking about: the chemistry between performers that makes a scene work.

You can't fake true chemistry between performers. Either it works, or it doesn't. As a director, I am responsible for matching guys up so that it does.

I don't want to brag, but I agree that directing the actual sex is my strong suit. I can get guys who otherwise wouldn't click together to hit on all cylinders. I can't tell you exactly why that is or specifically what I do to get it (it depends on the guys), but I think it's something I've learned over the course of my career. There's really no substitute for experience in this kind of thing.

Maybe it's that I make them feel comfortable on the set, or maybe it's just that I'm good at matching up partners. When you cast someone in a scene, you have to consider what kind of guy he likes in deciding who you're going to pair him with. Sure, there are some guys out there who are so professional, you can throw them in with anyone and get a convincing scene. But it rings truer, more genuine, if there's an attraction there that goes beyond work and film.

The porn star Aiden Shaw is a good example of how casting is so important. Aiden is one of the pickier guys in the industry in terms of who he'll work with. That is, there are some guys he just won't. When you cast Aiden in a scene, he normally demands to handpick his partner; with me he'll sit down and go through my file of working actors and either approve or veto each name I run by him. He's not a prima donna or anything, he's just kind of choosy about his sex partners.

Well, after working with Aiden a few times, I got to know the kind of man he went for. So when I was filming *Boot Black 2*, I thought he might click well with Alex Kincaid. When I suggested Alex to Aiden, Aiden was pretty reluctant at first, but I kept after him. "Listen," I told him, "you need to trust me on this. Just give it a shot." Finally, I convinced him. So they did the scene, and for a director it was like hitting the lottery. They were *perfect* together! Alex turned out to be one of Aiden's favorite partners of all time, and their scene in the movie was one of the hottest I've ever filmed. They hit it off completely, both sexually and personally, and the chemistry of the scene was just unbelievable. It's totally obvious from watching the movie how into each other they were. You look in Aiden's eyes during that scene, and they say, *You're just the hottest fucking thing I've ever seen!* And that scene is one of the reasons why *Boot Black 2* remains one of my favorite movies that I've done.

When that chemistry between performers doesn't work, that's when you have trouble. When two guys either don't turn each other on or for some reason just don't like each other, it makes a director's job ten times harder. That's why casting is so very important.

If there's not a sexual attraction there, most guys are going to have problems getting it up. There are a handful of top-flight professionals who can pop a boner on demand, but for most guys there needs to be some element of actual desire. And if that's not there, if you're stuck with two guys who just don't hit it off, you do anything in the world that you can just to get through the scene. I mean, these guys are under contract by that time, so you can't easily replace them, and you have to somehow make it work. You do whatever it takes: magazines, videos, fluffers (attractive people on the set who can step in and get a guy up either manually or orally). Any director will tell you, these scenes can be a nightmare to get through, so you'd better cast carefully from the very outset.

Take, for instance, Joey Stefano. Joey was another one who was really picky about who he worked with. He liked burly, scruffy, overtly masculine guys, guys like Jon Vincent and Ace Harden. I guess what I'm saying is that he liked straight guys; it was really hard for Joey to work with other gay guys. But in an oral movie I did for InHand called *French Kiss,* I had him paired with a gay guy named Storm. Well, Joey didn't like Storm at all; Storm was just too queeny for him. But Storm was a total pro, beautiful (he looked like Robby Benson) and able to get hard at the drop of a hat, so for a director he was good to use. And in *French Kiss* they happened to end up together.

Joey was not happy about this. And once we were on the set, to express his displeasure in a mature, adult manner, Joey decided to start farting. Throughout the filming, throughout the whole day, he farted and farted and farted. He would not be stopped. (This was a tantrum that took some careful planning. I don't know what he had eaten the night before, but you don't get that gassy just by accident.) He was mad at Storm for being too femme, he was mad at me for casting Storm, and he took it out on everybody and made all our lives hell that day. It was so disgusting that everyone eventually had to flee the set. We were left with just Joey, Storm, me, and the cameraman, and I don't know how we got through it.

But don't think Joey was just a bitch; he could be the complete opposite if he was turned on by his partner. In a film called *G Spot*, I paired him with Sergio Calucci, a Brazilian guy who had been in one of Kristen Bjorn's *Carnival* movies. Sergio was dark and masculine and just Joey's type (and mine as well: gay but masculine), and Joey was so turned on that he ended up topping Sergio instead of the other way around, which was how we had it scripted. They fucked in this dark, dirty garage, and it ended up as one of Joey's hottest scenes ever. It was only when he *wasn't* turned on that he made your life a stinking hell.

Generally, I have a lot of control over casting my performers, although some companies are more choosy than others. Falcon is one of the pickiest; regularly each month I fly up to San Francisco and sit around their conference table with Chuck Holmes (the owner) and John Rutherford for a photo-picking session. We'll consider whatever movie I'm doing for them at that moment, and we'll go through a book of photos and try to reach a consensus on which guys we want to use. As you can imagine, with three well-developed egos each having a say, this can be a pretty antagonistic process. A lot of times someone will favor a certain guy for a certain scene, and others there will try to shoot him down. Sometimes it's not even really based on any actual objection; we just play devil's advocate to make sure there are good reasons for selecting a guy. If one of us is in a bad mood for some reason, it can get pretty testy, but you can be sure that by the time a guy passes muster with all of us, he's right for the part we put him in. I think this process is one of the reasons why Falcon's flicks are among the best put out today. The guys are chosen so carefully that there aren't going to be any mistakes.

A lot goes into matching the right guy to the right role. For one thing, I think it's important to get a little variety in my movies. That is, I like to mix in some older guys, some younger guys, some hairy guys, some smooth guys — basically a wide range. Of course, for viewers who have very narrow, specific tastes, this means that they're not going to like every guy or every scene in a flick, but it also means that every flick will have at least a little something for pretty much everyone.

Personally, I'm not the pickiest person at the selection sessions. I like all kinds of guys, so I'll cast all kinds of guys. I'll use, for instance, someone like Mark West, who's more than forty years old, to balance out most of the other performers, who are in their twenties. Also, since so many models are smooth or shaved, I'll occasionally throw in someone who's hairy and more natural. (The recent trend in the industry has been toward smooth and shaved guys, but that seems to be changing. Hair is coming back, and more and more people seem to be wanting the "natural" look.)

There are other ways to mix and match. For instance, you could take some pumped-up, gym-perfect body like, say, Scott Randsome, and balance him with someone like Hank Hightower, who's built pretty well but not in that hours-at-the-gym kind of way. By that I mean, maybe he doesn't have the flat, rippled stomach, but he's still very, very sexy and turns a lot of people on.

You can also vary dick sizes. Of course, some size queens will want every dick they see to be ten inches or more, but again, I think it's better to have some variety. An awful lot of guys appreciate a nice, manageable cock that will fit in their mouth, so it's not vital to me that a performer have some enormous, ponderous piece of equipment. Those guys can't always get it totally hard anyway.

There are so many guys to choose from nowadays, more than there have ever been before. This makes casting both easier in one sense (because there's so much variety) and harder too (because there's so much variety). It's like shopping in a supermarket versus shopping in a convenience store: You may have a much, much bigger selection, but that makes it more difficult to find the product that works best for you. You can choose from two brands of pain reliever, or you can choose from twenty brands. This is the director's dilemma.

I have a few personal favorites, maybe five to ten guys I would use over and over if I could because they're sexy, they're easy to work with, and they're known performers who will give me what I'm looking for without a lot of coddling and fuss. They're friends, and they're true professionals. But while that might please me and make my job easier, it wouldn't be too wise from a marketing point of view. So I'm always looking for new guys and new combinations to keep things fresh and exciting.

Most guys are represented by agents, and you usually have to go through their agent to get somebody signed. This can be the ugliest part of the business because it involves negotiating over money. Let's face it, if I wanted to squabble over finances, I'd be wearing a business suit and sitting in some office building somewhere. But porn has become such a big-money business, it's come to be unavoidable.

Making It Big: Sex Stars, Porn Films, and Me

So if I want to cast someone for a movie, I call their agent first. Oh, I have a few stars with whom I'm close enough to call directly, but I still end up, before it's all over, fighting over fees with their manager. The vast majority of guys working now have agents, although some — like, for instance, my personal assistant, Jordan Young — still don't. In Jordan's case, he's my right-hand man, and he knows that I'll look out for him and won't let him get screwed over. But for most guys, agents are their only protection against some of the more unscrupulous elements in this industry (and you'd better believe there are a lot of them).

The hardest part of negotiating with agents is when you're also friends with them on a personal level. That was the case with me and David Forest, superagent to the stars. David was the biggest agent in the industry in the mid 1990s, and he represented me in addition to most of the working A-list stars of that time. From a director's stand-point, David could be somewhat difficult to work with in booking a movie. He was from a traditional background of booking bands and nightclub acts (he represented the '80s metal band Quiet Riot), and he brought that sense of impor-tance to his negotiations over his clients and their movies. Sometimes he acted like he was booking Madonna's next world tour when he was really only booking some little-known porn performer for one scene in some obscure movie. But then, it is the agent's job to get the best possible deal for his clients, so I guess that's what made him so good at what he did. What was aggravating about David from a director's or a studio's point of view was precisely what made him so good when he was representing a performer. (And when he was booking me for live shows around the country, you can bet I appreciated that quality in him.)

David not only got the big bucks for his clients but was the best there was at booking people to go on the road. That's a major source of income for both porn stars, who go out dancing and stripping, and for me when I go to do live shows. Let's face it, the guy in Cedar Rapids who doesn't ever get to Los Angeles or New York to see porn performers in person is going to come running to see them doing go-go at his local gay bar. Touring is a major, major source of revenue for those of us in this industry.

Depending on the studio you're working for, budget constraints can be the major factor in casting a film. Some studios give you carte blanche to pay what you have to to get who you want. Others give you a certain amount to work with, and you have to stay within that. For instance, when I've worked with VCA or when I did *Lost in Vegas* for All Worlds, I didn't have any financial limits. I was free to do things like, say, rent the helicopter from which we filmed the Las Vegas skyline shots for *Lost in Vegas*, and I was free to pay my performers pretty much what they asked for. As you might guess, this is the preferred situation to be in for a director. The freedom to pursue your vision results, I think, in better pictures. But with the smaller studios and low-budget movies, you can't do that; you have to make do with what you have. For instance, David Forest sometimes asked for $2,500 for a scene for one of his guys when I could have gotten two or three lesser names for that kind of money.

The moviemaking process.

The creation of a porn movie begins with someone coming up with a concept. In the past, before I had a personal assistant, I would turn that concept into a script myself, carefully considering just how many guys I was going to need. I would factor in how many two-way scenes I had planned, how many three-way or orgy scenes, and how many guys were going to do more than one scene in the film. Once all of that had been decided, we usually ended up with a cast of eight to twelve guys. Now, since Jordan joined me, I can come up with the concept and describe it to him, and he'll write the script for me accordingly, which makes my involvement that much easier. He's really very good at it.

Once you have the idea fleshed out, you turn your attention to the cast. Sometimes, when you're writing a script, you just know that a part will be a perfect fit for a certain performer. Other roles are more open, and you can consider any number of guys for them. When I cast, I use what I call my "active file," a book full of Polaroids of guys who are currently working and available to use. I take this book with me on the road (and to my casting sessions at Falcon), and I'm constantly adding people to it and deleting people from it. In one recent week, for example, I added five new guys to it; since I'm meeting people all the time, there's never a shortage of new faces to consider.

By the same token, I delete old names just as fast. Most recently I removed one guy who had been deported back to Belgium and another who was sent to jail. Porn stars aren't the most stable people sometimes, so there's a constant flux of available performers. On any given day there are maybe fifty different people in this book, and there are actually more than that available. Names I know, people I've worked with before and am sure of their professionalism and availability, might not necessarily be included, but I know of them and that I can call them. Cory Evans and Jake Taylor, for example, are two popular performers who aren't in the book. The book is for people I'm not necessarily personally familiar with.

When I wrote Cory Evans's role in *My Sister's Husband*, I knew from the outset that he was the guy I wanted for that part. When I did *Lost in Vegas*, on the other hand, I knew the kinds of characters I wanted, but I didn't have any specific people in mind. I ran through a lot of different ideas before I finally cast the drunk (Alec Danes) and the prostitute (Dave Russell). I gave one of the other prostitute roles to Jordan because he wrote the script (and is a good actor and a good performer as well). I gave him the concept and got him started, but he actually authored the script, and he added the part of the naive hooker who was killed. So he's the one who got that part.

Jordan's scene in *Vegas* was with Logan Reed, who was at that time his real-life boyfriend. When you start casting real-life boyfriends together, that's where you get into some dangerous territory. You might think on the surface that it would work well, but that's almost never the case. Sure, the lovemaking is authentic — authentically sweet and tender and kind and gentle, exactly what you *don't* want in a porn film. For porn you want dirty and raunchy and sleazy. It's hard to be a dirty porno sex pig with someone you actually love. That was the case with Jordan and Logan, although they eventually got rolling and did a great scene. It just took a while for that "porno drive" to kick in, and that's time you can't always spare on the set.

One real-life couple who can perform together convincingly is Eduardo and Sam Carson — they're both just pigs! Also, Ryan Wagner and Bryan Kidd, who were a couple for a long while, did a good oral scene in *Lip Lock*. But both of these are exceptions to the rule.

Once your script is written and your cast is set, then you start scouting locations. Finding the right locations is really one of the most difficult parts of this process. Personally, I like to use a lot of strange and different locations rather than just shooting in a hotel room or someone's living room. I go more for things like sex clubs, bars, warehouses, exotic places like that. In fact, I like nothing better than going out of town to shoot. I love seeing different cities and sleeping in motel beds; it inspires me and really gets my creative juices flowing. I find it extremely motivating to be away from my home and familiar surroundings, away from the constantly ringing telephone and the mundane hassles of day-to-day living. It's an escape, kind of, and an incentive to do some good work.

If you can get your cast and crew together and get out of town, it gives you the chance to really bond and have some fun with the people you're working with. In 1996 I went up with John Rutherford to shoot a Falcon flick near the Russian River in Northern California. And it was like being on a road trip with a group of close friends: We stayed in a remote cabin way out in the woods, and at the end of the day, when the work was done, we would all sit around a fire and laugh and talk and just get to know each other. I even barbecued for the whole gang. It was one of the best moviemaking experiences I've had because it brought us all very close together. By way of contrast, it makes going to someone's house in Los Angeles, shooting by the pool, then going home to your own bed seem very boring and impersonal. I like being around people; I'm very codependent, so the more people around, the better I like it.

The only thing about shooting on location is, you need a really good cast and crew who can all get along. If there's a lot of bickering and infighting, the whole thing can be spoiled. And it takes only one bad seed to do it.

When we were filming *Idol Country*, that bad seed was Ryan Idol. Now, Ryan's not really a bad guy, but he's known for being kind of difficult to work with, for pulling attitude sometimes. And during the filming of *Idol Country*, we were at each other's throats the entire time. We shot a lot of it on a farm up near Sacramento, and he was very, very demanding about what he wanted and what he would do. Usually I'm pretty accommodating about these things, about stars (especially major ones) and their little quirks, but this situation was over the line. Ryan was not working with the team at that point. I mean, we're all in this together, and we need to work together toward the common goal of a good finished product. But at that time Ryan Idol had his own agenda. He was having tantrums virtually every day on the set. At one point, when Steve Marks had spit in his ass, Ryan screamed at us, "Nobody spits in Ryan Idol's ass!" and threatened to come after me with a baseball bat if I left that in the final cut. Things got so bad that when we were finally finished, I swore I'd never work with him again. I don't necessarily feel that way anymore, since I think he's matured and mellowed out a little, but that set was just a really unpleasant experience for all of us. No one man is bigger than the rest of us, and there's no reason for anyone to behave like that much of a diva. If I can't, damn it, nobody can.

Making It Big: Sex Stars, Porn Films, and Me

I have developed plenty of contacts through my years in the business, so finding good locations is easier for me now than it is for a lot of people. The name Chi Chi LaRue carries a little clout as well. But for whatever reason, there is rarely a shortage of available locations for my films. A lot of people like the prestige of having a film shot in their house (or on their land or whatever), and it is kind of cool to see the finished product and know, *That's my couch those guys are screwing on, and that's how it got all those strange stains!*

A standard location fee ranges anywhere from $200 to $1,000 a day. Some people will do it free, though; Michael Trygstad, the guy behind Wet lubricant, is one who's let me use his house without a location fee. We compensated him with product placement, leaving bottles of Wet around the set and making them highly visible in the film. (He has an immense place in the Hollywood Hills, by the way. The personal lubricant business has been very good to him.)

Still, you have to be careful; not every place lends itself well to shooting porn. Generally, you want to be in as secluded an area as possible, especially if you're as naturally loud as I am. I don't scream — I *project.* But if I'm directing a flick, you *will* know I'm there.

On one occasion we were shooting in the backyard of this house in Hollywood when the owner of the house got a rather indignant call from the lady who lived next door: "Hello, I have my young niece and nephew visiting from New York, and there is something going on over there where the director of this so-called movie keeps yelling things like 'Fuck that ass!'" Well, that wasn't good; that's the kind of thing that can bring the law down on you, private property or not, so we — well, *I* — had to tone it down that day. I'm not ashamed of what I do, but I don't want to force it on people who don't want to know about it; that's not fair to them. I especially don't want to give any minors an explicit sex education before their parents want them to have it.

Incidents like that one are pretty rare, all in all, but it's nonetheless wise to do what we do in private, secluded locations.

Nothing is more crucial to a good moviemaking experience than a good, qualified crew. For me, that means people I've worked with before and whose abilities I'm sure of in advance. A weak link in the crew can really damage a movie, so it behooves you to know what you're getting. I hire my own crews (as opposed to letting the studio assign me one) because I want to know that.

A good crew works as a team, with no petty jealousies or individual agendas. For me, the fewer people running around the set, the better I like it. Too many cooks may not spoil the broth, but they sure water down the taste. And a big crew can really be a drain on a movie's budget. For me, the ideal crew is a party of five: me, the director; Jordan, as my personal assistant; a cameraman; a production assistant, or PA; and a makeup artist.

That can vary depending on the studio. On Falcon sets, for instance, John Rutherford will likely be there to work the camera, while on Catalina or other sets, their own people will be there. Every studio has different preferences and requirements.

Still, I have my favorites I prefer to work with, and some others I refuse to work with. If there's a bad experience on a set, I'm not likely to work with that person again.

John Rutherford is one of my favorites to work with because he's an outstanding director as well as a great cameraman. He and I help each other out when we work together, because he knows as well as I do what goes into a good movie. If I'm not "feeling it" quite right that day, he'll step in and pick up the slack. Then if he's the one who's not quite "feeling it," I can step in for him too. For some people that would be too many cooks, but John and I are able to put our egos aside and function well together for everyone's benefit.

Bruce Cam, a well-known camera whiz in this business, is another guy who's valuable to have around, although he's a little more opinionated than John, and we're a little more likely to see things differently. But with the multiple cinematography awards he's won, it's hard to argue with Bruce. You're lucky to have him around.

Once you have your cast, crew, and location and the start of shooting is imminent, it's time to stock up on whatever supplies you're going to need. Certain stuff is going to be standard on the set of any porn movie: condoms (a must in the 1990s), douches (cleanliness is next to godliness when you're talking about anal sex), lube, paper towels, snacks, and whatever props you're going to need (dildos, tit clamps, hot wax — it depends on the movie). I'll normally go out and buy these just a day or two before we start filming, and if we discover a need for anything while we're actually shooting, then I can send the PA. *Production assistant* can be a nice term for *gofer.*

Great Lengths

As you can imagine, we go through a lot of condoms. How many you will need depends on your top man. A great top, like Daryl Brock, can be fine with one or two: He stays hard and is enough of a veteran and a professional to give it to you right the first time. Other guys, however, who aren't perpetually hard can go through as many as two boxes of twenty-four in a single fuck scene! They're up and put it on, then they're down and take it off, then they're up, then they're down, up, down, up, down, etc. And when they go down, they'll pull off the condom and throw it away, since they're never reused. Nothing is funnier, in fact, than watching Chris Green, a onetime performer himself who now frequently assists me on my sets, going around with his rubber gloves and picking up condoms that have been strewn wildly around the room.

You also need to have your wardrobe prepared by the time shooting begins. I usually oversee the wardrobes myself; one, because I love to shop, but two, more importantly, so I can make sure the clothes fit right with how I see the scene. Since I pay for most of these outfits out of my own pocket, I want clothes that can be reused from film to film.

For *Roll in the Hay*, I had to outfit the cast in flannel shirts, jeans, and cowboy boots; for the *Total Corruption* flicks, it meant a lot of police uniforms and accoutrements (billy clubs, badges, hats, sunglasses). For a lot of flicks, the generic ones, anything tight and sexy will do, but for movies with specific themes, the right costumes are very important.

I'm not really into props, but in the right circumstances they can facilitate a scene. In *Alley Boys*, for instance, a Catalina flick I directed under the name Taylor Hudson (when I first started directing for Catalina, they didn't think Chi Chi LaRue sounded masculine enough, so they created a name for me by combining Elizabeth Taylor's and Rock Hudson's. And they were worried about *my* masculinity?), we shot at this warehouse that had an enclosed area in the back. It had previously been just an alley behind the building, but it had been covered and fenced in, so it was perfect for filming. The platforms on which all the rimming in that movie occurred were already in place, and they were perfect for those scenes, so I had no reservations about using them. They were at just the right height for guys to lie back on with their legs in the air, and guys who were kneeling on the ground had their faces right at butt level for easy ass eating.

In my *Boot Black* films, Bruce Cam specifically designed the wall of water that we shot through to create that shimmering, dripping effect. Bruce has also used things like ceiling fans to create odd effects with shadow and light; he's very, very talented at dreaming stuff like that up.

Technology is improving all the time, making it easier and easier to create special effects, even in porn movies. But anyone who thinks that computer effects are going to replace the basic human element isn't getting what porn is all about. Look at Gino Colbert's *Night Walk*, for instance: a fabulous film, a landmark in the history of gay porn, and the special effects were pretty incredible. But in my opinion the sex in *Night Walk* left a little to be desired. It was too much about the cool effects and not enough about the hot male-to-male sex. Too many half-hard dicks.

Great Lengths

The critics loved *Night Walk,* and it was expected to spawn a whole flock of imitators. But if people produce a hundred more just like it, it's going to get real old real fast. I just found it a little too sterile. The accolades for that movie should really go to the computer whizzes who did the backgrounds and special effects. The real skill of being a director, I think, lies in directing *people. That's* what porn is all about, and no amount of morphing gargoyles or virtual-reality sex will ever change that.

Once all the preliminaries have been taken care of, the shooting can actually begin. I'll usually get under way around 9 or 10 in the morning and do one scene (or at most two) a day. It doesn't move as quickly as you might think.

First there's the makeup and grooming of the performers. Most of these guys don't require a lot of makeup, but if they have visible blemishes, such as scars or big zits on their butts or cigarette burns from a kinky trick they took home the night before, we'll have to cover those up. For many years we've been shaving guys down to the bare essentials (a small patch of pubes), and while the natural look seems to be making a comeback lately, we still need to remove any stray hairs and trim back what's too long and bushy. Normally we'll trim pubes and the perineum, the area between the balls and the ass crack. Then, once all that's finally done, the actual shooting will begin.

In film as well as in real life, there are several different elements to gay sex. Let's take them one at a time:

Oral sex: Personally, this is one of my favorite things to do, both as a director and as a faggot in my own right. Oral sex is *the* single most important element of gay porn. You can sometimes get away with movies with no butt fucking or no rimming, but if there's no cock sucking, you're in deep trouble.

For the head giver, the same qualities that make one good in real life make one good on film. But there's one additional factor that may not come into play in a dark bedroom but is important on a lighted film set: Beyond all else the sucker must *look* like he's enjoying it, like he's savoring every precious second that beautiful dick is in his mouth. The expression on his face is going to be very visible to the viewer, so you can't have any distortions like sneers, grimaces, or scowls; he must communicate his pleasure at sucking dick to the home viewer who's watching. This is done with the eyes and with grunts and exclamations, little "mmphs" of pleasure.

Most vital of all — and I cannot stress this enough — is what we in the industry call "good length." This refers not to the length of the dick being sucked but rather to the amount of dick moving in and out of the sucker's mouth with each stroke. There must be a distinct up-and-down motion, with as much of the cock as possible sliding out on the upstroke and in on the downstroke. This is easier with a bigger dick, of course, but even a moderate-size dick can display good length if the sucker goes all the way down to the base, then all the way back up to the head.

It's wise to vary a sucker's speed. A slow and teasing suck with a lot of tonguing around the head, up and down the sides, and around the piss slit balances out the more hot and frenzied bobbing. Some guys just move up and down, up and down, like they're working out and can't wait to finish their reps and get done. That's all they do, and it gets boring. It's better to mix it up. Go fast and hard for a while, then try slow and easy.

I tell suckers not to forget the balls and the area behind them. Balls are very erotic, and seeing them licked and nibbled and rolled in and out of a cocksucker's mouth provides a nice complement to the dick, which is, of course, the main course.

The dinner analogy is a good one, in fact, when you're talking about oral sex. The dick is the entrée and deserves most of the diner's attention (just as it receives most of the cook's). But for a well-rounded meal, you need several courses, and so it's important to remember your side dishes, such as the balls, nipples, asshole, and perineum. For a healthy, happy dining experience, be sure to clean your plate!

The skilled cocksucker has admirable control over his throat muscles and can go all the way down on even the largest dick without gagging. It's a definite no-no to go down so far that you throw up all over your partner. Among the best I've worked with are Damien (maybe the all-time greatest; that boy could get a dead man hard), Matt Bradshaw, Derek Cruise, Bryan Cruz, Chad Donovan, Chris Green, Brian Maxx, and Jordan Young.

The suckee, the guy who's receiving the blow job, must also communicate his pleasure to the viewer. In his case this can be primarily verbal: His mouth is not otherwise occupied (unless it's a sixty-nine or three-way scene), so he's free to moan and growl and gasp and scream and break into song. Again, body language is important. It's a must when you're being blown for your eyes to occasionally roll back up into your head. Your arms and legs should flail as much as is feasible but not so much that you whack your partner or knock over a camera. Also, thrust those hips; it's really hot to look like you're fucking a face. The hands should clutch wildly at whatever's within their grasp: hair, carpet, pets, shrubbery. Every blow job, when it's received on film, should be treated by the recipient as the best one he's ever gotten.

Anal sex: Oral sex may be more common (and it's definitely easier to do on film), but nothing is as closely associated with gay porn as anal sex. Guys are known as "tops" or "bottoms," and there aren't too many in the industry who can be, as the French say, "convertible." But for a lot of viewers, blow jobs alone just won't do it; they're just a warm-up for the real action, which involves the pounding of an upturned butt.

A lot of what makes oral sex good also makes anal sex good. The primary concern for both partners is communicating their pleasure to the viewer. Again, this is done both verbally and through body language.

The most important thing to have is a good top. A good top can not only get hard on demand but stay hard for as long as it takes to film the scene. You may think that's not so tough, but a good fuck scene can take as much as four or five hours to get right. (In contrast, a good oral scene may be done in an hour.) There are breaks and interruptions you can't plan for, and they can be really distracting to someone who's not a complete professional.

A good top gives you the same "good length" described in the oral sex section and can be as tough or as tender as the film calls for. Certain films have rougher tones — i.e., rape or punishment scenes — and require hard, painful, brutal fucks. Other films can be sweet and romantic and call for gentle, loving fucks. Some guys are more suited to one of those roles than the other, so one who can pull off both can be very valuable to a director. Among the best tops I've worked with are Matt Bradshaw, Daryl Brock, Tony Davis, Sam Dixon, Cory Evans, Ace Harden, Chase Hunter, Mike Nichols, Jeff Palmer, Joe Romero, Aiden Shaw, Jake Taylor, Ryan Yeager, and Kurt Young.

A good top alone, however, is no good to anybody. A good top requires a good bottom, the yin and yang of gay porn. Bottoming ain't no picnic either.

First of all, most porn performers are hung better than average. So anyone who wants to bottom in porn must be able to take *really big dicks* up their ass. Also, since these scenes can take so long to do properly, the bottom must have stamina. A bad bottom is one who stops your filming every five minutes screaming, "No! Ow! Take it out! Take it out!"

Bottoms, of course, must be clean for their scenes, and this is done by giving them enemas before filming. This becomes standard practice after a while, and to most guys it's as routine as brushing their teeth in the morning. You don't even think about it, really, until you have an unfortunate occurrence where someone is *not* quite clean.

The ass is a very versatile thing, and dicks aren't the only objects that can go up them. As the years have gone by, I have gotten more into the other aspects of ass play. It's an area where I've learned an awful lot from John Rutherford. John is an anal aficionado, and so, especially when working with Falcon, I've expanded what I do with people's butts.

It was John who turned me on to the pleasures of finger fucking and dildos. It was John who led me into things like chains and zucchini. It was John who taught me what was hot to watch about anal sex.

For example, when I was doing *Family Secrets*, there was a scene where Steve Cannon was to be dildoed by Jake Taylor and Sam Crockett. When we started the scene, though, John stopped us and stepped in to show us how to do it better, how to manipulate the dildo to get that "good length" and end up looking hotter on film. And when I looked at the finished product, he was right — it was a fucking amazing scene!

Among the best bottoms I've worked with are Jake Andrews, Jake Cannon, Max Holden, Tom Katt, Bryan Kidd, Joey Stefano, Alex Stone, Ryan Wagner, Adam Wilde, and Jordan Young.

A truly gifted performer is one who can go both ways, who can top and bottom with equal skill. There aren't a lot of these guys around, so they're very valued in the industry. Among the best of recent times are Drew Andrews, Rob Cryston, K.C. Hart, Hank Hightower, Steve O'Donnell, Logan Reed, Donnie Russo, and Zak Spears.

The thing about anal sex nowadays is that condoms are so necessary. For a lot of people, this diminishes their enjoyment. But all the major studios have come into line on this, and I think it's really important. We are in a position to influence a lot of people, and it would be grossly irresponsible, considering how many members of this industry we've lost, to show unprotected sex now. It took us a while to get everybody on board, but now it's almost impossible to find a movie where condoms aren't used for the fuck scenes. I think it's a credit to this industry that we've addressed this issue. Someday, God willing, we'll be able to show unprotected anal sex again without the fear of anything being spread.

Rimming: This is something that's not to everyone's tastes, but I just adore it. You see a lot of rimming in my movies. To me, it's really stimulating to see someone's face buried up a hot ass, and it's even hotter to see the close-up tongue action. Also, if you've ever had it done to you, you know how great it feels.

Rimming also requires cleanliness, of course, though usually a good shower will do it in place of a complete douching. A good rimmer, like a good cocksucker, will show you how much he's enjoying it. It's the gay-porn equivalent of cunnilingus in straight porn. Watch a straight porn actor giving head to a woman, and similar techniques can be applied to produce good rimming. The tongue should be worked over, around, and up inside the asshole with a variety of speeds and motions. Gentle biting of the ass cheeks can provide a nice complement.

Some guys, however, balk at sticking their tongue up another man's butt. Some guys simply refuse to do it (although I don't recall anyone ever objecting to having it done to him). Some guys who wouldn't normally do it will do it for me. And some viewers just aren't turned on by it. But there is a market, as evidenced by the success of some of my rimming flicks.

Take, for instance, *Alley Boys*, that flick I did for Catalina in 1996. There is no anal sex in this movie, but there's all the rimming you could ever want. I just piled guys on the platform I mentioned earlier with their legs in the air, then had the rimmers kneel on the ground and go at it in a very long session. Critics and butt fans alike loved this movie, and it remains a special one to me.

Making It Big: Sex Stars, Porn Films, and Me

While sex is sex pretty much the world over, doing it on video does change some things. There are a few components to making porn that vary from your normal bedroom routine. Foremost among these is:

The come shot: Nothing in porn — not the blow jobs, not the fucking, *nothing* — is more important than the come shot. It's the big payoff, it's what everyone is waiting for, and that's why they call it the "money" shot. You know how unsatisfying it is to have sex and not get to come? Well, don't you get the same feeling of incompleteness when you watch a porn scene without the big geyser at the end? It's the natural, inevitable conclusion to everything else you've worked for. If it doesn't happen, it's just not right.

When you're talking come shots, it's tempting to say that more is better, but that's not always so. More is good, no doubt, but for me (and most of the industry), *farther* is better. It's all about distance. A guy doesn't have to cry me a river if he can send a stream flying across the room.

When a guy comes, the amount produced and distance shot is something that's only partially under his control. I mean, some guys can blow five times a day and produce a good load every time, while others can hold off for a couple of days and still not produce a whole lot. There are biological reasons behind this that aren't really the point here. There are, however, things you can do as a performer to increase your distance and volume.

Some guys swear by certain foods, saying that egg whites or seafood give them bigger orgasms. Others take vitamins or natural products like yohimbine. A myth that is really widespread among porn viewers is that zinc is the cause of guys' gushers. That's not true, at least for me; some guys may take it beforehand, but no one on my sets is force-fed zinc or anything else to make sure they come buckets.

What I have found — and I think other directors will back me up on this — is that the most important factors are the length of time a guy keeps it up and how stimulated he is. If you have been hard and working it all day long on a set, you're going to come a lot more forcefully than you would after a quickie ten-minute jerk-off.

It's also wise to abstain from coming for one to two days before you're scheduled to do a scene. This ensures that you've stored up as much as your body can produce and that you're horny when it comes time to pop. This is a really fine line you have to walk, however. If you wait longer than a day or two, you may come too fast, and on a porn set that's a major offense. Even worse, you may come in having abstained for a week and being just insanely horny, and then...you can't come. Believe it or not, this happens. It can happen no matter when your last orgasm was, of course, but it seems to become more likely the longer you wait. You wouldn't think it would be a problem, what with the increased sensitivity you get after going a few days without, but for some reason it does. So I have found that one to two days is the optimum period of abstinence for moviemaking purposes.

Among the guys I've worked with, several stand out for the quality of their orgasms. If you've seen *Download* (not my film, but a good one), you know that Cole Youngblood is one of them. In that movie Cole did a scene where he actually did eight streams of come! Watch it, if you haven't already; it's one of the hottest come shots ever captured on video.

Logan Reed is another new guy who can really pop a load, and K.C. Hart always provides dependable gushers as well.

Where a guy comes is pretty important too. It's not acceptable to come in someone's mouth anymore (God, I'd love to show that in a video if I could), and coming up someone's ass, even in a condom, is no good because the viewer can't see it. This is why most porn-video come shots happen with guys jerking themselves. They can bring themselves off more quickly and more reliably that way, and it allows them to aim it where you need them to aim it, be it on someone's back or stomach or face or coffee table.

I also find it very erotic to see guys eating their own come. (There is a known risk to eating other people's, so it's not often done.) Again, some so-called "straight" guys won't do it, but there are guys who won't normally but who would for me. I remember one scene where I had Kyle Brandon come in Sam Crockett's hand, then Sam fed Kyle's come back to him. Afterward Kyle told me, "Oh, I don't believe I did that, I've never done that. But I did it for you."

Dialogue: Okay, we both know that dialogue is not the major aspect to any porn movie. Most of you probably watch porn with the volume down and the CD player on, and that's fine. But someone has to attend to things like dialogue and plot, and as the director, that's me.

Most porn flicks have some semblance of a plot, however weak. There needs to be a little something there to grab on to, something beyond just the sex. There are people who pay attention to such things (mostly the critics), and they'll raise hell if there's not some attempt at doing this. Now, honestly speaking, we're not going to weave a lot of suspense or intrigue into one of these things, and we're not going to be nominated for any Academy Awards. But it's nice to have some common theme uniting the sex scenes and something to break up all the sex.

The flip side to this is that, as you are all (sometimes painfully) aware, these guys are not actors. That is to say, they may perform in movies, but they are not trained thespians who cut their teeth on Shakespeare. Sometimes, as hard as they try, bless their little hearts, they just aren't real convincing in delivering their lines. A director's task is to help them through that as well.

As a director, I know in my head how I want a line delivered. I know the inflections and the enunciations and the expression that's supposed to be on the face of the guy saying it. The trick is communicating that to the performer. Sometimes it's not very easy. Some guys pick it up very quickly, but others require hand-holding and being walked through, syllable by syllable. Filming the dialogue, believe it or not, can be just as time-consuming and much more frustrating than filming the sex.

I am not real great at directing dialogue, but I've tried to learn from those who are. Jerry Douglas, for one, has helped me immensely. Jerry is an acclaimed dramatist who has directed much more than just porn, things like off-Broadway plays, so he knows what he's doing in terms of that. Jerry and I are actually direct opposites in regard to dialogue; if a line is delivered close to the way I want it, I'll be happy with that and take it. Jerry's more of a perfectionist and will make guys repeat their lines over and over until they satisfy him. That aspect of his work is apparent in *Flesh and Blood*, which won Best Video of 1996 at both of the industry's major awards shows, the Gay Erotic Video

Awards and the Adult Video News Awards. (He also won Best Director at both, beating out me and *Lost in Vegas*, the bitch.)

If you can get a performer a copy of a script in advance, that provides an advantage in doing the dialogue. Unfortunately, it's pretty rare that you can do that. More common, in fact, is for me to be sitting at my computer the night before filming is to start, finalizing the dialogue then.

If you can get the script done in advance, you can do read-throughs with the guys who'll be delivering the lines. I was able to do this with Dave Russell and Alec Danes in *Lost in Vegas*; it allowed them to work out any bugs and be a lot smoother with their lines when we started filming. And in *Songs in the Key of Sex*, Randy Mixer, the poor guy, had to learn all of these songs to lip-synch, so he had to start rehearsing his part well in advance. But these are rare instances, and performers usually won't know their lines until they show up for filming and you tell them.

Dirty talk during sex is something that's pretty important in video. The fact is, people get off on it, even if it's just "Fuck that ass. Yeah, fuck that hot ass." And you better believe if we don't script the dialogue in advance, we're not going to script the dirty talk. Generally, it doesn't require quite as much coaching as the nonsexual dialogue; since most guys do it in their own bedrooms anyway, they can improvise pretty convincingly on the set.

When a guy comes, it's important to let the viewer know. Who knows, a viewer might have wandered out to the kitchen for a snack, and they should be alerted so they don't miss the come shot. So I encourage loud orgasms — as long as they're natural-sounding. I don't like fake screaming, and believe me, you can tell when it's fake.

The late Tyler Regan, one of the stars of *Secret Sex 2*, was one of the loudest screamers in the business. And when we did *Lost in Vegas*, Michel d'Amours nearly blew the lid off the hotel where we were filming. I had to stand over Michel saying "Shut up! Shut up! Shut up!" for fear that the other people on the floor would think someone was being murdered.

Group scenes: I've always believed in the more the merrier in porn scenes. Two is good, three is better, and orgies are the absolute best. There is just something so wild and decadent about orgies; they really capture what I think this industry is supposed to be about.

Each of my *Boot Black* movies ended with orgy scenes, and to this day they remain among my favorites that I've done. If they're done right, orgies can be very easy to shoot: You just move the camera around, and wherever you point it, there's something hot happening. I don't think you can have too many guys in an orgy. I had about ten in the *Boot Black* finales, which I think was a good, manageable number. More recently I did a scene with fifteen (All Worlds' *Dirty White Guys*). That too will eventually be surpassed.

You cannot script an orgy. Well, you could, but I don't think it would work well. It needs to be natural, spontaneous, unrehearsed. Basically I just tell the performers to go to it, and we'll see what happens.

Casting is important in that everyone must be totally into it. You don't want to cast any straight boys for group scenes; they'll get squeamish and look unconvincing. What you want is a group of pure gay sex pigs, guys who would be into it even if the cameras weren't on. Like Wolffe, for instance, in the first *Boot Black:* He was perfect. Too perfect, in fact, because he was so excited that he came too soon, in about two minutes, and had to do the rest of the scene soft. He still did all of the sucking and everything I asked him to, but he couldn't get hard again.

In general, you try to coordinate the come shots. I didn't do that in the first *Boot Black*, which made it hard on Dave Kinnick, my cameraman. Everybody was popping at separate times, unannounced, and Dave actually missed a few come shots. Normally that's an unforgivable thing in a movie, but orgies are the one time you can maybe get away with it. If nine guys come, odds are, you're not going to miss the tenth.

Behind the camera: Without a firm script, it's hard to tell in advance how long a movie will be. They should be a minimum of sixty minutes, but usually however long they work out to be is how long they are.

As the director, I watch everything happen from a monitor in a room adjacent to the one where the sex is being filmed. A common misconception about porn is that there are all these people running around just out of sight while the performers are doing their thing. That's usually not true. I've told you about the crew, that it's relatively small, and there just aren't a lot of visitors and looky-loos allowed to hang around and get in the way. Since the sound equipment is so sensitive and picks up a lot of extraneous sounds (phones ringing, doors slamming, cars going by outside), it's important to have as controlled an environment as possible.

On most sets only the cameraman is actually in the same room as the performers. (And there's usually only one of him. Catalina will often use two cameras, but they're the exception.) By watching on a monitor, I can see how each shot is framed and know what it's going to look like in the finished product. And by being so close, I can offer comments and instructions without actually interrupting filming.

As far as camera angles, each cameraman has his own style and technique, and each brings his own unique individual talents to his projects. I'll know in my mind what I want to see, but sometimes these guys will show you something in a way you hadn't imagined before. Some directors aren't open-minded to stuff like that, but if an idea is good, I'm not going to turn my nose up at it.

Personally, when filming sex, I like to see it all: When a person is being blown, for instance, I like to see his face along with his dick during his come shot. I like long shots, but extreme close-ups just don't do a lot for me; they're too clinical, too sterile. For all you know when you see a long, tight close-up, it could have been switched in from another movie.

The dick is not necessarily the most important thing when you're filming sex. That's why I rarely do glory hole scenes: I want to see their faces, their bodies, their expressions. I would never suck a dick through a glory hole for this same reason: I want to see a guy and touch him and experience more than just the one part of him. A man has many wonderful parts.

Generally, we go back afterward and do things like zooms, pans, and cutaways, and they can be mixed in later during the editing process.

Then what?: For each sex scene, each of which runs about fifteen to twenty minutes, we will need approximately sixty minutes of raw footage. So by the time a movie is filmed, you end up with three to four times more actual footage than you're ever going to need.

That's when you pass things along to the editor, who will cut out the bad parts and mix and match the good ones to make the scenes as strong as they can possibly be. Now, some directors don't like to give up this control; they like to oversee and butt their big egos in, telling the editor how to do his job. I'm not one of those. If you're going to give a person a job to do, I say let him do it. After all, the editor's not looking over my shoulder while we're filming, telling me what makes good sex, so why should I tell him how to do his job? I will go through the footage and note things I think are especially good or especially bad, but after that point it's up to him.

When the editor is finished doing his thing, he'll give me what's called a "rough cut," and I'll go through that and suggest any final changes. Then it goes back to the editor, who'll finish up things like the sound track. That involves not only adding in music where necessary but deleting any of my voice that's been accidentally caught in the filming process. Since I'm a big, loud drag queen, this happens fairly frequently; getting all my comments out of a sound track is probably an editor's worst nightmare. I talk all the time during filming, and it can't just be filtered out. The editor will actually have to stop the sound track, delete the section, and replace it with music or dubbed-in lines from someone else. (Some films are done with all music, no dialogue at all. I hate those, but there's a place for them, and I've done my share.)

The editing process generally takes anywhere from two weeks to two months.

Marketing the product: The box cover may be the single most important factor in marketing a video. You need to show on the cover the one guy (or two, maybe three) who is either the star of the movie or the prettiest boy in the cast, and you're depending on him to sell that product from the shelves at the video store. That's all the advertising you can do besides ads in certain print publications, so it has to be effective and immediate. A good box cover can make the difference between a movie's success or failure, and choosing the cover model is not a decision that should be taken lightly.

In the event that you have a major-name star — like, say, Jeff Stryker, Ryan Idol, or Ken Ryker — the decision is a no-brainer. Those guys could sell *commercials* if you put their sexy picture on the box.

Since I did art direction during my early days in the industry, I think I can tell what makes a good box cover. Most times I'll suggest some performers and some poses, then leave a still photographer to snap a series of Polaroids. I get approval rights on these, and the best one will become the movie's box cover.

The only studio that does things differently is Falcon. When doing a Falcon flick, we'll take individual photos of every guy in the cast, and the best one of those will be the box cover. For Falcon it doesn't necessarily have to be the star.

With other companies I get a lot more freedom. For the *Lost in Vegas* cover, for instance, I came up with the concept, rented the props, and picked the models — basically the works. The result was a very distinctive box that showed stars Dave Russell, Logan Reed, and Alec Danes in briefs in front of a black background with big neon playing cards and gaming tables.

A good box cover is stylish, is different, and will catch your eye from the rack at the video store. (Nude or almost-nude men are a must, of course.) Among the companies around today, I think Vivid Man has just about the best box covers, certainly the most creative. They used to fall into the trap of airbrushing too much, taking the character out of people's faces, but they seem to be doing that less lately. I don't like too much prettying-up to be done; it leaves the models looking too feminine, too plastic. Conversely, other companies don't airbrush at all, which is also not good. You don't need to see every wrinkle and pore and pimple and nose hair on a guy at close range.

Some guys make doing box covers easy: Zak Spears, Jake Andrews, Lex Baldwin, the late Joey Stefano — these guys were (or are) so photogenic, they simply couldn't take a bad picture. Lex may have been the easiest to shoot of any guy I've ever worked with. Everything about the man was perfect: his face, his body, his dick. He was simply blessed.

Other guys are cute in person or on film but for some reason don't come out so well in still pictures. Maybe they don't know how to hold their heads right or use the light correctly. With so many beautiful men around today, though, that's rarely a problem. Other guys photograph *better* than they are in person.

Once changes are made to the rough cut and the movie is in its final version, it could be available by mail order in as quickly as a week. Films are generally offered by mail order first, both as a perk for a company's hard-core fans and because the companies can charge more money that way. After they're out by mail order it can be as long as six months before they hit the shelves at your corner adult bookstore.

My only involvement after this point is to put on a dress and a wig and get out and promote the thing on the road. Depending on the budget of a flick and the fanfare surrounding it, I'll do a major-market appearance or two or sometimes even a whole tour. When *Idol Country* came out, my agent, David Forest, booked Ryan Idol (another of his clients) and me on a cross-country tour. The fact that the tour was a borderline disaster, with Ryan and me at each other's throats, didn't detract from the success of the movie.

Ryan didn't totally have his act together at that time, and it came to a head one night in New Orleans at a Bourbon Street club called Oz. For whatever reasons, Ryan chose not to strip that night, as the crowd had been promised, and instead told everyone how much he hated everything about the porn biz. Well, when he got backstage I ripped into him pretty good, telling him that if he was going to talk down the porn industry, that I wasn't going to be on the road with him, that it was my business too, and now I had to go out and promote his stupid movie and justify that I'd made it. That evening probably wasn't pleasant for the crowd at Oz, and I know it damn sure wasn't pleasant for Ryan Idol, but he did keep himself more in line after that. Everything was okay between us by the next stop in Indianapolis — which was, in fact, the very night I discovered Ryan Wagner — and Mr. Idol and I were able to remain good friends.

Other aspects: Like I said before, a good porn flick is all about the sex. You can't fake the sex; if it's not good, then you're doomed from the start. Beyond that, however, there are other production values that go into making a film good.

Location and story line are important, both of which we've already discussed, and personally, I kind of have a thing for special effects. Not car crashes and explosions and *Terminator*-type stuff but artsy, MTV-ish rock video effect. In *Sex in Wet Places*, for example, I mixed in four loops of black-and-white footage. Sepia tone, slow motion — anything to be different and stand out in a genre where the sameness can be mind-numbing. That's why I introduced drag queens into some of my videos. They're funny, they're entertaining, and they really break up the monotony. Some people might not like it, and I'm under no illusions that hordes of people find us incredibly sexy, but as long as it's not too big of a distraction, it can be something to have a little fun with. After all, gay men pay good money to watch us lip-synch in nightclubs, so surely no one's going to object to a brief comic-relief scene in a porn flick.

I first cast drag queens in *Jumper*, a film that caused a lot of controversy but also won Best Gay Video at the 1991 Adult Video News Awards. I've also appeared in drag in films more times than I can count. One of the best experiences I've had on film was my pool wrestling scene with Sharon Kane in *Revenge of the Bi Dolls*. That was a fun movie, which I define as one you can watch, then rewind and watch again without the sex scenes.

I can't tell you that they've all been winners. Early in my career (and even more recently), I've directed some real stinkers. In my early days with InHand I would just slap things together with no regard for the big picture. One of those that still haunts me was called *To the Bone*. It starred Joey Stefano, Andrew Michaels, and Brett Winters as members of an oral-sex anonymous club who sat around and told their stories. I look back at that one now, and it seems really stupid, though at least some of the sex was good. Matt Gunther and Steve Kennedy did a scene together that was incredible, but for the most part it was boring, boring, boring.

Private Parts for Mustang (not the Howard Stern film; mine was originally called *The Diary*) was another one that was a real horror story. It starred a bunch of new people, and nothing went right; every single scene was like pulling teeth. The stars couldn't get it up, couldn't get along, couldn't come. By the time we finished that one, I was certain that my career was finished, and I didn't want to go on.

Newcomers to the industry can be a real headache, but it's a situation everyone has been in at one point. I remember one rookie — who shall remain nameless here to spare him further embarrassment — who had never douched before but was supposed to as preparation for his first bottoming scene. Well, things were crazy on the set that day, and no one ever explained to him how to fully complete a douche. So this guy, the poor thing, filled his butt with water and thought he was supposed to hold it in! No one had ever told him that you're supposed to let it go and leave it all in the toilet! So he comes out and starts his scene, and as he's getting fucked, the top (who shall also remain nameless, as shall the film; I could never name the names in this story!) pulls out of his ass, and *everything* comes pouring out. Water, shit, the works. It was a catastrophe, the top freaked out, and the poor bottom was humiliated. I did the best I could to reassure him, but actually I was fighting not to die laughing. On the upside, the guy eventually recovered his dignity and went on to a successful film career.

Other films I've slept through even while directing, and I mean that quite literally. It was a Catalina flick, and while the sex was going on, I wandered upstairs, lay down for a moment in a spare bedroom, and actually fell asleep! I awoke to find Catalina's Josh Eliot standing over me screaming — a terrifying sight if ever there was one. But it got my attention and scared me into a renewed dedication to my work.

As a result of that embarrassing scene, I now try to get as much as I can into every movie I direct. It's not always easy. The projects come continuously, one right after the other, and it's easy to get burned-out after long periods of uninterrupted work. But then, when you do a film where everything works right and you *know* it's a killer, you're completely rejuvenated and ready to go again.

I actually feel like I've done some of my best work lately. *Lost in Vegas*, which was released in September 1996, was maybe my all-time best. *Total Corruption 2* and *Alley Boys* are other recent efforts that I think came out well. *Alley Boys* was one of those without much of a plot, but the cast was really hot and worked well together, resulting in some nice, raunchy sex.

Since *Lost in Vegas* didn't do as well as I had hoped it would at the 1996 awards, I'm taking that as a challenge to do even greater stuff in the future. I can top that. You don't ever want to make Chi Chi mad.

LESBO A-GO-GO
OR
WHAT DOES A GAY MAN KNOW ABOUT STRAIGHT AND LESBIAN PORN?

YOU MAY BE SURPRISED TO LEARN that a big fag like me has directed straight porn. It's true, though. Early in my career I worked with women. My very first time on a set was for a straight flick, *Tracy and the Bandit*. Later, once I had broken into the business in a real way, I freelanced for a while and directed some films for companies like Soho and Las Vegas Video. Drag movies, bisexual movies, solos, boy-girl, boy-boy, girl-girl — I've done it all.

Recently I've gone through a long hiatus without working with women. That wasn't something I did intentionally; it was just that as I achieved so much success doing gay films, all of my energies were pulled in that direction. The success built on itself until I ended up doing nothing but gay films. Hopefully, with the blessings of companies like Catalina and All Worlds, I'll be able to get back to working with the girls eventually.

Compared to working with the guys, working with the girls is a breeze. Obviously, you don't have to wait for a hard-on, and you don't have to be worried about your star not being able to get it up. Even if the partners in a scene hate each other, the scene is a snap if they can act at all. Girl-girl scenes go just like *that*. I made *Lesbo a Go-Go* in four hours, start to finish.

Of course, just as some of the guys can be prima don-
nas, some of the girls can be too. Any beautiful person can
become arrogant if he or she doesn't watch it. Jeanna Fine,
one of the best-known and one of my favorites, can be one
of the biggest divas in the world. When Jeanna arrives on
the set, she comes in and takes the place over. She'll
announce, "We're going to do this this way, not this way,
and I'm not going to follow this script." As you can imagine, she's a director's nightmare. (Not that that's stopped
her from working. She had major nonsexual roles in two of
the flicks nominated for Best Video at the 1996 Gay Erotic
Video Awards: All Worlds' *Flesh and Blood* and *Our
Trespasses*. She won for the latter.) I tend to let Jeanna get
away with more than some people do because I know she's
good and the film will usually be better for whatever it is
she does. Some directors, though, are put off by her abra-
siveness, which I can also understand. Some won't even
hire her anymore because they're afraid of her reputation.
She's a good sexual performer, though, if you can deal with
her attitude.

Most of the other women I've worked with — Bionca,
Tiana, Angel Kelly, Patricia Kennedy, Madison — aren't in
the business anymore. Sharon Kane, a good friend with
whom I've done so much wonderful work over the years,
is the exception, and that's because she still looks fantastic for her age. She must be at least...well, wouldn't you
like to know? (I'm not telling her age; she's a friend. Aren't
you listening?)

The only female star I ever "discovered" was Tracy
Wynn. Her boyfriend brought her to me and wanted me to
get her signed, so I took her in to Vivid. Tracy was gorgeous, but Paul Thomas at Vivid was put off by her for

some reason and wouldn't even consider her. So I ended up doing two movies with her for other companies. One was a kinky bisexual/cross-dressing flick for Catalina called *Steel Garters*, and the other was a vehicle designed specifically for her called *Introducing Tracy* for Pleasure Productions. She did a scene with T. T. Boy in that one, and one with Nick East and Jon Dough. Sharon Kane, Nina Hartley, and Victoria Paris all had roles. If you're a straight guy who somehow started reading this book by accident and have stuck with it to this point, there's a flick for *you* to check out.

Basically, the gay and straight porn industries are very much the same, with the obvious distinction of who fucks whom (the agents are the same, though; they fuck everybody). They do feed you better on the straight sets, a result of their bigger budgets. And straight films are made more quickly for the reasons outlined before. Three to four sex scenes a day is normal for straight films, while in a gay flick you're lucky to finish one a day.

Very few guys move back and forth between the industries. Even at this late date, there's a good amount of homophobia on the straight side and a lot of blacklisting of guys who have done gay films. A number of guys will start doing gay flicks even though they're not gay, and once they discover that they can't fake being into it, they'll move over to the straight side. Then a box cover will come out, and word will get around that they've done gay, and the jobs will dry up. And they'll be forced back to the gay side that way.

Girls who do bi films get blacklisted the same way. It's totally stupid, because all of the fucking in gay films is safe now, *all* of it, and in straight films these girls are still eating come, being fucked without condoms, taking it up the ass, you name it. We'd be crucified if we tried that in gay films. No fluids are ever exchanged in my films, and condoms are used in every single anal penetration. Still, doing gay is a good way to get out of the straight business. It's sad to say it this late in the 1990s, but it's homophobia, plain and simple. Some of the guys who do straight porn still think you can catch AIDS just by walking into a gay bar.

It's true that guys in gay porn are generally better-looking than guys in straight porn. For all our shortcomings in the gay community, no faggot will ever pay money to watch some of these guys fuck. I have a theory that straight guys don't want to see guys who are better-looking than they are fucking these beautiful women. They want to see guys who look like they do. Or, even better, guys who are uglier than them and can make them feel studly. Of course, there are some handsome men doing straight porn — T. T. Boy, Alex Sanders, Rocco — but by and large, most of them couldn't cut the mustard for me or for you reading this book.

Gay men, on the other hand, appreciate male beauty and want to see it. It's been shown in studies that most consumers of pornography, gay or straight, are men. Women just don't use pornography in the same way men do. Men are more visual; they get their stimulation visually, while women get theirs mentally or emotionally. I've spoken to a lot of lesbians who have watched lesbian videos, and they hate them! They feel like dyke films are made for men, and they don't like that they star these perfect, beautiful Barbie-doll women with huge breasts and tiny waists and flawless features. They're just not real. They're not lesbian videos; they're girl-girl videos made for men. If I ever put women in my movies, it's designed to appeal to straight and bisexual men, not lesbians.

My plan for the long-term future is to venture back onto the straight side of porn and dabble in that a little more. I'd love to make a straight flick with subversive gay twists, like maybe a woman fucking a man with a strap-on. I'd love to make a straight version of my *Boot Black* films, and I think I still have the contacts on that side to make it happen. Chris Mann, the guy who gave me my first chance at Catalina, is now at Video Team, another major straight-porn player. All it would take is a phone call. I wonder how he feels about drag queens in nonsexual roles.

On Your Knees, Punk
OR
The Many Stars I've Discovered

Oh, the men I've known. Oh, the men I've loved. There have been many, too many to count — hundreds, thousands maybe, way more than I can keep track of (is your mouth watering yet?).

The best part of this job, being one of the premier gay porn film directors in the world, is the beautiful, beautiful guys I've been so fortunate as to work with. No one has a right to have known as many buffed, gorgeous men as I've directed; it's almost unfair for one man to be so lucky and to have so much. It's an embarrassment of fleshly riches.

And the best thing is that they come to me now, lavishing me with gifts and favors (sexual? Wouldn't you like to know!), trying to gain my directorial benevolence. As the number one, most famous director in gay porn, I hold their fortunes in the palm of my sweaty little hand.

Okay, so I exaggerate a little. I hardly run the industry. You can see, though, what an appealing situation it is to be in. Because I'm known and people want to work for me, I have a lot of freedom in who I can cast. It's a luxury, and I'm privileged, I know that. I'm not saying that I have the power to keep someone out of the business if I don't like him (I would never be that malicious), but appearing in a

Chi Chi LaRue movie is certainly a good way to establish your credentials.

Thus, I get a lot of people coming to me wanting to break into gay porn. I get letters, I get photos, I get people coming up to me in bars and restaurants and on the street. "Chi Chi," they say, "just give me a shot. Please, just one shot." And I say, "On your knees, punk."

Just kidding. I don't believe in the casting couch, never have. It's an abuse of power, and it's not ethical. I won't tell you that such things don't go on in this industry (or in any industry that operates out of Hollywood), because they do. It's almost a prerequisite for a lot of producers. But that's not the way I do it.

In my early days in this business, when I was working in promotions and screening models for possible use by my companies, I certainly had the opportunities. I used to have potential new discoveries come over to my house and take off their clothes to pose for Polaroids. I could have told any one of them that they had to put out to be considered. But I never did. That part of the job felt dirty enough as it was, and I didn't want to cross that line of professionalism. Too many guys do, and I think it's vile. Especially if you look at some of the directors involved.

In determining if someone has what it takes to make it in gay porn, I look at several factors. There are three that are the most important: body, face, and dick. Body and face are pretty self-explanatory; we need a body that's at least moderately toned, if not bulked up to bodybuilder proportions, and we need a face that people won't cringe at. It doesn't have to be spectacular, but it can't make little children cry. Then as far as dicks go, well, we need one that works. And one that's not grossly misshapen or anything.

It can't make big lecherous drag queen directors cry. I'm not a size queen, so it doesn't have to be enormous. What I look for is if a guy can get hard (and if so, how quickly) and if he can come. Generally, I say that if a guy has two out of these three attributes — body, face, and dick — then he's someone I can work with.

When these guys would come over to my house back in my days of screening new discoveries, I'd have them strip and get hard for pictures that I would then take back to my bosses for consideration. If a guy was to work in gay porn, he'd have to be able to get hard pretty much on demand. When I snap my fingers, you jump to attention; that's the way it works. We can't waste time on the set for guys who need hours to flog themselves into some semblance of hardness.

My way of testing them was this: I would give them whatever stimulation they felt they needed — not physical stimulation but magazines, videos, lingerie, whatever they wanted — and then leave the room. (I didn't want to put the extra pressure on them of sitting there slobbering and watching while they whipped themselves up to full glory.) Then when they were ready, they would call me back in to take the pictures. This didn't *always* work; some guys do need the "human touch" to really get into it. But if that's the case, then they can find fluffers on the set. It's not something I'll do for them.

I have what I guess is a pretty good track record of discovering new performers and/or turning average nobodies into stars. A lot of the guys I've helped along the way have become some of the biggest names in the industry: Joey Stefano, Ryan Yeager, Zak Spears. There are a lot more, including quite a few of gay America's current favorites.

On Your Knees, Punk

People have told me that I have my finger on the pulse of gay porn consumers. I'm not sure about that, but I do know what I like.

Because I have such a long list of discoveries, people think that I have the power to make them in this business. So when a naive little rube from the wheat fields of Kansas wants to take his stab at greatness, guess who he calls. Right: me.

There's no way I can put all these guys who want to be in my movies in my movies. Nor would I want to. Nor would you want me to. Some of them just don't have what it takes, and no way in hell, even after six months of not getting any, would you ever want to jerk off to them.

But once in a while I'll come across a guy who has that special something, and I'll know I've found a true gem. Sometimes you just know by instinct even before you ever get them on the set. It's all about star quality, that great, indefinable aura of glamour and fabulousness. If you have that trait, you can't hide it. Heads will turn when you walk into a room, and prospective sexual partners will throw themselves at your feet. If you have it, you could dress in a feed sack and still radiate *star*. If you don't have it, you can't fake it. You'll just never have it.

With the late, great Joey Stefano, I knew it from the second I laid eyes on him. That's usually the case; star quality seldom lurks under the surface. Sometimes you can cultivate it, learn to use what you have a little better, but mostly it's a natural thing. Joey (his real name was Nick Iacona) fairly glowed with it. Even Madonna knew it; she absolutely adored him. His death in 1994 was by far the greatest loss suffered by the industry since I've been a part of it.

The biggest stars I've discovered or broken in to the business have this star quality in common. Here are capsules and film recommendations for some of the best and brightest.

Joey Stefano: Okay, so I didn't personally discover Joey. I have to give credit where credit is due, which is to Tony Davis, a major porn player of the late 1980s and early 1990s. Tony brought Joey to me, and Joey promptly eclipsed Tony's fame, leaving him in the dust. All I had to do was the easy part: show Joey to the world.

Tony was in New York City to dance at the Show Palace. There he met Joey, who wanted to break in to the business. So Tony brought Joey with him to Los Angeles and introduced him to me.

I was shooting the box cover for *Sharon and Karen*, the bisexual and transvestite flick I was making for Las Vegas Video. And I remember that when Joey first walked into the room, I stopped dead in my tracks. I felt like someone had thrown ice water in my face. I got chills, goose bumps the size of little nipples. I remember thinking, *Oh, my God, it's the next Tom Cruise.* Joey had that same dark hair and brooding look, the same smoldering intensity, that same striking beauty. Something in my head was screaming, *S-u-u-uperstar!*

Joey is one of the few people in my life I think I've actually been in love with. And I think it happened that first day, pretty much instantaneously. Sharon Kane (the *Sharon* of the film's title) and I both latched on to him immediately. As I got to know him and what a beautiful, wonderful person he was on the inside as well as on the outside, my feelings only increased. A long, emotional roller-coaster ride began for me that day in 1989, and it didn't end until Joey's death five years later.

The first couple of weeks after I met him were simply a matter of finding the right way to get Joey started. He was too good to just throw into any old flick; he needed a vehicle befitting his status as the next porn superstar. He needed a film that would adequately display his talents (which were not, may I add, confined to his striking good looks. He was sexual dynamite as well).

Joey had long been eager to break into porn, and he even had a list of guys he wanted to work with. Of course, most of them, like Chad Douglas and Cole Carpenter, were retired from the business by that time, but Joey took that disappointment with grace. Anyway, I finally found him a movie that would do him justice: *Buddy System 2*, the sequel to the Ryan Yeager feature *Buddy System* that I had done earlier for Vivid Man. Actually, Joey also had a scene in *Sharon and Karen*, and I truthfully don't remember which one he did first. They were both filmed at about the same time, and they're not always released in the same order in which they're filmed. Plus, he worked with Andrew Michaels in both movies. Joey worked with Andrew a lot, actually, because I had a much smaller circle of stars I could use in those days. Besides Joey and Andrew, there were Ryan Yeager and Tony Davis, and the four of them appeared in virtually every movie I did for a while in the early '90s.

Soon after that I took Joey with me to Catalina, and we did my first really outstanding movie, *Billboard*. Joey was *so* easy to work with then; he could have been a model for performers in the industry. He could get hard at will, he could take direction, and if he was really turned on by a partner, his sexual performances were pure magic. Unfortunately, he was easier to direct in the early days than he was after a little time in the industry; as his personal life deteriorated, it began slowly to spill over into his professional performances.

Besides *Billboard*, Joey did bang-up jobs for me in films like *Songs in the Key of Sex* and a hard-to-find InHand flick called *Fond Focus*. As time went on, though, the temptations of the fast-paced porn world began to take their toll on him. His drinking and drug use increased, and he got in this downward spiral that no one could seem to break him out of.

The beginning of the end had come on a trip to New York around 1990. We were staying with my friend Scott (the Weather Gals' June), and Joey went out to the store and came back with a bottle of peach schnapps. He had been completely sober when I'd first met him, but on that night he finished that bottle. From then on it degenerated into more and more booze, then more and more drugs, leading finally to the hard stuff: cocaine, speed, ecstasy, and heroin, the use of which eventually killed him. The next four years were a painful slide downward as he gradually became less and less in control of his life, a descent that has been well-chronicled in at least one book about his tragic end.

Still, Joey could do no wrong in my eyes. I was blinded by my affection for him, and anything he did to me, no matter how cruel or thoughtless, I could always find it in me to forgive. We never did have sex, though he was a sexual compulsive who would go out when he was bored and pick up tricks off the street. It was a long period of hell for me; many times I would drop him off at his place or at a friend's, then drive home crying to myself out of frustration and my love for him.

When the end finally came in 1994, I was on a set, shooting for Falcon with Danny Somers, Steve Marks, and Chad Conners. We were waiting for Joey, who was supposed to do a scene. The night before he had promised me he'd stay sober, but as time went by and he didn't show, I started to get a really bad feeling.

I called home to check my messages, and there was one from Crystal Crawford, a fellow drag queen who's also involved in the porn industry, telling me that Joey had overdosed and was in desperate condition at Cedars Sinai Medical Center. John Rutherford and I jumped in his truck and rushed immediately to the hospital, where we met Crystal and Sharon Kane. Sharon had to pass herself off as Joey's fiancée for us to be allowed in to see him. Then a doctor came out and told us that Joey had "expired." The euphemism didn't register on me at first; I just couldn't comprehend. I had to ask again: "Is he dead?" He was, gone of an overdose — heroin and special K, an animal tranquilizer — at the tender age of 26. Whether it was a suicide or a tragic accident is something that's never been fully determined.

Joey was also HIV-positive, and this might be a good place to discuss models who have HIV. It has been charged that I knowingly cast Joey with actors who were not infected. That is absolutely not true. If it becomes known in this industry that someone has HIV, even though all the sex is now safe, his career is pretty much over. No one will cast him, and most guys won't work with him. I am not saying that no one in this business has HIV; some certainly do, and there's always a certain amount of gossip about people's status. If there are guys who are positive and working now, it's because they've been able to keep it a secret, and directors who cast them don't know about it. We can't pry into people's medical records, so we have to take them at their word. If HIV ever got spread on the set of a porn film, it would be an awful, tragic thing and a lot of guilt for a lot of people to live with for the rest of their lives. It's in no one's interest to let that happen, so we go about our business as if *everyone* was HIV-positive. HIV is not going to spread on my set.

I think Joey's death is the hardest thing I've had to experience in this business. It was just so unfair that one so beautiful and so talented would be taken from us so abruptly and at such a young age. There's a lot I wish I had told Joey, not that any of it would have made any difference. To this day I count him as my greatest discovery, my greatest contribution to this business. I still miss him, and I still cry sometimes thinking about him.

Recommended films: *Billboard, Buddy System 2, Songs in the Key of Sex.*

Zak Spears: Zak is from my neck of the woods, Minneapolis, so we've always had a really good rapport. Also, he's so fucking hot, and I think it's really important to have good relationships with guys who are really hot. Don't you agree? Then, on top of all of that, he's an auto mechanic. So of course I invited him to live with me in my home, which is usually so full of porn stars that we've dubbed it the Porn Motel, and fix my car whenever it broke down. You wouldn't believe how some unethical mechanics will try to cheat a man in a dress!

On Your Knees, Punk

Zak is another one who always wanted to do porn. I met him through a mutual friend, porn star Joey Morgan, one night at the Gay '90s nightclub when I had gone back to perform there. His voice — deep, resonant, and sexy as hell — grabbed me immediately. I hadn't seen him without his clothes on, but I remember thinking, *If he has any kind of a dick, he's going to be a superstar.*

So I asked him then and there in the bar to take off his clothes. And to my surprise he did, pulling off his shirt and even opening his pants. I knew then that we had a winner both in terms of physique and personality. When he did that without so much as a second thought, I knew he was going to be fun to be around and cool to work with. And looking at his long torso, all his body hair, his long arms, and that handsome face...well, he's the kind of guy who makes my job easy.

The funny thing about Zak's discovery was that about six months earlier he had sent pictures to all of the major studios. And Falcon, Catalina, and the rest — every one of them — had all rejected him because he was too hairy. So when he went on to stardom, I took a certain pride in finding one the others had missed.

A few nights after that first meeting, I went over to Zak's house to appraise the rest of the package. I had him strip, and I took some Polaroids of him naked and hard. And I was delighted to see that his dick matched the rest of him: 100 percent perfect. I flew him out to L.A. for his film debut a month later.

His first film was *Model Behavior*, and I had him paired with Wes Daniels, a big star of that time. Like a lot of guys, though, Zak had an attack of nerves when it actually came time to do the dirty deed. Zak was supposed to top, but he had what we in the industry call "wood" problems. To put it bluntly, he couldn't get it up. So I switched their roles and had Wes fuck Zak, which turned out all right. Then the next day Zak showed up for a scene with Alex Carrington, and the nerves were gone. He took to it like he'd been doing it his whole life. He was a different person: wild, uninhibited, an animal. Again, perfect. He tore up the screen and never looked back.

Zak was the original studly, hairy man in porn. Before Hunter Scott or Hank Hightower, Zak set the standard for hairy guys. Even today, when someone is really hairy, who are they compared to but Zak Spears? And his voice! Oh, God, he has one of the deepest, sexiest voices ever to grace a porn movie. His personality was great too; he was a sweet, innocent, childlike soul who worked regularly after *Model Behavior* — even for Falcon, which doesn't go for hairy guys — and never did a single bad scene. He's out of the business now, unfortunately, and working as a personal trainer in L.A.

Recommended films: *Model Behavior, Total Corruption, Posing Strap.*

Alex Stone: I met Alex at the Four Star nightclub within a couple of years after coming to L.A. I was just about to start directing, and we hit it off really well. He loved drag, and we had similar senses of humor — basically he laughed at everything I said, which I loved, because I get off so much on entertaining people. The best way to suck up to me is to laugh at my jokes.

Still, he had to be persuaded to make the leap into porn. I thought he was good-looking, and I'd asked him several times to do a movie for me. But he never gave me a firm response — he always hedged. So when he finally decided to do it, it took me by surprise. I was onstage at the Four Star doing a show, and he came up to me and passed me two pictures of himself naked and hard. I was so excited, I almost passed out. I jumped off the stage and ran after him, chasing him across the bar, and when I caught him I asked, "Are you ready?" He said yes, and so I put him in *Flexx*, the first movie I directed.

Alex was basically a top then, although he's versatile now. He's had some peaks and valleys in his career, dabbling in drug use and piercing parts of his body, but he's cleaned up for the most part and now looks as fresh and clean as the day I first met him. He's a true pro to work with, and I still use him when I have a role that's right for him.

Recommended films: *Flexx, Lip Lock.*

Michael Brawn: Another big one of the early '90s, Michael dropped by Catalina while I was working in promotions and screening models there. Michael was a radio announcer from Chicago who walked in sporting a big, grisly mustache and enough bronzer on his face to make him look Latino. Despite that, I had him take his clothes off, and he had a fantastic body and a huge dick — there was definitely potential. So I told him to go back to his hotel, shave his mustache, and get rid of the bronzer, all of which he did. And the next day he came back, and he looked like a totally different guy. He was gorgeous, like a god. I immediately put him into *A Friendly Obsession*, and he went on to a successful career.

In general I like facial hair, and I especially love goatees and 5 o'clock shadows. It was just that the mustache didn't work on Michael. Some guys can wear them, and some guys can't. You have to be able to judge.

Recommended film: *A Friendly Obsession.*

Making It Big: Sex Stars, Porn Films, and Me

Steve Marks: Like Michael Brawn, Steve was from Chicago, where he too had a background in mass media. Steve was actually a television weatherman who was let go by his station for some reason or another. I didn't actually discover him, but I helped make his name by casting him as the country cousin in Ryan Idol's *Idol Country.*

Steve had done one film for another director before I met him on the set of *Hard Body Video Magazine No. 4,* where I was shooting segments with Aiden Shaw and Peter Bishop. He was kind of impressed by the fact that I was Chi Chi LaRue, and I was impressed with his fresh face and blond hair and great personality. I thought he'd be perfect for the cousin role, which was clear in my mind but not yet cast. And he was. We quickly became close, and I had him move into the Porn Motel for a period. He worked a lot for a while before leaving the business in 1995.

Recommended films: *Courting Libido, Idol Country, Secret Sex 3.*

Jordan Young: What makes Jordan unique is two things: First of all, he's half Korean, so he fills a niche in the industry for people who want to see Asian men. To my knowledge, there are no other porn stars of Asian descent making gay movies at the present time. (Ryan Wagner claims some, but he doesn't really show it in his appearance.) Second and more important, since Jordan moved in with my gang of porn boys in the fall of 1995, he's become my personal assistant, and I couldn't function now without him.

We call my house the Porn Motel because at any given time there will be three or four porn stars living there with me. At the time of this writing, Jordan, Chris Green, and Dino Phillips are all under my roof, either temporarily, because they have nowhere else to go, or more permanently, as paying tenants. Adam Wilde and Dax Kelly have just recently moved out. Jordan is the shepherd to my ever-changing flock.

He was dancing in Denver in 1995 and was being represented by an agent, Dan Byers, who I thought wasn't really doing him right. Jordan was a big porn fan who wanted to break into the business and had even been in contact with John Rutherford. But Dan had told Jordan that because of his Asian descent, he'd never be more than a bit player, a filler in movies that showcased other, bigger stars. I knew that wasn't true. Jordan has striking good looks, and I knew there was a niche there for Asian guys because a lot of people were always telling me they wanted to see them.

So I flew him out to L.A. to do a movie, *Night Watch 2* for Mustang. He was a talented bottom and a natural performer, and he was fucked in that film by Cory Evans and Mike Nichols, earning everyone's immediate respect by taking two of the best tops in the business.

Still, it was uncertain that he'd stick with it. Jordan had done some modeling, both print campaigns and runway appearances, but essentially he was a farm kid from a small town in Wyoming who was scared to death of the big city. So at that point he did his film and flew straight home. It took another five months for me to convince him to move out here permanently. But since then he's made himself an indispensable part of my business dealings and a damn good friend too.

Jordan handles all the little business items that could bog down someone like me, who's not a detail-oriented person. He pays the bills, organizes appointments, runs errands, gets supplies for the set, and picks up the occasional model at the airport. He keeps the house clean, which is a full-time job in and of itself. (If you want to dispel that stereotype that all gay men are neatness fanatics, just come over to my place sometime.) Basically, Jordan started as the guy who would pick up around the house because he couldn't stand it being dirty, and his role has grown into being my right hand. (Well, no, he doesn't have to do *that* for me.)

In addition, he's a creative mind who's destined to do more in this business than just take big dicks up his ass. While Jordan has appeared in about fifteen or twenty films to date, he's written probably close to a dozen as well. Plus, he writes a column for *Skinflicks*, "New Kid on the Cock," and is even authoring mainstream independent film screenplays.

I think we've become such close friends because we're so much alike in so many ways. We like the same music, we like the same food, we have very similar tastes in men. We have a lot of the same emotions — we're both pretty sensitive and get hurt easily. And we have *the very same* sense of humor. Sometimes just a look between us can set us off, and we'll both just be rolling on the floor over some stupid, insignificant little thing. Everyone else around will look at us and look at each other, like "What the *hell* are they going on about?" And to them I say, "Nothing. Never mind."

Recommended films: *Lost in Vegas*, *Total Corruption 2*, *Night Watch 2*.

Ryan Yeager: After I moved from InHand to Vivid Man early in my career, Ryan was one of the first boys I broke in to the biz. A friend of mine who shall remain nameless, someone within the industry, got these teeny little photos of a boy in the mail. They were small and fuzzy, and you couldn't really tell much from them; the guy looked cute, but you couldn't be sure. But because my friend was unhappy with his employer, he passed these photos on to me, a competitor. I thought they were worth a follow-up, so I called Ryan up, and we clicked well over the phone. The photos he'd sent weren't real enlightening; one was a runway shot, the other a smiling facial portrait. But he was a nice, sweet guy, and we bonded from that very first call.

I was actually making movies for both InHand and Vivid Man along about then, and I put Ryan in a flick called *Buddy System* for Vivid Man. It was a cute script, all about a military camp, and it turned Ryan into one of my staple stars. I paired him with Andrew Michaels, with Ryan as the bottom. He was naturally a top, though, and it was hard for him to get fucked, so we had to fake it. Yes, I admit it now, that scene was faked. We didn't use a stunt dick; we just didn't show any actual penetration. Still, it came out pretty good.

After that, Jim Steel and I wrote a script for Vivid Man that showcased Ryan, a '50s-era flick called *Davey and the Cruisers*. To this day people still love that film. I had a role in it too, though it really wasn't my film, it was Jim's, and it was one of my favorite experiences. Ryan also did a film for Jim called *Air Male*, and he and I went on to become very good friends.

Ryan later starred in *The Rise*, which in 1990 won me my first Adult Video News Award for Best Director, and Stan Ward later wrote *Jumper* specifically with Ryan in mind. That one won Ryan a Best Actor and me my first Best Video award, both from *AVN*.

Ryan's dick was not huge, but he was a fantastic performer who deserved to be as big as he was. He got hard quickly, and he could always give me a second come shot whether I needed it or not. Sadly, Ryan eventually hooked up with a boyfriend who pressured him to get out of the business, and I'm not in contact with him anymore. I believe that Sabin, of the *Gay Video Guide*, called him last year about presenting at the Gay Erotic Video Awards, and Ryan told him rather curtly that that part of his life was in the past. Too bad.

Recommended films: *Buddy System, Buddy System 2, Davey and the Cruisers, Jumper.*

Andrew Michaels: Another star of my early years, Andrew was just a nice, cute little straight boy from Orange County, Calif. I was at Vivid Man and had advertised in the local gay rag *Frontiers* seeking new faces, and he answered that call. (It was at about the same time that I found Joey and Ryan.) I didn't get a lot of memorable guys from those ads, but Andrew was a good find. I put him in *Sharon and Karen*, and he worked a lot after that, though not for very long. He was in some kind of accident, I believe, and won a big financial settlement, so he no longer had to work for a living and quit the business.

Recommended films: *A Friendly Obsession, Billboard.*

Aiden Shaw: One of a very few major British stars in the industry, Aiden has a big, uncut dick that makes him stand out. He originally came over to my house along with a lesser-known video star named Danny Cocker. When I first met him, what struck me was how much he looked like Richard Gere (though to my knowledge Aiden has never been rumored to need any small animals extracted from his body cavities). I immediately wanted to put him into a film.

But though he was interested in doing video, Aiden was shy about taking his clothes off. He didn't want to undress with me there watching him. So I had to leave the room, and he would call me back when he was naked and hard. When I returned he wasn't shy at all, and what I saw was a fantastic body and that great big uncut dick, and I knew I had a winner on my hands.

For his first movie I put Aiden in *Ripped*, where he did a three-way with Wes Daniels and another actor. It was the start of a beautiful relationship between Aiden and Wes, who went from rolling around in baby oil on the bathroom floor to becoming actual real-life boyfriends for quite some time.

Aiden and Wes went out for a while, and then Aiden returned to London, where he was originally from. Even after that they maintained a long-distance relationship for a short time, but it eventually folded under the pressures of Aiden's other pursuits.

Those "other pursuits" mark him as one of the most intellectual, special people I've ever worked with in this business. Aiden is smart and talented and very artistic. Okay, he's a little bit weird too. He's known around London for his escort work, and he has started a band called Whatever that plays the club scene there. They have kind of an alternative, progressive, artsy sound that's very distinctive. In addition, he's written two books, one on prostitution, about his days doing escort work, and another of poems.

As I've mentioned, Aiden was one of the pickiest porn stars I ever worked with. He had to okay every single partner he worked with for every single scene he did, a behavior that a lot of guys couldn't have gotten away with.

Aiden got away with it because he was that good. I knew that if I paired him with someone he liked, the resulting scene would be something truly special. Take a look at his scene with Mark West in *Roll in the Hay* or his performance with J.T. Sloan in Ken Ryker's first film, *The New Pledgemasters.* He also did that great job with Alex Kincaid in *Boot Black 2.*

Aiden is no longer doing porn but is living in London and performing with his band (sometimes he'll even strip onstage) and pursuing his fledgling career as an author.

Recommended films: *Midnight Sun, Roll in the Hay, The New Pledgemasters, Boot Black 2.*

Damien: Damien had been a bartender at the West Hollywood disco Studio One before becoming one of the hardest-working actors in porn in the early 1990s.

I had seen him at the club now and again, and I'd always thought he was cute. I had even gone so far at one point as to propose his doing a movie, but he'd shrugged it off without ever giving me a real answer. But then he called me one day totally out of the blue and told me he wanted to do a film. So I had him come over, and we did some Polaroids.

I wasn't disappointed; he had a gorgeous body. He also, unfortunately, had this long, flowing hair that video companies didn't like. I didn't care; I thought it was beautiful, but the companies wanted it short back then. Plus, Damien had one of the most beautiful dicks I have ever seen. And on top of all of that, we really, truly got along well and became close, close girlfriends. We understood each other's senses of humor, and he laughed at everything I said. We were really good, really tight friends for a long while.

Unfortunately, Damien was also a little bit flaky about the business. He was on again, off again about whether he really wanted to be a part of it, and he said some things to a lot of people that weren't exactly true. For instance, he once lied to me about being mugged in New York. I don't know where his money went; he didn't do drugs, but I'm certain he just wanted more cash from me and had never really been robbed. In all, Damien was a little shady, I guess, but he had a lot of good qualities and wasn't a bad guy by any means. He lives in San Francisco now, and we still talk on the phone once in a while. In fact, he's even asked me about working again, and if he's serious, I know I can find a place for him.

Recommended films: *Bad Break, Inner Circle.*

Wes Daniels: Wes was a friend of Damien's, and I met him through Damien not long after Damien had started in the business. We were at a barbecue beach party with Sharon Kane, just sitting around drinking, and into the party walked these two boys. One of them just grabbed your attention and wouldn't let it go: He was unshaven and well-built and and just reeked of sexual charisma. It was Wes. But not knowing him, I jokingly said to Damien, "Look at that piece of trade that just walked in," never dreaming that I'd actually get him into films.

I left the party and went on home, and Damien and Wes ended up going home together that night. At some point Damien asked Wes if he'd be interested in doing movies, and Wes said he would. A week later I had him in a flick. And since Wes had been dating Damien, I put them in a scene together. (Hey, I wasn't born knowing that it's a bad idea to put lovers in scenes together. I had to experiment and learn from experience just like anyone else.)

So they were filming their scene, and Wes was being a real trouper, and Damien was being a real shit, full of attitude and pissiness and generally making things hard on everybody. The scene called for Damien to suck off Wes while Sharon Kane was lying there asleep on a bed with a face full of cold cream. And for all his shittiness, I have to say, that boy Damien could suck cock like nobody's business. He may be the best I've ever seen. When he brought Wes off, Wes shot so hard and so far that it hit Damien right in the eye (karma on the porn set if ever I've seen it). And the remarkable thing was that no one broke up, no one even giggled. In fact, no one broke character in the slightest. It was brilliant, and it preserved a fantastic scene that eventually made it into the movie.

Like Damien, Wes was really compatible with me, and we became really good friends. I used him a lot for a while before he got out of the business and retired to North Carolina. He did a show recently at the Eros Theater in New York, so he hasn't cut off that part of his life completely, but for now Wes isn't doing any more films.

Recommended films: *Jumper, Songs in the Key of Sex.*

Hank Hightower: Anyone who knows Mr. Hightower (his real name, believe it or not. With a name like Hightower, what other career could you have but porn star? It just sounds like a big dick) will tell you that he was truly one of the nicest people who's ever been in the business. An absolute, genuine sweetheart of a guy. And because his look was fairly unique — that is, he had a thick coat of body hair in a business where everyone else shaves down — and he wasn't a prima donna, he worked a lot.

Hank's discovery was a happy accident: He came to a bar called Capone's in West Hollywood to hear a friend play the piano, only his friend wasn't playing that night, so he sat down to have a beer instead. I was there with Wes Daniels and Chris Green, and I was out of drag, so Hank recognized Wes but not me. I thought his look would be perfect, though; there weren't a lot of guys in porn who had that look at that time. Actually, I thought he was a hustler. Capone's was always full of hustlers. So I called him over and told him who I was, and we got to talking. He lived in Long Beach and wasn't really working at the time, so I made him a proposition and gave him my card. He was kind of reluctant at first, but a couple of days later, he called me up and said he was ready to do it. I got him onto a set soon after that and was able to satisfy any doubts he had. After that he took to it easily.

One of the biggest reasons for Hank's success was that he was such a pleasure to work with. He would do anything you asked of him, he took direction very well, and he wasn't a complainer — he'd leave the set with the same smile he brought onto it. He was always cheerful and fun-loving, and he put the others around him at ease.

One of my favorite Hank stories came one night after our trip to a leather bar called the Eagle for the International Mr. Leather contest preliminary round. Hank and Donnie Russo (another well-known porn leatherman) and I went back to my house, smashed out of our gourds. Hank and Donnie were being very friendly with each other, and at one point they were in the bathroom together to take a leak. But then they got turned around and ended up peeing on each other, and I had the presence of mind to chase after them with my video camera.

At that time I favored women's leggings to wear. I thought they made my legs look small. Which they did, but they also made my upper body look larger by comparison, giving me the appearance of a giant lollipop. Plus, on top of that, I was wearing a tight lycra jumper I had just purchased at Bullock's, and I had put a leather jacket on top of it. So I had on this full ensemble of fabulous clothes, and here I am, frantically racing around trying to film these two hot porn stars peeing on each other. If you think this is a situation where I'm in some jeopardy, you're right. Donnie suddenly spun around, aimed his dick at me, and cut loose, sending an arc across the bathroom toward me. And though you can't see me on the tape, you can hear me shouting, "Oh, my God, don't, *you'll pee on my new jumper!*" He got me, but I don't remember if the jumper was ruined or not.

Due to his unmatched professionalism, Hank worked steadily through early 1996. He stopped working later in the year after moving to San Francisco with his lover, *The Advocate's* former editor in chief, Jeff Yarbrough. Who knows if he'll ever make a return?

Recommended films: *Total Corruption, Total Corruption 2, Lost in Vegas.*

Grant Larson: Grant is from Illinois, but I met him when he came to our nation's capital for the queer march on Washington in 1993. He came up to me in a club and started chatting me up, and sparked pretty well. He was wearing a pair of tight white shorts and a cock ring on a chain around his neck, so I thought, *Now here's someone I can maybe work with.* I started talking dirty to him to see what kind of reaction I'd get, but I couldn't rattle him. So I suggested that he come to L.A. and do a movie — he was running a painting and interior design firm back in Illinois — and I think *that* kind of shocked him. A little while later he called me from Illinois with some more questions. I basically told him the truth; not all of it was very pretty, but I didn't want to mislead him, so I told it like it was. I think he was impressed by that. And he ended up coming out in July of 1993 and becoming one of the bigger names in the industry for a while. He went on to win a Best Actor at the Gay Erotic Video Awards and a Best Erotic Performance at the *Adult Video News* Awards.

Recommended film: *Idol Country*.

Ryan Wagner: This one I found in Indianapolis. Or, rather, he found me. Ryan worked hard at being discovered — in fact, you could say he wouldn't let me *not* discover him. He had always wanted to be in porn, had grown up dreaming of it, and he just wouldn't be denied. He had come to this bar where Ryan Idol and I were performing, hoping to meet me and get his shot at glory. But apparently he hadn't been able to find me, and by the end of the evening, he was in a corner crying into his beer, brokenhearted. Meanwhile, Ryan Idol and I were outside signing autographs before we left. And I noticed this cute little boy standing off to the side, looking like he wanted to come up and say something to me but not quite having the nerve. So I made it easy on him and called him over: "Hey, what are you waiting for? Come over and talk to me!"

Given the invitation, Ryan told me that he might be interested in doing a movie. But since I was flying back to Los Angeles first thing the next morning, I told him I needed Polaroids at my hotel by 4 a.m. Well, he went home, shaved down, got a Polaroid, took the pictures, and got them to me before I left, sliding them under my hotel room door in the middle of the night. And two weeks later I called him from California and told him I had him cast in a Falcon movie (*Greased Up*) and to get his ass out to L.A.

Good bottoms are always in high demand, and because Ryan is such a good one, there's never any shortage of work for him. His exotic looks — part French, Japanese, and Brazilian — don't hurt either.

Recommended films: *Hard Hats, Like Father Like Son*.

Marco Rossi: Marco is a straight boy, but I liked him anyway, and we did some good work together. (And whenever a star of gay porn tells you he's "straight," you have to take it with a big grain of salt anyway. How straight can you be with a dick in your mouth?)

Originally from Queens, N.Y., Marco is full-blooded Italian; father was actually from Naples. I met up with him through Damien after Marco was brought out from Miami to dance at the White Party, a big porn event held each year in Palm Springs. Well, Damien told me that he had found this cute Italian boy and suggested that I put Marco in a movie, and even though I hadn't seen so much as a single picture of him, I took Damien's word for it. Damien knew talent, and who am I to turn down any cute Italians?

Score one for Damien. Marco had a hot body and a dick he could keep rock-hard, even if it wasn't that huge. I knew he'd be successful. I put him in a flick called *Mirage,* where he did an oral scene with Johnny Rey, and his career took off like a rocket after that. He worked regularly through the mid '80s before getting out of the business. He still does escort work, and rumors keep flying about a comeback project if the price is right.

Recommended films: *Total Corruption, Idol Country, The Look of a Man*.

Randy Mixer: Randy had actually done a film with Wes Daniels, *Alley Action,* before I was introduced to him. (That was for All Worlds, and he appeared under the

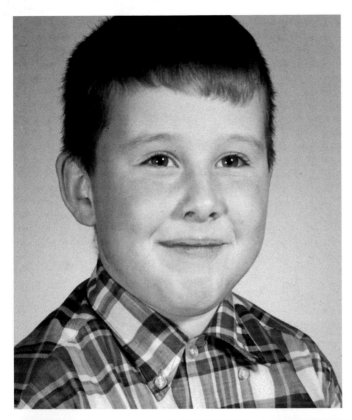

Me as a young boy
(left); me as a drag
queen (lower left); a
promotional flier for
a Weather Gals show

A few of the men in my life (from left): Alex Stone, Hal Rockland, Hank Hightower, Jordan Young, Ryan Idol, and Zak Spears

Joey Stefano (above); me with Sharon Kane (lower left); Falcon's John Rutherford

silly name Cody Feelgood.) Wes brought him to Studio One one night and introduced us, and I knew right away that I wanted him to work for me. He was part Cherokee and really just very wholesome-looking, and he had the most beautiful lips I think I've ever seen. Plus, he had the added talent of being able to suck his own dick. Anybody who can suck his own dick is certain to be a hot commodity in this business (not to mention great entertainment for parties).

Two days later the perfect opportunity to cast Randy came up when Arik Travis canceled out of his planned role in *Songs in the Key of Sex*. *Songs* was written by Stan Ward specifically for Travis, a beautiful Latin guy with a great voice who could sing his own material. Original songs had been written specifically for this movie, and most of the recording had already been done, so when Arik canceled, it really put us in a bad position. Out of desperation, I called up Randy and offered him the lead role, which he accepted. I got Chris Green to rerecord the songs (Chris is a talented musician), and Randy just lip-synched to them in the movie.

He was living in San Diego then (he'd been kicked out of the Navy for being gay), so after he'd done a lot of driving back and forth, I asked him to come to L.A. and stay with me. He ended up doing more than twenty flicks, though *Songs* is really his signature piece.

Recommended films: *Songs in the Key of Sex, My Cousin Danny.*

Bryan Kidd: Like his long-time real-life boyfriend, Ryan Wagner, Bryan is an accommodating bottom. Unlike Ryan, though, Bryan has also topped for me on occasion. And, like Ryan, I didn't so much discover Bryan as he discovered me. He was the aggressor.

Making It Big: Sex Stars, Porn Films, and Me

I met Bryan at my birthday party in 1995, where he'd been brought by another porn star, Adam Wilde. When I first saw Bryan, I thought he looked like a cute little paperboy (he's one of those guys who's in his mid twenties but looks much younger). When we met that night, he expressed an interest in being in movies. I told him, "Let me see your stomach." He raised his shirt. He wasn't shy, that was good, and ooh, was his body nice. Then I told him, "Let's get some Polaroids of you, and we'll get you in movies." So he came back to my house for an after-party party later that night, and he actually ended up being the evening's entertainment. We got him up to my bedroom and got his clothes off, and he settled back and let a group of us have our dirty little way with him. He did a private sex show for us, and we just took advantage of what he had to offer. Bryan is one of those guys who really gets into being enjoyed. If you're into him, that by itself is enough to make him happy. He's totally uninhibited and wants only to please. In fact, I'd even caught him being blown by Jazmine, another porn-associated drag queen friend of mine, in the bathroom at the party earlier that night.

By the next weekend I had Bryan in a scene with Mike Nichols in *My Sister's Husband.* It was his first sex scene, and I assigned him one of the biggest dicks in the business, but he handled it like a pro. In fact, he's a pro every time he steps in front of the camera. He's a good sexual performer, and he's even good at delivering his lines. Plus, he's versatile, which all too few guys are. I even had him flip-flop in his scene with Joshua Sterling in *Under Covers.*

Bryan and Ryan Wagner became a couple soon after he got started. They had danced together in bars in Indianapolis before coming to California, and they did several scenes together on film. They live in San Diego, and both work steadily.

Recommended films: *My Sister's Husband, Cockfight, Like Father Like Son.*

Lex Baldwin: Lex was one of the most "gay for pay" people I've ever worked with. I don't think he liked having gay sex, though he did like the money it provided him.

I was doing a film called *Straight to Bed*, which was a JO film featuring several male stars of the straight porn industry, people like Randy Spears and Cal Jammer and T.T. Boy. Well, I ended up one performer short, and we needed one more guy to finish the film, so T.T. Boy suggested his brother. That's right, Lex Baldwin is T.T. Boy's brother. T.T.'s only reservation was that Lex shaved his pubic hair, but I was willing to give him a look. "Is he cute?" I asked. Said T.T.: "I can't tell that." Sheesh, straight guys!

Well, Lex was cute. When I first saw him, I thought he looked like one of the famous acting Baldwin brothers, probably Alec. And I really, really love the Baldwin brothers. Needless to say, Lex got the part. And yes, that's where his name came from.

Despite being straight, Lex did a good job for me with his JO scene, and we even put him on the back cover of the box. While we were out doing that, I took him to lunch and gave him my full "let me make you a star" get-into-porn spiel, and I gradually persuaded him. Catalina signed him as an exclusive soon thereafter.

Once in the business, though, Lex never really became what we had hoped for. He never warmed up to the idea of having sex with men, even as a top, and we had to stunt every fuck scene he ever did. He just didn't want to stick his dick in another man's ass. It's very, very rare to use a stunt dick, in case you're wondering, but we had to do it regularly for Lex.

Also his involvement with gay porn caused problems between Lex and his brother. T.T. was upset that Lex was doing gay films — and probably, quite honestly, that Lex was making a lot more money than he was. There's simply more money in the gay industry these days, and Lex was making in one film what T. T. Boy had to do five to make. So Lex, I think, disliked the family conflict and disliked the gay sex, so he didn't stick around long. He did some good work, just not nearly enough of it.

Recommended films: *Straight to Bed, Power Tool 2, King of the Mountain.*

Chris Green: For someone who's done only one hard-core sex movie, *Courting Libido,* Chris has carved out a career in the industry that's been a lot more durable than anyone expected. He's talented, he's versatile, and he's a hell of a nice guy. Also, Chris, like Joey Stefano, is a person I've actually been in hard, painful love with.

I met Chris several years ago at the Queen Mary, a drag bar in North Hollywood, and we got along well from the start. We had so much in common, especially our musical tastes, which both ran toward KISS, Joan Jett, the Runaways — glam rock like that. We talked and really were compatible, and I thought he was just adorable. At that time, though, my schedule was really busy, my social calendar full to bursting, and as much as I liked him, I didn't really want or need any more friends. I didn't have time for the ones I had, and more new friends would mean more phone calls and social engagements and, inevitably, neglect due to my busy schedule. But Chris started calling me and wouldn't stop; he wanted to be friends, and he was very persistent. I liked him so much that I eventually gave in, and we became great friends and have been ever since. He's a longtime resident of the Porn Motel.

The more I got to know Chris, the better I liked him until finally I was head over heels in love with him. And, as was the case with Joey, it was unrequited love; he just didn't feel the same way about me. I went through a year of sheer hell, wanting him so badly yet not being able to have him. It drove me nuts, and I never did have him sexually. There was one night when something might have happened, when we were dancing at a club called Arena and started kissing on the dance floor. And I don't mean just *kissing*, I mean groping, grinding, tongues everywhere, prelude-to-crazy-wild-fucking-type kissing. It was heavy, and we were both getting incredibly hot there on the dance floor. Alexis Arquette even walked by and told us, "Find a motel!" So we got out of Arena and went back to my place. That's when the sex could have, should have, and would have happened — except that I, the dirty drag queen sex pig, suddenly had a brain cramp of colossal proportions: I suggested we go back out to another club, the Probe. Sex was probably inevitable that night, but I gave it up to go back out and do more drinking. Idiot!

Now, though, I look at that stroke of idiocy as a blessing. If Chris and I had had sex, it would have put a strain on our friendship that I'm not sure we would have been able to overcome. It would have gotten all tense and uncomfortable between us, and everything would have been ruined. We probably would never have spoken again after that night. So I guess it was all for the best. Everything happens for a reason, so maybe it was the hand of God that night acting through my stupid drunken brain.

My crush on Chris lasted for one very long year. We'd go on the road together and have major fights in places like New York or Washington, D.C. He'd go out and pick people up, and that would make me insanely jealous. (Why I keep doing this to myself with people like Chris and Joey is a question a good psychologist could probably have a field day with.) But eventually I got over it, and we settled into the comfortable friendship we have today.

Sometime after all of that was finally settled, Chris told me he wanted to do a fuck movie. He had done several nonsexual roles for me and in fact had become somewhat of a porn star without ever having sex. In the *Hard Body Video Magazine* series, he had undressed gradually, film by film, and had ended up naked but never actually performed with another guy. So he had somewhat of a reputation already when I cast him as the lead in *Courting Libido*. It was awkward to direct him, because we were such great friends, but in the end it came out well. And right after that Chris did a photo shoot for *Advocate Men*, which gave him the cover, so his name was made. His performance in *Libido* won him Best Oral Scene honors at the Gay Erotic Video Awards, so he was obviously a natural at that, but he never did another sex scene. He'd made it through crafty marketing, and he's still a familiar face around the porn circuit.

While he still makes occasional nonsexual film appearances (check out his hilarious role as a cowboy named Sue in Catalina's 1997 *Hung Riders II*), most of Chris's time now is taken up by his band. Chris has long pursued a music career and is the driving force behind the Johnny

Depp Clones, a West Hollywood-based glam band that usually includes me too. He did the music for *Songs in the Key of Sex* and has done some other work, but we're all still waiting for another Best Oral-worthy performance.

Recommended film: *Courting Libido.*

Adam Wilde: A relative newcomer who until recently lived with me in the Porn Motel, Adam is now based in Columbus, Ohio, where he is determined to become a top-flight agent in this business. I guess being a porn star isn't sleazy enough for him.

I met Adam through Chris Green after the gay pride festival in West Hollywood in 1995. Adam had done a three-way with Chris and another porn star, Chad Donovan, and Chris brought Adam home and introduced me to him. He was blond and willing and really wholesome-looking, so I put him immediately in *My Sister's Husband* and *Total Corruption 2.* When Sharon Kane moved out, leaving a free bedroom in my house, Adam moved in with Chris and Jordan and me, and he stayed for a year.

Wilde has been a very common name for porn stars and was especially overused back in the '80s. There was even another Adam Wilde working in straight porn in the '90s, and the common name caused the straight Adam a good bit of trouble. He was upset that the gay Adam had stolen his name, and the straight Adam reportedly even lost work because women thought he was doing gay films and wouldn't work with him.

The gay Adam did a lot of movies in a very short time before striking out on his own. He left for Ohio at the end of the summer of 1996, though he still plans to fly back for the occasional film performance. (He'd better, as good a cocksucker and bottom as he is. He won Best Bottom at the 1996 Gay Erotic Video Awards.) He has started the Wilde Collection, a group of boys he plans to represent.

Recommended films: *My Sister's Husband, Total Corruption 2, Studio Tricks.*

Scott Bond: Remember how I found Andrew Michaels through an ad in a local L.A.-area gay rag? Well, Scott was the only other good find I ever made through that ad. More often than not, it brought the scariest, freakiest, most disgusting guys imaginable to my door. From eighteen to sixty, you could not possibly imagine some of the men who think they can do porn. How they get so misguided, so deluded, is something that's just beyond me. I eventually quit running those ads because what they brought me was simply too grotesque. (Though I did keep some snapshots of some of the most incredible ones to break out and show friends in private. Yeah, I know. I'm a cruel bitch.)

When Scott called in response to the ad, I didn't let my hopes get too high. My enthusiasm had been squashed by some of what had been calling, and I wasn't expecting anything special. So when Scott asked to come over, I told him, "Come right now." I was getting ready to go out of town, and I just wanted to get him in and out and get it done with. Well, to my surprise, Scott walked in, and he was spectacular. He had a beautiful face and the whitest, smoothest skin and a dick that was this dark-brown color, almost like it belonged on a black man. It was a unique-looking contrast, so I cast Scott immediately in *The Rise*. He performed with Ryan Yeager, and he was fantastic.

The Rise was the only film Scott did for me, though he later did some for other directors. But if nothing else, he did restore my faith in casting calls. It makes all the weirdos worth it if, at the end of it all, you find someone like Scott Bond.

Recommended film: *The Rise.*

Dirk Fletcher: I met Dirk at the Gay '90s nightclub in Minneapolis when he came up and told me that he was a fan. Since he was good-looking, I asked him if he wanted to do a movie (if you've noticed, this is something I ask of just about every good-looking guy I ever meet. It can't hurt to ask, right?). Very nonchalantly, Dirk said that he'd be interested. So I brought him out to L.A., where he did *Boot Black* and *Courting Libido*, and then he decided he'd had enough and went home.

Dirk may end up working for me again. He calls me up every once in a while and asks if I have any projects for him, and I always tell him, "For you, baby, I'll find something. Just come on out." He hasn't yet; he doesn't want to make his sole career out of it, which is something I think is smart. Guys who keep one foot in the nonporn business world can generally keep their porn involvement in better perspective. But obviously the idea is still simmering somewhere in the back of Dirk's mind. It wouldn't surprise me to see him again sometime.

Recommended films: *Boot Black, Courting Libido.*

Ian Sharp: Another of those one-hit wonders, Ian is notable just because he was so good in his only film effort. I met him through Greg Gilbert, a location finder with whom I've worked in the past. Greg came on the set one day with Ian, who was his boyfriend. I was doing the first *Hard Body Video Magazine* for Mustang, and I had a spot open in an upcoming film, so we set about persuading Ian to take a shot at filling it. It took three hours of heavy sales pitch and more money than would normally be paid to a no-name making his debut, but we finally got him to agree, and he made his only porn performance in *Hot Ticket*, where he was paired with Bo Summers. He was really good, but that was all he wanted to do, and no amount of financial incentive or persuasion on my part could convince him otherwise.

Recommended film: *Hot Ticket*.

Hal Rockland: A more recent discovery, Hal followed his older brother, Vince Rockland, into the business. I met Hal two years ago in Las Vegas when I was there for the Adult Video News Awards. Vince had driven up to be part of the show, and he came to my door with Hal in tow. I remember thinking, *Good heavens, he's gorgeous!* and knowing that someone would sign him as an exclusive the moment they could. So I brought him to Falcon, which signed him up and put him in *Saddle Tramps*. Vince was also in that movie, and the two of them appeared in a threesome together, though they didn't actually do anything to each other. (Tyler Regan was the lucky filling in the Rockland sandwich.)

Saddle Tramps contains a fabulous rimming scene that is among the most difficult I have ever had to film. The problem with the Rockland brothers is that when they get rimmed, they laugh; they just find it too ticklish to bear. So it was very hard to get that scene right. It took a lot of takes, and I had to scream at the actors a lot more than I usually scream on the set.

Hal's discovery actually triggered some unpleasantness between me and Dan Byers, the same visionary agent who had told Jordan Young that he'd never be a star. Dan called me up in a rage after we did *Saddle Tramps*, shrieking to the effect of "How dare you steal this one from me! I've been working for six months on getting him!" Well, what can I say? I didn't know. Sorry. Fortunately, Dan got over being angry, and everything is okay between us again now. He's even booked me some live performances since then.

Recommended film: *Saddle Tramps*.

Mark West: The thing that makes Mark unique among this bunch is his age: forty-two. He's one of the oldest guys working today in a genre where age is the premium and thirty is considered too old by many. I didn't discover Mark, Catalina did, but I kind of adopted him because he was a good friend and so easy to work with.

Mark has this incredible rugged, masculine appeal that just drives me (and a lot of other guys) nuts. Let me tell you, I think these companies are missing a bet by not looking for more hot, in-shape older men. I think Mark looks like the Marlboro Man. He was sensational in *Roll in the Hay* and both *Saddle Tramps*, and any other older guy who came to me and wanted to do movies would definitely be considered if he looked anything like Mark. My tastes run the gamut, and you don't have to be eighteen or nineteen to impress Chi Chi and get a shot at a movie.

Recommended films: *Roll in the Hay, Saddle Tramps, Saddle Tramps 2*.

Sharon Kane: Didn't expect to find an actual woman here, did you? And one who's not even a drag queen! I'm including Sharon here because of her unique role in the gay porn industry. She's done a lot of straight films, but now, probably because of her age and, possibly, overexposure, she works almost exclusively in bi and gay films (in nonsexual roles). A lot of people call her an honorary gay man.

Sharon is a dear friend and a fantastic entertainer. She was one of the first women of porn I was exposed to (in *Pretty Peaches* when I was sixteen) and has always been one of my favorites. I followed her career closely through my teenage years, and when I came to L.A. and got into the porn biz myself, I finally got to meet her in person.

It was at the offices of Vidco Video, and Sharon had just had her first nose job. When I first met her, her face was all bandaged up, and she had two black eyes. Even then I thought she was beautiful. We ran into each other again at an *Adult Video News* convention in Las Vegas, and it was there that she tried to seduce me. Yes, really. Sharon has a thing for gay men, which I didn't know at the time. We were at this party and started making out, working our way into some really hot and heavy necking. I thought it was very strange that this straight woman was coming on to me so strong, and it was clear that I could have taken her then and there if I had wanted to. Unfortunately, I didn't want to fuck her — I wanted to *be* her.

Now we're so close and work together so often that sometimes when I'm on a set, it's weird to look around and not see her there. She's someone who I know I'll love for the rest of my life. Like a fine wine, she's only gotten better with age. Her body is still fabulous, and she has inner beauty as well. She's a loving, spiritual person who always has time to help others. And I've never seen a woman who could seduce more gay men. Sometimes I tell her she's a gay man who somehow got stuck in a woman's body (she hates that).

She's also a talented songwriter and has written the

scores for films like *The Hills Have Bi's* and *Idol in the Sky*. Hopefully, someone will discover that someday and give her a much-deserved recording deal.

———————

You may have noticed that many of the guys we've discussed are no longer active in the porn business. That's true, and the sad fact of it is that most porn careers don't last very long. When they're older a lot of these guys don't look back fondly at their film careers. And while they're doing it, rarely do they stick around for very long. They get jaded and burned-out quickly, and a lot of them just get too jealous to function. Their looks are their biggest asset, and there's always a newer, younger, cuter guy coming down the pike to take their place. They constantly feel a lot of pressure.

It would be nice if everyone could take doing porn for what it is, enjoy it while they're doing it, and then get out with no regrets, but that doesn't seem to happen. A lot of them end up wishing they'd never done it. I sympathize, but they're adults, and we all have our choices to make. Nobody is forcing anyone to do anything. It's a question of free will. And while some are weak and end up consumed by this business (like Joey), others survive and come out stronger for it.

Moreover, there's never any shortage of guys willing to give it a shot. I'm finding new ones every day. Some of the ones climbing the ladder currently are Dino Phillips, Dax Kelly, and Kyle Reardon, and there will doubtlessly be more by the time this sees print. Dino's been around for a couple of years (I actually found him dancing in Phoenix), but he just recently joined us in the Porn Motel. He has an unusual, appealing look with very dark hair and rather fair skin (His best film for me was *Hard Body Video Magazine No. 2*). Dax and Kyle are even newer. I met Dax in Denver through a drag queen named Kinsey Rappor, who had sent me photos of him. I flew him out to do *Photoplay* for Catalina, and he made quite an impression with everyone who saw him. He has very light skin, what I call "butter" skin, just smooth and pale and flawless, plus strawberry-blond hair and a great body. I met Kyle at the same time, and he was notable because he had this dick that got totally hard in about two seconds and stood straight out in photos, really grabbing your attention. He was in *Photoplay* with Dax (in fact, they shared the box cover) and another film called *Hard Hats*, so their careers have been linked even though they're not really friends or anything. But they're both stars in waiting and will be successful in video as long as they want to be.

This is not a complete list of my discoveries and protégés, all of whom I can't even remember. These are just some of the best and most successful. I can't always pick a winner; I passed on Cole Youngblood three years ago because the pictures he sent me were so blurry that I couldn't tell anything from them. Now he's working non-stop and is bound for superstardom, and I'm kicking myself for missing out on that eleven-inch dick.

But that's okay. The next big-dicked superstar could always come knocking on my door tomorrow.

"Just Let Me Put My Mouth on It for Three Strokes"
OR
These Are a Few of My Favorite Films

One of the questions I'm most frequently asked is, "Chi Chi, where can I find a really good dry cleaner in this town?" But another, more interesting question that I'm asked even more often is, "Chi Chi, how many films have you made during your long and interesting career?" Well, that second one is a very good question, and I wish I had a better answer than the one I'm going to give you, because that answer is, basically, "Beats me." The honest to God truth is, I don't know how many. I haven't kept track. On a guess, I would say at least 100, maybe as many as 200; 150 is probably a safe estimate. It's hard to say. If somebody out there has actually kept track and has a better answer, please let me know. (Then again, if somebody has nothing better to do than to track my career that closely, maybe I don't want to know about it. You probably have a shrine wallpapered with pictures of me and my old wigs and dresses and would want to be my friend and then stalk me until you finally killed me. Now that I think about it, never mind.)

When I look back over my career, I like to think I've accomplished two major things: First, I pioneered the casting of drag queens in nonsexual roles in gay porn films. It was done to a lesser degree before me in films like

Dynastud from HIS Video, but I was the one who first did it in a high-profile way. To the surprise of a lot of people, it caught on and became popular, and now it's very common. And second, I helped directors to become recognized. In the old days directors were anonymous, just names on video boxes and in the credits that you never even remembered once the movie was over. Usually you didn't even know who directed the film you were watching, and if you did know, you didn't care. And that was fine with directors then; guys like Matt Sterling and Toby Ross weren't in it for the glory, they were in it for the sex.

That's all changed now too; people like John Rutherford and Jerry Douglas and Jim Steel are major celebrities in their own right. They want to be known; they want the notoriety of the performers. And for the most part they've achieved it; nowadays, the name of a superstar director can be almost as important as the name of a superstar performer in selling a movie. Look at the way HIS Video promoted 1994's *Idol Country:* "Chi Chi LaRue's *Idol Country,* starring Ryan Idol." I was billed equally with Ryan Idol, who's hardly a B-list nobody. And the director's name becomes even more important when there's *not* a superstar performer like a Ryan Idol in the cast. A name like mine or John Rutherford's can guarantee a certain amount of sales even if the cast is composed entirely of unwashed trade plucked off Santa Monica Boulevard.

All this means that directors are under a lot more scrutiny today than they ever have been before. We put ourselves out there, and now we have to bear up to the unblinking glare of the spotlight. For me, that's not been a problem, though I think being a public figure is easier for guys like John or Jim Steel who are good-looking in their own right. There's no part of life that isn't easier for pretty people.

Both John and Jim are good-looking enough to turn on models on the set. That's something I think I'm safe in saying I've never done. When we were filming *Score,* Joey Stefano wasn't turned on to his partner, so he looked at Jim Steel to get himself excited. John Rutherford is another one who can usually get what he wants because he's so damn fine; he could be in these movies if he wasn't directing them. Oh, and Gino Colbert! Gino and I have had our differences, but there's no denying how damn sexy he is. I used to watch him in films before he started directing, and he was one of my favorite performers. He was so nasty and so dirty — a little bit dangerous — and he had a total overpowering sexual magnetism. When I finally met him, I told him how hot I thought he was, and we became friends for a while. He even used to make these joking sexual propositions to me. So it's kind of sad that he's so bitter toward me now that he keeps bashing me in the media. (I really don't know what it's about except that it's entirely one-way; I have never had any problem with him.)

As a basically insecure person, I don't like not being liked. I want everyone to like me. It bothers me when people like Gino Colbert take cheap shots at me in magazines and on television, but it's part of the job, and it comes with the territory. If you raise your head high enough above the crowd, somebody's going to throw rocks at you. Look at Princess Diana; look at Elizabeth Taylor: These are good people who have never done anyone any harm, yet jealous, petty little people take shots at them in the press. So in a world where even people like that are vilified, what can I do? You're just not going to please everybody, no matter how hard you try.

In the ultracompetitive world of gay porn, this is especially so. Directors simply have to make decisions, sometimes very difficult decisions, about casting their movies, and these decisions are always going to leave some people unhappy. You have to choose what's best for the film and the company that's paying you. You have to determine who and what will make your movie as profitable as it can be. There are models out there today who simply don't have what it takes. They're working because they'll work for next to nothing, but it's not on merit, and they won't be working for me. Telling guys that I don't have roles for them is about the hardest part of my job. But there are other directors who will be happy to pay them an insulting $150 for a sex scene.

Look at Crystal Crawford, for instance. Crystal can make an entire movie on a budget of $2,000. (In contrast, *Lost in Vegas* ran upwards of $80,000.) But the way she does that is to pay one guy well, maybe $1,000 for the top star, and round out the cast with nobodies and has-beens who will work for $150 or $200 apiece. She hires her friends, who will work for next to nothing, and she'll race through filming in one day to get the product out quicker. Of course, it's an inferior product; you see it and just want to bury it in your backyard. But there's a place in the industry for that too, as the sales of those videos demonstrate, and Crystal has made her name in that way, so who am I to criticize? What can you say except more power to her?

"Just Let Me Put My Mouth on It"

The latest trend in gay porn is the big-budget extravaganza. It pretty much reached its peak with *Night Walk*, the slickly promoted 1996 collaboration between Gino Colbert and straight porn's Michael Ninn that topped out with a budget of six figures. *Night Walk* did very well, and its end result was that other studios jumped onto the big-budget bandwagon. But *Night Walk* was hardly the first big-budget gay production. More accurately, it was the culmination of a trend that started several years before.

Catalina was making some pretty pricey films as far back as the mid 1980s (*Powertool*, for one, had a pretty hefty budget by 1986 standards), and the amount put into films escalated in bits and pieces over the next several years. For my part, my first big-budget blowout came in 1991 when I approached VCA's Russ Hampshire with the script for *Jumper* and asked for $25,000 to shoot it. That was a figure that was still pretty much unheard-of in those days; most of us would be lucky to make that in a year. To my surprise, Russ said yes and gave me the money. It wasn't as though I needed the money at the risk of a bad movie; I had made good films on small budgets many times before and am still doing so. *Billboard* and *The Rise* for Catalina, *Fond Focus* for InHand, and *G Squad*, a bisexual flick for Soho, were among those that had turned out all right without costing much. But like any director, I wanted to see what I could do with that much money.

I've always believed that my "one-day wonders" — the low-budget, produced-in-a-hurry, rush-'em-out quickies — are as good as or better than anyone else's one-day wonders. I can go into someone's house, paste plastic up on the walls, move some chairs around, put up some candles, install a bench or two, and have a set for a porn movie that you wouldn't even recognize if it was your own living room. For *French Kiss*, the oral flick I did for InHand, I created the set out of Sabin's house (Sabin is the publisher of the *Gay Video Guide*), and nobody knew the difference. Then we just went in and got the sex done, and the finished product was a good one.

Still, with more money I can do bigger and better and more shocking things. And more than anything else in the world, I love to shock. Putting drag queens in gay porn was shocking — me in *Davey and the Cruisers*, Jizelle Climax in *Jumper*, Crystal Crawford in *Courting Libido*. (*Courting Libido*, in fact, was shocking on any number of levels. In one scene, Chris Green walks through an alley and encounters drag queen Crawford with her dick hanging out.) If it's new and shocking, you can bet Chi Chi had a hand in it.

My biggest-budget flick to date, *Lost in Vegas*, is also, I think, one of my best. It received eleven nominations at the year-end Gay Erotic Video Awards, the most of any film. Though it didn't win, at the time of this writing, *Lost in Vegas* has still probably been the most significant film of my career.

I'd have to call *Lost in Vegas* and *Idol Country* my favorites out of all the movies I've done. Yet I can't say which one I like better. You can't really compare them to each other, because they're so vastly different. One is happy, the other is sad; one is outdoors, the other is in; one is in the country, the other is in the city. *Lost in Vegas* starred a whole long list of heavyweights, while *Idol Country* was primarily a vehicle for one superstar. They represent totally opposite ends of the spectrum in every way.

Also, for pure, basic, uninhibited, raunchy sex, I have a soft spot for my *Boot Black* movies. *Soft spot* is probably not the best choice of words, since the thing about the *Boot Black*s was that they were about sex and nothing else; not much plot, not much pretense, just a vague notion of a concept and a bunch of sex pigs wallowing around in the mud. If these films don't give you a hard spot, sweetie, you must be dead from the waist down.

I also have a fondness for *Flexx*, the first movie I ever directed, since it was the one that really cemented my place in this business. None of us really knew what we were doing for that film, and it showed; *Flexx* is not a movie you'll want to watch for the cinematography, the editing, or the seamless camerawork. If you look back at it now, in fact, it's a bit funny. On its artistic merit, you might call it a bad movie, but it's kind of dear to me just for personal reasons.

Not only was I learning on the job in my directing, but the rest of my crew was learning on the job as well. I've mentioned the pointless cutaways of table lamps, ugly ceramic statues, and cheesy silk flowers — hot, hot, hot! It's hard to watch it and not laugh, seeing these mundane pieces of furniture pointlessly added in between all the sex. But watching *Flexx* now is like going back and rereading a paper you wrote in school. It's a glimpse back into when you were just learning.

Fortunately, I learned more and more about the business as I went along, and my films got better. By the time I did *Billboard* for Catalina (starring Joey Stefano), I pretty much knew what I was doing.

Billboard is the film in which Scott Masters tried to sabotage me. As I told you earlier, Scott felt threatened by my ascent at Catalina, and he set out to make sure that *Billboard* was so bad that I'd never get another shot at directing. So he went to the crew and told them to under-cut me, not to help me, not to give me any special shots, like Catalina's trademark penetration-from-underneath shots. Members of that crew didn't confess the truth to me till years later.

I've learned a lot also from people like John Rutherford, Catalina's Josh Eliot, and Studio 2000's vet-eran John Travis. John Travis is the best at special shots, like certain close-ups of various sexual acts. He's very picky; he'll demand ten insertion shots instead of the two or three that most of us make do with. Maybe that's a bit excessive and maybe it makes the models bitch and moan, but it makes for a better movie, so I have to admire that.

John Travis paid me one of the biggest compliments I think I've ever received in this business when he told me after the *Lost in Vegas* premiere party at the Love Lounge in West Hollywood how wonderful the film was and that he wished *Vegas* could have been a Studio 2000 project. That really meant a lot to me, coming from the guy who discovered Jeff Stryker and was responsible for the classic *Powertool.*

Another film that stands out in my memory is *The Rise* for Catalina, for which I won my first Best Director award (from the *Adult Video News*). Josh Eliot helped me write the script; we just sat down at his house and collab-orated. No one in this business can write a script like Josh Eliot can. Watch any of the *Bi Dolls* movies if you don't believe it. Clever ideas just pour out of his head; there's no way to stop them. So between us we came up with what I thought was a really good script, and we put Ryan Yeager in it, and he turned it into a phenomenal success.

The credit for *Jumper*, my first big-budget flick, is all due to VCA boss Russ Hampshire and screenplay writer Stan Ward. Russ read Stan's script and liked it, so he entrusted me with an awful lot of his money. Admittedly, it was a very good script (Stan has a long track record of writing very good scripts), but it was still something of a gamble on Russ's part. He trusted me because he had seen *Flexx* and *Billboard* and *The Rise*, and so he knew what I was capable of, that I could do quality films and wouldn't take his big investment and bring him back a piece of amateurish crap. I didn't; *Jumper* won Best Gay Video that year from the *Adult Video News*.

I was pretty happy with most of my projects for VCA. *Total Corruption* (another Stan Ward script) earned the first five-star review ever given by the *Adult Video News*. It was originally written for a porn star named Chuck Barron, but he ended up not doing it. His role was given instead to a newcomer named Greg Ross, and the cast also included the always adorable Zak Spears and the maddeningly inconsistent Phil Bradley. Phil didn't always click on all cylinders when he was on the set, but when I put him with Zak, he really came alive. And this turned out to be one of his best performances. The cameraman was industry veteran Dave Kinnick, and I was very impressed by him. (So much so that I used him later in *Boot Black*. He also shot and edited *Hologram* and won the Gay Video Guide Award for Best Editing for his work there. He can be really picky and whiny and annoying, but he's outstanding at what he does.)

I worked closely with Gender on several significant films as well. *Jumper* and *Hologram* both bear her marks, and she scripted most of *Courting Libido* (I reserve credit for the alley scene). Now I'm working very closely with Jordan Young, perhaps the best scriptwriter I've collaborated with yet.

Roll in the Hay, a flick I did for Jocks, is a special memory to me because of the craziness that surrounded its filming. It starred Aiden Shaw and Mark West, and we shot it at this farm in Sacramento that was owned by this horny old guy who loved to watch the boys doing their thing. This guy was following us around every moment of every day, and he just couldn't miss even a minute of the damn sex. Well, just watching would have been all right if that was all he had wanted to do. But this old farmer insisted on standing right behind me the entire time we were shooting, and he filmed the proceedings himself with this little handheld video camera. I guess he wanted his own home movies to jerk off to. (And I'm sure they were *so* much better than our finished product!) Anyway, this farmer had a crippled old dalmatian that was tied up nearby while we filmed, and it would not stop barking. It wanted attention, but it couldn't walk, and so what it did was bark. Incessantly. For hours and hours on end. The dog was ruining the shoot and driving us all simply mad. Finally I told the farmer, whose name was Henry, to go and shut his damn dog up. But Henry wouldn't miss even a few seconds of the sex; he just had to be there for all of it. So we ultimately interrupted the scene, and I told him, "Henry, if you do not go and stop that damn dog's damn barking this very minute, we are packing right up and moving this damn shoot somewhere else." Reluctantly, he went to try and quiet his dog. But even that didn't work; as soon as Henry left the dog to return to the set, the dog was off and barking again. Finally, since Henry couldn't be deprived of watching the sex, we had to dispatch Gender to spend the rest of the afternoon with the dog, petting it and keeping it quiet.

We got back at Henry, though, and had a little fun at his expense. Henry kind of had the hots for Chris Green, who was part of our crew for that film. Well, John Rutherford told Henry that Chris had a nine-inch long, beer-can-thick dick. And as the filming went on, John kept tweaking Henry with this little tidbit of information — which was, by the way, absolutely false. "Henry, have you seen Chris's dick yet?" "Henry, you really wouldn't believe the dick on this guy." "Henry, you simply *must* see Chris's dick!" By the time John was finished with him, Henry was going just bonkers with lust! Well, the fact is, Chris Green *does not* have a nine-inch long, beer-can-thick dick; his dick is more like seven inches and has a pretty normal thickness. It's not a bad dick by any means, but Ken Ryker he's not. But Chris was happy to just play along and never volunteered this information, so we just let poor old Henry tie himself up in knots over this imaginary monster cock Chris supposedly had.

Henry also made a couple of funny attempts at getting in on some of the action. He volunteered to fluff, but I think he would have taken any old job we could have given him, even picking up used condoms after the filming. His best-known line from that shoot, which we still throw around today to get laughs, is, "C'mon, just let me put my mouth on it for three strokes!"

Making It Big: Sex Stars, Porn Films, and Me

Roll in the Hay was originally supposed to be a Mustang film, but the chemistry between all of us was so good and the end product was so good (somehow!) that it was upgraded to a Jocks release. (By way of explanation, the company commonly known as Falcon releases its biggest-budget and best-quality products under the Falcon name, while smaller-budget, lower-profile films are released under the banners of Mustang or Jocks. Since I've done a lot of work with smaller budgets, I've directed many Jocks and Mustang titles.)

Despite all the madness that surrounded the filming of *Roll in the Hay,* we went back to Henry's farm to shoot *Idol Country* in 1994. By this time, thankfully, Henry had a boyfriend, but that didn't improve working conditions as much as we thought it would. Instead of one person watching us, now we had two. And like Henry, you'd have thought his lover had never seen men having sex before. They both stared, slack-jawed, like they were witnessing the miracle of birth or some divine creation. Again, they camped behind me with their little camera and made their own little private home version of my movie, and again they couldn't be pried away from so much as a second of the action even if their barn was burning down.

So anyway, one day Henry was sitting behind me and filming away while Jake Andrews and Trent Reed were doing their scene. And then Henry calls to his lover, who was standing nearby, "Honey, come down here, I want to suck your dick!" And I was thinking, *Oh, my God, they're going to have sex right here behind me.* And let me tell you, even Chi Chi was a little skeeved out by that idea.

"Just Let Me Put My Mouth on It"

But Henry's lover was also wrapped up in what Jake and Trent were doing, and he didn't want to miss a second of it either, so what he told Henry was, "Not now, honey. I'm watching hot men have sex right now." Well, this really set Henry off, and the old guy went storming back into the house, wailing, "You don't love me anymore!" And then the lover looked at me kind of ruefully and said, "Oh, God, I guess I'd better go take care of this," and he followed Henry back up to the house, and we didn't see either of them for quite a while after that. I know how it was resolved, though, because I had to go up to the house a little while later, and there I found Henry and his lover in the midst of, well, "making up."

Truthfully, Henry and his lover were very sweet and were wonderful hosts to us. But as you might imagine, it's pretty common for us to have to deal with gawkers who want to watch what's going on on our sets. I don't mind this as long as it's under control and the performers aren't distracted and the spectators aren't interfering with the work in progress. Actually, it can be kind of flattering; I think the highest compliment that can be paid to a director is when someone new to a set gets aroused watching what's going on. It doesn't happen to me anymore, of course, though it did once; it used to really drive me crazy. Now it's just work, and I want to perfect what I'm doing. But if people like Henry and his boyfriend get aroused, then I know we must be getting some pretty good sex out of whoever's performing.

Every movie I've ever done has been kind of special to me in some way, and it's really extremely difficult to say what my all-time favorites are. So rather than giving you a long, boring complete videography to deal with, here are capsule summaries of a few of what I feel are the most significant.

Lost in Vegas: I really feel like, from top to bottom, in terms of cast, editing, production, cinematography, and all-around quality of the finished product, this is the best  movie I've ever done. If you've never seen one of my films and want to view just one to get some idea of what I'm all about, this is the one I recommend.

Lost in Vegas is loosely based on the Oscar-winning 1995 feature film *Leaving Las Vegas.* Jordan Young saw *Leaving Las Vegas* and told me how much I'd love it, so he and I and Mickey Skee, a writer well-known around the porn industry, went back to see it together. Well, if you saw it, you know how incredible it was: the acting, the concept, the realism — it was a fantastic movie. And right there in the theater, I knew we could adapt it into a porn flick.

I told Jordan to write the script, since he loved *Leaving* as much as I did, and he did a great storyboard and outline, which we presented to All Worlds. Now, it was not shaping up to be your typical feel-good porn flick; *Lost in Vegas* dealt with heavier topics, like alcoholism, prostitution, and death. Real downers. Such a film would have to be handled really deftly to be successful, and a lot of studios would have been afraid to back such an ambitious project. All Worlds was not afraid. Big boss Rick Ford liked the idea, and he told me with no reservations to go for it.

Rick has always been one to take risks, and I really

admire and respect him for that. He'll do films about incest (*Flesh and Blood*), murder, serial killers — topics that more conservative companies wouldn't touch to save their lives. He's been very supportive of me, and in this case I think he trusted my judgment and track record. We've had our differences in the past, and we've gone through long cold periods where we didn't even speak to each other, much less work together (the result of a planned collaboration that fell through). But the more I work for him now, the more highly I think of him. He has been wonderful to me.

Lost in Vegas is about a hard-core drunk, Alec Danes (playing the Nicolas Cage character from *Leaving*), who goes to the big gambling mecca in the desert and gets involved with hooker Dave Russell. After trysting with another prostitute (Hank Hightower), Danes is thrown out onto the street and, after some hot sexual adventures, is finally reunited with Russell and gives up the booze that's been ruining his life.

It's a violent movie: Russell is beaten badly by a trio of jocks he picks up and Jordan, playing another hooker, is actually beaten to death. But the ultimate message is a positive one: That the love of a good man can be all the strength you need to conquer even the greatest adversity.

Videographer Bruce Cam deserves a lot of credit for *Lost in Vegas*'s appeal; his helicopter shots and montages of the skyline and Nevada desert make the film visually striking and very memorable.

Idol Country: This 1994 film is about a snooty city boy, played by the title character, Ryan Idol, who bets a pile of money with buddies Marco Rossi and Grant Larson that he can survive for three days on the Minnesota farm of Rossi's cousin Steve Marks. While he's there, bumbling around like a character from *Green Acres*, stepping in cow chips and toting around bales of hay, Idol falls in love with

Farmer Pete (Marks). Farmer Pete feels much the same way about Idol. The climax of the film comes when they finally get together.

This film is noteworthy because it marked the real-life heterosexual Idol's on-screen rimming debut. Ryan was strictly a top throughout his early career but eventually consented first to sucking dick, then finally to rimming in later films. It can be told now that he commanded an unprecedented fee — well into five figures — to munch Marks's manhole in this movie.

Boot Black and **Boot Black 2 (The Spit Shine)**: The first *Boot Black*, from 1994, was the story of a guy (Jake Andrews) who shined patrons' leather footwear at the Eagle, a sleazy leather bar based loosely on the late, great West Hollywood club of the same name. My version was about all the sexual antics that occurred there. For the 1995 follow-up (it wasn't exactly a sequel in the sense of being a story that continued; it was really just a second movie based around

the same theme), Rob Cryston became the title character, and we conceived another club, but the raunchy, nonstop sex was pretty much the same. *Boot Black 2* is noteworthy for the eight-man (Cryston, Andrews, Dave Logan,

Michael Parks, Casey Jordan, Rick Drake, Jeff Austin, and Kurt Manning) orgy at the end that was called a "marvel of choreography" by *Advocate Men*. *Boot Black* also included a climactic orgy.

My Sister's Husband: Somehow one of the top movies of 1996 despite a lot of friction on the set, this was the last film project I worked on with Gender. Gender's lack of professionalism in creating this script was the straw that broke the back of a relationship that was already badly strained. She regularly showed up for filming with just a few hand-scribbled notes, and one day she even showed up with nothing, saying she didn't feel like writing anything and telling me to  "just have them say what you want." Yeah, that's the way to put out high-quality movies. The film surprisingly turned out okay, I think, mostly due to a fabulous cast and crew that helped save it from Gender's indifference. It drew a slew of nominations for the Gay Erotic Video Awards, and Adam Wilde won Best Bottom, based in large part on his performance here.

The film was based on a very hot concept that many of us have been through: attraction to a forbidden family member. In this case it's gay boy Wilde who has the hots for Cory Evans, the husband of Wilde's sister, Sharon Kane. Wilde comes to town for an extended visit and is tempted painfully by Evans at every turn, watching him do things like washing the car and taking a shower. There's a really great scene where Evans takes young Wilde to a strip club and dancer Brook Waters (a star of straight porn) gets up close and personal in Wilde's face. Wilde flees to the toilet, where he has a hot threesome with Jake Taylor and Dino DiMarco.

Finally, Evans confronts Wilde over all of Wilde's staring, and the two of them get it on in the movie's climactic scene. In addition to Wilde's well-rewarded performance, Evans turned in a really superstar topping job as well.

Total Corruption and **Total Corruption 2 (One Night in Jail):** The first *Total Corruption* came out in 1993 and tells the tale of an honest, naive rookie police officer, played by Greg Ross, who is partnered with deviant sex-pig pigs  Donnie Russo and Phil Bradley. Russo and Bradley both abuse their authority by forcing those they arrest into sexual situations. Ross is offended and complains to his supervisor, Zak Spears, leading to a scorching three-way between those two and Bradley. In a subplot Ross is also tormented by an unrequited love for his ex who turned straight, Scott Baldwin, and though there is plenty of hot sex throughout this film, these situations are never quite resolved.

The popularity of *Total Corruption* (police drag is always a winner) led to a 1996 sequel, *Total Corruption 2 (One Night in Jail).* The hero of the second film is not a cop but a civilian, played by Scott Randsome, who is busted by officers Tom Katt and Blade Thompson during a sexual tryst with Karl Bruno in L.A.'s notoriously cruisy Griffith Park. While Randsome is arrested, Bruno escapes, leading Thompson to exercise his corruption with Jordan Young in a popular park tearoom. Randsome, meanwhile, has some not-altogether-unpleasant experiences back at the jail with cell mates Vic Hall, Taylor Perelli, and Adam Wilde and nasty sergeant Hank Hightower. Finally, Katt, the good cop, smuggles Randsome out of the clink and back to his apartment to hide out forever as his love interest.

Alley Boys: Another 1996 project, this is an all-oral movie about the public-sex happenings in some anonymous Los Angeles alley. The two mainstays of the  alley are Steve O'Donnell and Tony Cummings, two of the best new performers to come along in the mid '90s. Among the visitors who come and go are Eric Marx, Kurt Houston, Jake Holloway, Eduardo, Matt Easton, Sam Crockett, and Adam Rom. There are just two long scenes in this film, the first with five guys participating, the second with six.

We did this film in two days in a warehouse with an alley set, including the convenient platform we used for the rimming. I've done quite a few all-oral movies (*Lip Lock, French Kiss, In Your Face, All You Can Eat*), but this may be my favorite. Like many of my Catalina films, it was directed under the name Taylor Hudson.

 **Roll in the Hay:** This was about a boy (Rob Cryston) and his buddies (Aiden Shaw, Dave Logan, and Tim Baker) going to visit uncle Mark West on his farm. Sexual exploits between the visitors and the uncle's sons (Christian Fox and Ty Russell) ensue, with Cryston chasing Fox, Baker pursuing Russell, and Shaw stalking West.

West and his "son" Fox team up on Russell in one more-or-less incestuous scene, and that, coupled with

West's fine performance, led one reviewer to label this film "well over the top." Like many of my Mustang and Jocks flicks, this was directed as Lawrence David.

All About Steve: Winner of the 1995 Gay Erotic Video Awards' Best Sex Comedy honor, this flick gave the blue treatment to the classic *All About Eve.* In HIS Video's ver-sion, porn heavyweight Marco Chandler (Jason Andrews) sees his popularity being surpassed by that of rising newcomer Steve Harrington (Derek Cruise). The fading diva Andrews runs off to New York with Tony Hampton, and the new discovery Cruise steps into his vacated role in the current project he blew off. The various foolings-around culminate on awards night with a surprise ending I won't give away here; you'll just have to watch it to find out.

The awards-show scene was especially realistic because I rounded up a bunch of actual industry folks to serve as extras and appear in the background. People like Sharon Kane; directors Josh Eliot, Sam Abdul, Steven Scarborough, and Jim Steel; the Tom of Finland Foundation's Durk Dehner; and industry insiders Levvy Carriker, Mickey Skee, and Dave Kinnick all helped out. In fact, I even talked Dave, Mickey, and Sam into sitting at the same table, even though Sam really disliked Dave. Dave's camerawork was exceptional here, and Johnny Rahm did a noteworthy scene with Cruise. Zak Spears, Hank Hightower, and an uncredited Cliff Parker are among the others in the cast.

Mirage: This 1993 movie was also memorable for its filming, another tale of bug-eyed gawkers horning in on innocent pornographers minding their own business. We were filming in Palm Springs at a resort called Mirage, and the owners, who were very proud that we had selected their

establishment as the backdrop for our little project, were telling people who called for reservations, information, wrong numbers, whatever, what was going on there that day. So as the filming went on, we collected a crowd of about fifty people who were standing around the perimeter just watching. It was like a football game — they were hooting and cheering and applauding and really, *really* getting on my nerves.

We were trying to film a scene with Tim Barnett and Dean Johnson in a Jacuzzi complete with a volcano and waterfall, and the scene wasn't going well. It was getting late, and it was starting to get dark, and the crowd milling around was starting to interfere with our being able to shoot; they were getting in the pictures, being too loud, and breaking the performers' concentration. There was ultimately only one solution: I had to clear the set and force everyone who wasn't supposed to be there, who wasn't part of the crew and didn't have a specific job to do, to get the fuck out.

Well, we finally got the crowd dispersed, and I was feeling all relieved and ready to get back to filming when I noticed several old men trying to climb up on the roof of an adjacent building. As we stood there and watched, we saw a whole handful of the lecherous old guys we had just tossed off the set actually boosting each other up onto the roofs of neighboring buildings so they could continue to watch even after we had cleared them away. I mean, really! It was Henry times ten! Had none of these guys ever seen two men having sex before? It continues to amaze me what lengths people will go to just to get a little glimpse of what we do.

Mirage was originally supposed to be a Mustang release, but it was eventually released under the Jocks label. We finished the hot tub scene as a night scene, and since we were fortunate enough to have a full moon that night, it came out gorgeous. John Rutherford was the videographer, and he did some of his (or anyone's) best work ever. It's a really simple story about two buddies, Daryl Brock and Cort Stevens, who take their newly single friend Kirk Jensen to Palm Springs for the weekend to help mend his broken heart. Damien, Rick Lawrence, and Johnny Rey were also in the cast. Dean Johnson turned in an extraordinary performance, and this film also marked the debut of Marco Rossi.

Lunch Hour: This was one of my earliest projects, a Catalina release dating back to 1990. Josh Eliot codirected with me (he alone did the sequel, *Lunch Hour II: Sweating*

Grease). The appeal of *Lunch Hour* to me is in the age-old concept of the oppressed worker rising up against evil management and throwing off his shackles, then finally getting his due. Here the workers at a machine shop, led by Matt Powers, strike back against their asshole bosses. There's some really good sex and an undertone of violence that struck me as really erotic.

Songs in the Key of Sex: Randy Mixer stepped into a role designed for Arik Travis and saved this 1992 HIS Video film with a sensational performance. He portrays a singer

in a nightclub owned by Sharon Kane, and Danny Somers plays his lover. Mixer becomes tired of the relationship and falls for another guy, Jason Ross, an alcoholic. Mixer enters into a horrible, destructive relationship with Ross but, in a happy ending, eventually reunites with Somers and gets a recording contract.

Chris Green ended up singing the original songs in Travis's place, with Mixer lip-synching to the lyrics on film. This was pretty much the first XXX-rated gay musical, with four original songs done by Chris and Sharon.

Courting Libido: In Chris Green's first and only hard-core sexual performance, he plays a patient given a libido drug by psychologist Steve Marks. The drug is meant to induce dreams, and so for the rest of the movie, Chris sees sex wherever he goes, not knowing if it's real or if his mind is just playing  tricks on him. The alley scene described earlier, which also included straight-porn stars Jeanna Fine as a hooker and Bianca and Tiffany Minx as lesbian lovers, remains one of my personal favorites.

Jumper: A vehicle designed solely to promote Ryan Yeager, who I knew could be a star. Yeager plays an angel after being killed in 1783 at the Battle of Yorktown in the Revolutionary War. Once he gets up to heaven, he wants to return to earth and help his gay brethren. God (the voice of Gender, of all people) gives him five days in which to do his good deeds.

In order, Yeager is able to help a snotty model (played by Adam Archer), a straight military boy (Danny Somers), a pair of lovers (Alex Thomas and Tom Farrell), and a

nasty, homophobic video producer (Wes Daniels in his first role). In a bittersweet ending, Somers is killed by fag bashers but gets to spend eternity with Yeager in the hereafter.

The sex in this film was described as "riveting" by the *Adam Gay Video Guide*, and Yeager's big role did indeed make him a major star.

The Rise: Another early effort, *The Rise*, a 1990 Catalina production, featured Ryan Yeager and Scott Bond as a pair of boyfriends living in a small town. One dreams of escaping and making a better life for himself, while the other is

quite content with their suburban middle-class existence. The dissatisfied one (Yeager) leaves, moves to the big city, and becomes a porn star. The other, gradually overcome by a change of heart, eventually follows him into the industry and becomes a porn star himself. Through a stroke of coincidence,

they meet on a film set and fall in love all over again — a happy ending.

A Burt Reynolds-esque newcomer named Vic Young-blood made his debut in this movie and drew a lot of attention, but unfortunately he didn't last long in the industry.

Flexx: It's a simple story: Alex Stone sits on his bed reading magazines, and the stories in them then come

to life, putting him in a variety of sexual situations. Those silly cutaways that I've confessed to are a bit embarrassing, but it's like a lesson in moviemaking to watch — a kind of how-to manual on what *not* to do.

Billboard: Another of very early (1989) efforts, this movie succeeded on the talents of Joey Stefano. Joey played a guy who paints album-cover billboards (we filmed it in an actual studio where that was done) and has to paint Vic Summers in a stage of partial undress. As he works on the job, Joey becomes obsessed with Vic until they finally get together at the end.

The *Adam Guide*, in its review of this movie (which I did as Taylor Hudson), said it was "proof that, with a decent budget, he (Chi Chi) could produce a fine little video." Well, with Joey, at least in those days, it was hard not to.

Secret Sex: There were actually three *Secret Sex* movies (more Taylor Hudson products for Catalina), but I'm counting them as one for the sake of this listing. The premise of 1994's *Secret Sex* is that in the distant future, the country's been taken over by the Radical Right, sex is illegal, and the official government sex police are charged with stopping a secret underground movement of free-sex radicals. The radicals run around in torn-up underwear, while the copulation cops sport tight black fatigues and berets. In one

memorable scene radical John Wood is worked over by cop Grant Larson, and in another Mark West and Aiden Shaw (those two always seemed to work well together) show why they're so concerned that sex remain free and legal.

The true stars of *Secret Sex*, though, are Zak Spears and Kurt Wolfe as cops who try to find out just what the appeal of this sex thing is anyway. Zak pounds Kurt with one of the all-time great on-screen fucks.

Spears and Derek Cruise return in *Secret Sex II (The Sex Radicals)*, in which the guerrillas finally defeat the sex police and bring their forbidden habits back into the light of day where they belong. A few of their revolutionary cohorts still remain in prison, though, so in *Secret Sex III (Takedown)*, they rescue the remaining prisoners and blow up the sex police's headquarters, thus freeing the nation from the grip of this ghastly menace.

The Coach's Boys: In every gay boy's most secret schoolteacher fantasy, a naughty coach, played by Scott Hardman, forces his athletes to have sex with him to make good grades and stay on the team. Damien and Zak Spears utilize a video camera to give the coach his deserved comeuppance.
A 1993 Mustang film that also featured Wes Daniels, Tanner Reeves, and Kevin Kramer.

Hard Body Video Magazine: A five-part series that was intended to be a behind-the-scenes video diary and help the viewer get to know the models on a somewhat personal level. It followed my escapades on the road through various cities and live performances.

The idea was one I'd been toying with for a long time, and I finally took it to Men of Odyssey, for whom I was working a lot around that time. I cohosted along with Chris Green, who took off more and more clothing and  came closer and closer to actually having sex as the series progressed, and Gender. You never really saw Chris doing it on camera, although we finally got to the point where he did get his dick sucked in the last one. He was naked, and you saw the back of a head covering his crotch, but you never actually saw his dick being sucked.

Gender exercised more and more influence as this series went along, which was something Odyssey and I should have never let happen. The series finally petered out despite its popularity when Odyssey decided there was getting to be too much drag in it. I would have done further installments, though on slightly different terms (they were essentially getting my entire life on video and weren't paying me nearly enough), but we never could resolve the drag issue. I maintain to this day that the drag presence gave us two audiences, one to watch the sex, the other to watch the drag. Odyssey obviously felt differently. That's okay, though, because we've worked together on other projects since. I may do additional behind-the-scenes looks in the future, though not necessarily like...

Naked Truth: An insider's look at the making of a porn video, this one didn't come out as well as I wanted it to. Basically, the performers — whom you see preparing for their scenes and in their natural element backstage, then you see the actual sex scenes — just aren't animated enough. Jordan

Young is the sole exception; he did a great job. But Catalina didn't want its personnel to appear on film, so that made things difficult, and the resulting footage just doesn't hold your interest like it probably should. I'm going to try this again, probably for All Worlds, but if you're interested in getting a peek behind the scenes, you can get it here.

Striptease: I filmed *Striptease* for All Worlds at an actual club called Wet in Washington, D.C., late in 1996. It came out great; we featured thirteen newcomers who were nude dancers at the bar (keep an eye out for some of them who will now be pursuing careers in porn; All Worlds even signed one to an exclusive contract). We also had a heavy-weight cast of professionals that included Cole Youngblood, Tony Cummings, Steve O'Donnell, and Chad Knight.

When I went to Washington (my trip coincided with the D.C. appearance of the AIDS quilt), I had just come off a Mustang shoot that was like pulling teeth. Things had gone terribly, and I was terrified about what disasters would befall us next. We'd used some new people on the Mustang set, and a three-way between two of them and Jake Andrews ran long, making me late from the very beginning. Then I got to the airport and had no confirmation of my reservations. *What next, a plane crash?* was all I was thinking.

Even once we got to Washington and got into our first scene, set in a motel room that overlooked the Capitol, it started slowly. Doug Jeffries is a pro who could handle his part, but his partner, a newcomer named Jay Anthony, was nervous, and it took him some effort to get up and running. But once he did, things turned around immediately. Jay got into it, Doug got into it, and the scene turned out sensational, better than I ever could have expected.

After that it was smooth sailing. We did the Wet orgy scene the next day, using about fifty guys who just happened to be at the club that afternoon as audience extras, and it couldn't have gone more perfectly. Audience members actually started sucking the dancers' dicks (legally a no-no even in D.C., but since we had rented the club and shut it down for a private function, it was okay), and one businessman in a silk shirt actually took a come shot in the face. The porn gods must have been smiling on us that day. I was actually jumping for joy, it was so good. *Striptease* is one you don't want to miss.

––––––––––

This is not a listing of all of my best movies, although it does include most of my favorites. You may have a preference for others you've seen or one I neglected to include. That's fine; this is a very subjective business.

I do know that I'm not done yet. I feel like I have a lot of good films left in me, a lot of unique and creative ideas I can't wait to try. I want to codirect with John Rutherford, something I haven't had the chance to do. We have such different tastes, I know we'd come up with some interesting contrasts. I want to do a *Davey and the Cruisers* sequel with Jim Steel for Vivid Man, because I know it would sell like hotcakes. And I want to do more straight and bi films, like that straight version of *Boot Black*. Plus, I'll definitely be a part of the third *Bi Dolls* movie in 1997.

I guess what I'm saying is that this list of my favorite

films is a good place to start — for now. It's not a final list, and it will change, but for a Chi Chi career retrospective, from the early to the late, here's a place to begin. Watch them; watch them all. And for God's sake, watch them at home, where you can satisfy yourself in privacy and comfort. Whatever you do, just don't try to visit us on the set.

Rats in the Cellar
OR
My Own Appearances in Film

WELL, PERHAPS DIRECTORS are a little better-known these days, but to achieve true stardom, you still have to get in front of the camera. And I have done that too. Besides directing, I've also made appearances in quite a few films, both my own and other people's. Now, before you get all panicky, let me reassure you that none of these roles has been sexual. Chi Chi remains fully clothed at all times. Well, there was that one cunnilingus scene in *The Hills Have Bi's* where I'm eating out a drag queen named Moist Towelette, who plays my lesbian lover. But that was just simulated. It's not like we have actual pussies to show or anything. Still, I think I did a pretty good job, and any real lesbian would have been proud.

I've appeared both in drag and out of it, more often in. I like to think these appearances have provided some comic relief in the middle of these usually very serious films. Let's face it, most porn flicks aim for sexual arousal, not good laugh lines. But does that mean there's no place for laughter in porn? I think not.

Drag queens in porn are common now, but it freaked people out very badly when it was first done. People just didn't react well to the idea. There were weeping and wailing letters to magazines, and other directors were afraid I was going to ruin the business by casting DQs. *What was she thinking?* they all wondered. But most people gradually came around, and the movies that the drag queens were in started selling. When other directors and other studios saw that, of course they wanted a piece of the action. So they all went out and signed drag queen directors of their own, and now Karen Dior and Crystal Crawford and Daisy Mae and everybody else with a wig and makeup and thrift store dresses thinks she can be a gay-porno film director.

It's not true, of course. Just because someone is given the opportunity to direct doesn't mean that she deserves it or will create a good product. Being a drag queen doesn't turn you into Steven Spielberg. Some of what these folks produce isn't worth the videotape it's put on. I'm not saying that I'm any great filmmaking genius either; all I'm saying is that I've done my time, I've studied hard, and I've learned some of what's good to do and what's bad to do. And I'm not afraid to admit that I'm still learning. I could go out today and direct an independent nonsexual film, and it would be the greatest challenge of my career, and I don't honestly know how it would turn out. I'm sure it wouldn't be sensational. But I bet I could come up with something better than some of the art-house tripe that's been released lately, just from what I know now. Which is, basically, how to shoot good porno. It's a lesson for all of life.

Appearing in these things from time to time has helped my directing, and directing these things for the last several years has given me some insights into performing. Would I jump in front of the camera to do a sex role if I had the body for it? Sure, why not? There's no shame in it. What's good for these guys should be good for me too. And truthfully it has been. Acting is a lot of fun, and it's a good diversion from time to time.

I'm a natural performer, have been ever since the Big Fig Newton improv back in junior high. Normally, I get my onstage adrenaline fix from touring the country and performing at nightclubs, but once in a while that just isn't enough. Sometimes I can't resist jumping in front of the camera. For the right role in the right movie, it can be a real blast.

Take, for instance, my appearance in Catalina's *The Hills Have Bi's*. It was a bisexual film (well, duh!) directed by Josh Eliot, who had directed me in a pair of earlier bi efforts, *Valley of the Bi Dolls* and *Revenge of the Bi Dolls*. *The Hills Have Bi's* was not a sequel to those, which have achieved kind of a cult classic status among fans of gay video, but I guess it was intended to capitalize a little on their enduring popularity.

The premise of *Hills* is this: Wealthy socialite Clarice (Sharon Kane) has a college-age son (Drew Andrews) who's engaged to marry Sara Lee (Lexi Eriksson), this sweet, beautiful little girl from the hills. Of course, Sara Lee's extended family is coming down out of the backwoods for the nuptials. This creates a very *Beverly Hillbillies* kind of conflict: Our whole bucolic clan arrives in L.A. and is thrown in with high society, and hilarious mayhem ensues. I play Sara Lee's lesbian mother, Mama, and Moist Towelette plays my lover, Muff.

Moist and I have some funny lines and some funny scenes. In one I'm eating the caviar hors d'oeuvres Clarice has had prepared for us, but, redneck that I am, I don't know what caviar is. When Clarice tells me that caviar is fish eggs, I spew out a mouthful that splatters across her face. It's just a brief scene, but it's great comic relief in the midst of all the sex that's going on, especially given the way Sharon can act by her eyes and facial expressions.

In the end Clarice divorces her unfaithful husband, Tyler (Sean Ryder), and comes to live with us in the back-woods. She gets a little trailer of her own, and that's how the movie ends. (Sort of begs for a sequel of its own, doesn't it?)

Hills was fun for a lot of reasons: I got to have big, flow-ing red hair, I got to work with Sharon and Moist, and the script was really, really funny. All three of my children — Sara Lee, Campbell, and Dinty — were named after foods (Campbell after the soup, Dinty after Dinty Moore beef stew). I fashioned Mama along the lines of the nurse-from-hell character from the *Bi Dolls* movies, so even playing hillbilly trailer trash wasn't too much of a stretch.

I think *The Hills Have Bi's* is pretty good, but it's not quite as outstanding as *Valley of the Bi Dolls* and *Revenge of the Bi Dolls*. Those were true classics, and *Revenge*, especially, remains my favorite of the ones I've appeared in. I got to act, I got to sing for the first time (I had lip-synched in *Davey*), and I even got to fight with Sharon. I'm eventually killed in that one when a thousand-pound sand-bag falls on my head. Still, somehow I don't think you've heard the last of my nasty nurse.

———

My very first on-screen performance was not in drag. It happened back when I was working in promotions for Catalina, and Vivid Man's Jim Steel asked me to appear in a film he was doing called *Mannequin Man,* a takeoff on the popular 1987 film *Mannequin.* I was to play the flamboyant owner of an adult bookstore. Since the adorable, juicy Eric Manchester was in the movie and he was one of my absolute favorites at the time, I was happy to give it a shot.

The film was to be shot in an actual adult bookstore down in San Diego, so, unknown to Catalina, I went down there after work one night to do my scenes. My character was a guy, but since he was supposed to be such a big fag, they gave me a quick coating of mascara and blush to make me look queenier. Well, we got started, and the shoot ended up running long — way long. In fact, it took all night, and the sun was coming up by the time we finished the next morning.

So Jim and I had to hustle back to Los Angeles so I could get to work at Catalina. We got in Jim's van and broke all kinds of speed records getting from San Diego to L.A., Jim sleeping in the back of his van, me at the wheel trying to stay awake and not kill us both. My hair was ratted, my makeup running, and I looked like hell, but it was rush hour, and traffic was insanely heavy, and there was no time to sleep or even go home and grab a quick shower. I went straight to work. I never told them where I'd been or what I'd done, but I do remember sleeping on the floor behind my desk for a good part of that day. It's a miracle I didn't get fired.

I can't say I was great in *Mannequin Man* (I only remember one line: "There are *rats* in the *cell-a-a-ar!*"), but it was a lot of fun to do, and it whetted my appetite for more appearances. So not too long after that, I had moved to Vivid Man, and I was talking to Jim over lunch, and we came up with the idea for the 1950s takeoff *Davey and the Cruisers*. Now, Jim, being a good friend and knowing my ebullient nature, thought it would be a good idea to cast drag queens as the girlfriends of the main characters. And that led to my first drag appearance in a film.

My character, Buffy, was the girlfriend of David Rockmore, a huge star of that time. I remember spending the whole movie putting on lipstick and drinking milkshakes and running around in a poodle skirt that didn't fit. We shot our scenes at this '50s-style diner in Van Nuys that was perfect; it looked completely authentic. (Because we weren't doing any of the sex scenes there, we didn't tell them it was for a porno flick. To this day I don't think they know.) Other girlfriend roles were played by my friend Kevin (Rose from the Weather Gals) and this DQ named Eva, and we called ourselves the Bonettes (like the Ronettes). We got to sing, and the script was good, and the sex was good, and the movie became a major hit. To this day I think it's some of Jim Steel's best work.

For the sequel (I'm still pressuring Jim to do it, but trust me, it's going to happen. I'll wear him down eventually) I want to depict where these people are in the 1990s, with drag queens as both the mothers *and* the daughters. I know it would be just huge.

By the time we finished with *Davey,* I had a couple of film appearances to my credit, and I was getting more comfortable in front of the camera. You know, acting is not as easy as a lot of people think. The hardest thing about it for me was learning eye levels; that is, where to point your eyes so that your face gets the best possible angle exposed to the camera. You have to turn your head just *so* to get into the shot; under no circumstances should you ever be turned so people can't tell who you are.

You can't ever look at the camera, of course, and while that sounds all basic and easy and fine, just try doing it sometime. It's like your head is magnetically pulled that way, and it takes all your effort (it took all of mine, anyway) to force yourself not to do it.

You also need the confidence to deliver your lines. This may sound silly in the context of porn flicks, but I know you've heard these soft-spoken guys who mumble their lines so soft and wimpily, you can't understand what they're saying. Or else they deliver them in such a flat monotone that they're unintentionally funny, and you just have to laugh. You really have to e-nun-ci-ate your lines in almost an exaggerated way for them to come out sounding right on film. If you see my film performances, you'll know that this is one area where I have never had much trouble. I'm a loud, crass bitch and a natural ham.

I've also benefited from things like appearing in the video for Madonna's "Deeper and Deeper." That really helped me learn to "find" the camera, to know where to be to be seen. You've all seen live remote reports on your local TV news where some clown goes behind the reporter and waves or does something goofy for the camera? Well, it's the same principle. You want to be in the camera's eye as much as you can. You can't be quite that blatant, of course, but as much as you're able. Before I did my scene, Madonna told me, "Here's your chance to act," and then when she came down the stairs, there I was behind her, visible and prominent. If you ask me, it was the best shot in the video.

After *Davey* I did a lot of straight films, including working with the fabulous, gorgeous Angel Kelly in a flick called *Little Miss Dangerous*. In the sequel to that, called

Even More Dangerous, I played a madame, the keeper of a whorehouse. After that I had a nondrag role in *Powertool 2*, where I play a big, butch cop who is revealed to be wearing pumps when his desk is moved away.

I've also been in drag to host my *Hard Body Video Magazine* series, which we've already discussed. More recently I did *Hung Riders 2* for Catalina, playing the nefarious saloon keeper and gold thief Miss Klitty. It's a very funny project in which Jordan Young (who plays my sidekick, Hip Swing) and I each poke a little fun at ourselves.

Then there are the *Bi Dolls* films. These were such enduring favorites that we eventually got the third installment we all wanted. It wasn't just me; porno fans the world over kept asking Josh and Sharon Kane about it. After a lot of resistance, Josh was finally persuaded to do the sequel: *Night of the Living Bi Dolls*, in which Sharon and I both return, was shot in early 1997. In this one we play zombies. As if drag alone doesn't require enough time spent putting on makeup.

Roses and Rim Jobs
OR
Fame: Its Upsides and Downs

It wasn't too long ago that I was coming home from one of my appearances on the road — it was in New York or someplace; I don't remember where — and I was on a Continental Airlines flight back to Los Angeles. I was out of drag, of course, and feeling tired and ready to get home. It had been a long and grueling trip, and I know I must have looked like hell; certainly I didn't feel very glamorous.

As we were making our way across the country, I noticed a pair of stewards in the back of the plane who kept staring at me. Not just idle glances, mind you, but prolonged, interested stares. Several times I glanced back, and each time I caught them staring.

I checked my hair. All in place. I checked my fly. Safely zipped. I checked my nose. Nothing dangling. I was presentable. My seat belt was on, tray table up, seat not reclined. I was a model passenger. Yet the stewards continued to stare. Were they cruising me? No, I'd seen the cruise look before, and this wasn't it. Still the stares continued.

I was starting to become uncomfortable. As I glanced over at them, trying to figure out what the hell they were looking at, they whispered between themselves. My discomfort grew. Had they somehow pegged me as a fag? Was

I about to be bashed right there on the airplane by employees of the airline?

Finally they started toward me. I braced myself, having no idea what to expect. They stepped up to my seat and bent over, addressing me in polite and quiet tones.

"Excuse me," said one of them. "But, um...who are you?"

"Larry," I said, still guarded.

"Uh, are you known by any other name?" he asked.

"Yes," I said, "I'm Chi Chi LaRue."

The stewards turned and faced each other, trading knowledgeable socks on the arm and breaking into huge I-told-you-so grins. "We knew it!" the first one said to me. "We just *love* your work!"

Well, I was floored. Here I was, out of drag, ragged and drowsy and beat up from my long trip, and these two young gay stewards (cute, I might add; I wouldn't have minded joining the mile-high club with either one of them) somehow knew me well enough to recognize me on this airplane.

Is there anything more flattering in show business than to be identified like this?

For me, incidents like this one are one of the most enjoyable parts of what I do. I didn't know these guys from Adam and Steve, but from magazine profiles and TV appearances and my own film guest spots, they knew Chi Chi LaRue well enough to identify Larry Paciotti out of drag on that late-night flight. It happens every so often, but not so often that I get tired of it. In fact, I'm flattered every time it happens.

What was remarkable about this celebrity sighting was that it occurred in a normal straight environment. It's a lot more likely to happen when I'm walking down the street in West Hollywood or just hanging out at a club somewhere — environments where the gays outnumber the straights. Any gay person can watch porn, of course, but when an incident like the one on that flight happens in such a totally normal place, it still just floors me.

I have to tell you, fame is everything it's cracked up to be and then some.

For the most part I like my degree of fame. I'm known, but I'm not *famous* famous. You certainly can get *too* famous; just ask Brad Pitt or Madonna or Dennis Rodman. But I'm not there yet, so for me the benefits still outweigh the drawbacks.

I get comped into clubs. I get flown around the country. I get to meet scads and scads of gorgeous men and see them naked. And sometimes, every so often, I even get to have sex with them. It's well worth the demands on my time and the occasional fan who recognizes you even when you look like hell.

The happenings of my life are major social events. Each November for my birthday, I fly to New York, where I have a wonderful, raucous celebration at some trendy club. Then I come home and have a separate party in L.A. for some 500 more of my closest friends. Then there are other people's parties, one or two virtually every weekend. This industry is one big, long party. And sometimes I feel like my life is that way too.

It's not all roses and rim jobs, though. Sometimes it all gets to be too much. You're not always in the mood to party or to deal with a fawning public, and sometimes, quite frankly, it gets to be a real pain in the ass. When I can't walk through a club without being pulled and pushed in a dozen different directions, or when I can't stop and exchange pleasantries with every single person who wants to talk to me, thus making them mad and leaving them with a bad impression of me, then I'm reminded of the downside to being so well-known.

Take my 1996 birthday party, for instance. We had it at Movie Tech Studios in Hollywood, and my friend Bradley Picklesimer, a decorator by trade, decked the place out beautifully. He covered the large open court-yard with a tent, and we set up bars and food and a dance floor. Hundreds of people jammed into a space designed to hold maybe half that many. If the fire marshal had shown up, he'd have shut us down in a heartbeat. My dear friend Keith Dunhill, who runs a wonderful club called King in New York and has always treated me like a queen when I've performed there, even flew five drag queen friends of mine to L.A. to help celebrate. (Keith would make some man a perfect husband. In the absence of that, I've settled for being his friend.) Fashion designer Thierry Mugler, a regular at these kinds of functions, also showed up. Everyone was relaxed, uninhibited, and having a gay old time.

And I, the birthday girl, the guest of honor, thirty-seven at last, had to work. Not directing but greeting, schmooz-ing, pressing the flesh. With 500 guests there were hellos to say, gifts to graciously receive, contacts to further. As any politician will tell you, this is work. This is my job. I had no time to relax and sit back and enjoy the festivities; I had to get out there and "Chi Chi LaRue" that crowd.

If there's a drawback to celebrity, this is it. Many of the people there didn't even know who I was and couldn't have cared less that I was turning another year older. They were just there to party. Some of them weren't even part of the industry; they were just along for the ride.

All celebrities have to endure the same thing. And I can't complain too much, because I know it's a lot worse for a lot of people who are much more famous than I am. One of them, RuPaul, came to my party in 1995. Now *there* is a girl who commands attention, and not just because she tops out at about six foot ten when she's wearing her big hair. RuPaul, supermodel, is a super*star*. All gay people know RuPaul. With her show on VH-1, a lot of straight people now do too. And when Ru walks into a room, the spotlight goes directly to her. She has that star aura, and anyone else around her, anyone who might have been the center of attention before, had better just be prepared to become invisible. RuPaul made *me* disappear at my own party. My moderate degree of fame was totally eclipsed by her superstardom.

But you know what? The same thing happened to RuPaul that happens to me in clubs and at parties: She was pulled into little tiny pieces. Not literally, of course, but every single guest there wanted a piece of her, a moment of her time, a conversation between *RuPaul* and themselves to tell their friends about. She was set upon by a hundred different people, and there was nowhere she could turn for relief. There was no escaping it. Ru knows the score and is a good sport about these things, but eventually she just got tired of it and left.

I felt bad about the way that turned out for Ru, but there wasn't really anything I could do about it. She got the spotlight off me for a few minutes, so I was just grateful for that. It wasn't through any fault of hers or mine, it's just the way people react to fame. It's human nature. Even in

Hollywood people aren't so bored with seeing celebrities that they can leave them in peace for some private time. If people would realize that these are human beings with regular lives to lead too, if they could just chill out and respect these stars a little bit, I think celebrities would get out to public events more often.

The ones I really feel for are the true megastars, the Jim Carreys and Sharon Stones. I mean, at least presidents get Secret Service protection. If you're Ace Ventura, pet detective, you can't run down the street to the 7-Eleven without an entire security contingent.

Look at Madonna and the media circus that surrounded the birth of her daughter. There were paparazzi camped outside of the hospital in a death race to get the first pictures of little Lourdes. There were helicopters buzzing her house and people scaling fences. I can just see reporters with cameras dressed up as nurses and trying to sneak into the maternity ward. If anyone has it rough, it's Madonna. All things considered, I think she handles it with remarkable good grace.

I was once at Arena, a popular Hollywood club, to see some singer perform. Madonna was there too. Now, I was smart enough to get up in the club's VIP room for a little privacy and room to breathe. Madonna came there too initially, but we couldn't see that well from up there, and we couldn't hear the music clearly. Madonna decided to get down on the floor, where she could see and hear the show she'd come to see.

Brave, yes, but foolish too. Madonna's faith that people would take her presence in stride was shattered immediately. She staked out her place on the floor, and an enormous crowd of gawkers instantly congregated behind her.

They stared and pointed and whispered like she was some kind of carnival freak, not one of the most beautiful, talented women in music. Put off by this drooling mob, Madonna moved over to the other side of the club. Predictably, like lemmings, the entire mob followed her over, this gigantic wave of people moving en masse across the dance floor. She scratched her head; they scratched their heads. She sipped her drink; they sipped their drinks. Madonna could have marched them all straight over a cliff, and they'd have gone happily to their dooms. That is the power of her fame.

Well, as you might imagine, this got really old really quickly, and Madonna didn't stick around too long. Her attempt at seeing a concert like a normal person had ended in failure, and she had to run back behind her walls and security fences and go back to the lonely life of a superstar, all because these people couldn't respect her enough to give her a little privacy.

If I ever become *that* famous, I hope someone just shoots me. One time I got off an airplane in Newark with boxer Mike Tyson, and he was surrounded by what appeared to be an entire football team. There was one of the toughest guys who's ever lived, and even he had to have a flock of security goons.

Porn stars have it worse yet. If I go out clubbing with guys like Tom Katt or Sonny Markham, they just get swamped by hormone-crazed fans. And because these guys are porn stars, people think they can take sexual liberties with them. People come up out of the blue and ask, "Can I suck your dick?" Sometimes people even just grab the porn stars' crotches, no "Hey, pleased to meet ya" or anything. That is really so gross and wrong; these guys are human beings and should be treated with the same respect and dignity as anybody else. Sometimes I'd like to see someone as muscle-packed as Sonny Markham just haul off and knock somebody's stupid block off. (Sonny, of course, is a sweet guy who would never do that, but you know what I mean.)

I, thankfully, am nowhere near the point yet of needing bodyguards or having my basket groped. I think I'm less famous than I am infamous. While a lot of gay people know me for my movies, if I went on TV, on Sally Jessy or Oprah, most of the viewers wouldn't know me from Divine. I'm still just a cult celebrity, and sometimes I'm really glad for that.

I'm famous enough within gay circles that if I ever need to be cheered up, I can go out and get that without being swarmed or overkilled. My situation is a lot like Sally Field's in the film *Soap Dish*. There was a scene where Sally was feeling low, so she and Whoopi Goldberg went to the mall so Sally could be recognized and fawned over and have her ego stroked back to health. I will own up to doing that sometimes. If I'm a little down for some reason or another, I can just go out to Axis or Dragville or the Love Lounge, any local club, really, and get the celebrity treatment. It's fun to be the center of attention, just not all the time. And on those nights, if it gets too hairy, I can always retreat to someplace like the Queen Mary, the drag bar in North Hollywood, where I can blend in among the DQs and trannys, and no one will bother me.

———————

Aside from fawning fans, fame has other perks as well. I never have to pay cover charges to get into clubs. I seldom have to buy my own drinks. I get to see the country on someone else's tab. I accumulate enough frequent-flier miles that I can always go first-class, and let me tell you, that is the only way to travel.

Being Chi Chi gets people wanting me who otherwise wouldn't. As Chi Chi, I've had sex with guys who wouldn't give Larry the time of day. They're starfuckers, I know that, but I can accept that and enjoy it on that level. I'm at peace with myself, so if all they want to do is fuck my celebrity, then I'll be happy to bend over and push.

I've never had to force any unwilling person onto the casting couch. If anything has ever happened, it's been initiated by the model and done by mutual consent. In fact, I'm very self-conscious about my body (as you would be too if you weighed 260 pounds), and it's very difficult to get me out of my clothes. I'd sooner have sex wearing a parka than get totally nude and reveal this big, fleshy pot of love. If I can just drop to my knees, keep my clothes on, suck a guy to ecstasy orally, and then move on to the next one, hey, that's fine by me. As long as it doesn't smear my lipstick.

I've lost a great deal of weight in the past year or so. Contrast the Chi Chi you saw in *Revenge of the Bi Dolls* with the newer, svelter Chi Chi who was in *The Hills Have Bi's*. The latter Chi Chi wasn't skinny or anything, but she was getting closer. And I'd like to continue on that path, if only for health reasons. I'm pushing forty now, and a heart attack's not out of the realm of possibility. Some people have told me that if I lost weight, I wouldn't be Chi Chi, but that's bull. I'd still be Chi Chi; I'd just be thinner and healthier.

I have had sex with some of the stars of this industry, but I'm not going to name names here. Sorry if this disappoints you, but I've never liked kiss-and-tell books, and I'm not going to write one. That's unfair to the other people involved. If they want you to know, let them tell you.

I will tell you who I *haven't* had sex with. I never had sex with Joey Stefano. I haven't had sex with Jordan Young. I haven't had sex with Chris Green. I haven't had sex with Damien or Aiden Shaw or Wes Daniels or Ryan Yeager. Not that I wouldn't have, had the opportunity come up. It just never did. (Except for Chris, as I related previously. Pardon me while I kick myself a few more times.)

This business, of course, is just bursting with boys who any gay man would be crazy not to jump. Scott Baldwin is one of the yummiest men alive. So is Sonny Markham. Ryan Idol is beautiful. Ken Ryker breathtaking. Sure, I've had sex with some of them, but you're going to have to find it out from them, not me.

I get to travel several times a month. I've seen most of the major cities of the U.S. Clubs fly me around to perform, as do video companies when we do model searches and video promotions. I frequently go out scouting for new talent for Falcon, All Worlds, and Catalina.

Generally, a model search starts a couple of weeks in advance, when the company I'm working with advertises in various local gay rags. They'll run an ad saying something like "Think you have what it takes to do XXX video? Our scouts are looking for you! Come to Club Come Stain on Friday the 26th at 4 p.m. and meet with our representatives. Fame and glory and lots of sex await you!"

We also prowl the circuit parties and hand out cards to prospective candidates. I've discovered a bunch of guys this way. Other times, bars will advertise that I'm doing a show and invite people to come down and talk to me. It's always a hit-or-miss proposition. A lot of times you don't find anyone interesting, but you never know when the next Ryan Idol is just around the corner.

Another great part of being a celebrity is that you get to hang out with other celebrities. Here's where I'm going to drop some names. I've met many of my very own idols: Cher, Madonna, Prince, John Waters, Bette Midler, Divine. If I weren't Chi Chi, most of these introductions would never have happened.

Even more gratifying, I've had some of the celebrities I respect the most — John Waters, RuPaul, Soft Cell's Marc Almond — come up to me and tell me how much *they* enjoy *my* work. Let me tell you, that alone almost makes it all worthwhile. Whoever would have thought that John Waters, creator of such film classics as *Polyester*, *Pink Flamingos*, and *Hairspray*, would get off on *Boot Black*? Sure, I know celebrities are human beings with sexual needs too, but you just don't think about it, you know?

It's almost like being in an exclusive club, the way celebrity social circles operate. You're often matched up with groups of people completely at random, regardless of what you might have in common or how well (or poorly) you might hit it off. The only common denominator is fame. For instance, I recall being at a charity benefit at L.A.'s Greek Theater a couple of years back (another perk: I got $1,000 tickets for a cut-rate $200 apiece) where Meryl Streep, Goldie Hawn, and Olivia Newton-John were performing. It benefited Greenpeace or some organization like that; I'm embarrassed to admit, I don't remember which. I got to meet all the performers backstage after the show, which was great, but my most enduring memory came before that, during the show, when Goldie Hawn was singing "It's Not Easy Being Green" and the entire audience sang along. I joined hands with Shelley Duvall, who was seated next to me, and sang along with her. I was in full drag at the time. Maybe it wasn't a special memory to Shelley (why, she probably breaks into song with big drag queens every day), but it was to me just because of the weirdness of the two of us coming together like that, the respected actress and the drag queen porn maven. Strange bedfellows indeed!

One of the better lines on my résumé is my appearance in Madonna's "Deeper and Deeper" video. I've known Madonna sort of marginally for a while now; we originally met at an underground club in L.A., and though we've never become fast friends or even speaking acquaintances, she knows who I am, and I most certainly know who she is. We have this strange sort of relationship where we're aware of each other's presence at parties and industry functions and other events, even if we never speak or acknowledge it. I normally do attend these functions in drag, so people tend to remember me. People usually react in one of two ways: If they're homophobic or just have never been exposed to drag queens before, they'll be scared to death, or if they're more open-minded, they'll be curious and think, *Oh, I'd like to meet that interesting person.*

Long before my appearance in Madonna's video, I had gone to the *Truth or Dare* premiere party and exchanged greetings with her there. Then I found out about a casting call for the video, and I went and was offered a role on the spot. Well, of course I jumped at the opportunity; who in their right mind wouldn't? A couple of phone calls later, it was all set up, and when I went to the set on the designated day, I was treated as one of the most integral parts of the video, even though my part wasn't that big. Madonna was very concerned with where I was supposed to be in each shot; she kept saying, "Okay, I want Chi Chi to stand over here," and "Right, I need Chi Chi to be over there." She never would address me directly, it was always through her handlers and crew, but I heard her keep referring to me and where everyone else was supposed to be in relation to me.

All of the buzz you hear about Madonna, how she works the media, how she can manipulate people and circumstances, it doesn't do her justice. It doesn't paint the full picture. It's all true and then some. She's a master manipulator, and I don't mean that in a bad way. She knows the right things to say and the right things to do to shape and control circumstances to her liking. If you're around Madonna at all, you begin to appreciate how good her people skills and marketing instincts really are.

Let me give you an example: At one point, midway through the filming, I took a break and left the set, and Madonna had them summon me back to shoot my shot on the staircase. At that point she addressed me directly for the first and only time all day. She asked me, "What's your name?" and I told her "Larry." Then she turned back around and said to one of her lackeys, "Okay, I need Chi Chi to stand over there." Well, Madonna and I had been introduced before, and she'd been referring to me all day. Madonna knew perfectly well what my name was. But she wanted to remind me, I guess, as well as everyone else on the set, that she was the star and it all came through her, that we were only there as we related to her. It wasn't mean or vindictive, and I don't think it was intended to be insulting. It was just her method of controlling the circumstances of the shoot. Things like that are probably a big reason why Madonna is where she is today.

(At about that time, with her *Sex* book in the works, Madonna inquired about coming on one of my sets. Strictly for research, of course, just to see what it was all about. Unfortunately, it never panned out. It's probably just as well. I don't know of too many gay boys who could get hard and perform for the camera with Madonna looking over their shoulder.)

I've also been acquainted with Prince ever since our early days in Minneapolis. When his band the Revolution were all wearing these strange asymmetrical haircuts, he suggested I do my hair the same way, and I went right out the next day and did it. He was very cool and always very playful; he'd sit with us at Rudolph's Barbecue and fling onion rings at my friend Carolyn. I think he was a bit obsessed with Carolyn, actually. She was a six-foot-two (at least a foot taller than him) model who was really striking, beautiful and statuesque. She really could have been a supermodel if she had wanted to pursue it. As everyone knows, Prince is very short, and every time he sat down with us, he'd ask Carolyn how tall she was.

He also came to my defense on one memorable occasion. One night at First Avenue I was all intent on seeing the new Joan Jett video, and I asked the deejay, who was a friend of mine, to play it. He had it all cued up and ready when in waltzed Prince with *his* new video, which he gave to the deejay. Of course they played that one instead and forgot all about Joan Jett. So, a little bit miffed, I went up to Prince and grabbed him (more playfully than angrily; I could never be too mad at him) and asked him, "How do you think you rate over Joan Jett?" At that point one of his security goons jumped in and tried to separate us, afraid that this big, hulking drag queen was about to pummel the tiny music superstar senseless. And Prince quickly told him, "Hey, take your hands off of him, he's okay."

Other celebrities I've rubbed elbows with were Cher, who I met through my friend Michael Schmidt on the set of her "Heart of Stone" video (he was her costume designer); RuPaul (more about her in the next chapter); Marc Almond, who I met through Michael Schmidt at a club in New York; and Joan Rivers, from when I made a pair of appearances on her TV talk show.

One of my most memorable celebrity encounters was meeting the fabulous Bette Midler at a dinner party. Zak Spears and I were invited over to Greg Gorman's house along with Bette, John Waters, and John Schlesinger, the director of *Midnight Cowboy*. We all just sat around a table having drinks and talking and laughing. Bette was very funny and exhibited exactly the same qualities that you see in her films: a great sense of humor, very upbeat and vivacious, and when she's provoked, a little of the caustic side you saw in *Ruthless People*.

It was back in 1993, and Bette was talking about her 1991 film *For the Boys*, which had been really viciously abused by critics and the media. She was still doing kind of a slow burn about that; she was really passionate in her defense of that film and, at the same time, about the fact that Disney never gave her good scripts to work with. So, her being such a great singer and all, I asked her, "Well, why don't you do another musical?" And Bette spun around and said loudly to me, "Honey, musicals don't make any money!" Color me squashed! She hasn't done another musical since.

All right, enough of the name-dropping. There are yet more perks to being famous, and another of those is having the ability to indulge some of my wilder whims. One of those whims is the band I'm in, the Johnny Depp Clones. The Clones are really Chris Green's band; he was the founder and is the driving musical force behind it, but I think I help give them a visibility they might not have otherwise. People who know who Chi Chi is get to know the band that way, and they may come to see us for that reason. In all honesty we don't devote enough time or effort to this project so that we can stand on our own musical merit. We're not that great. Chris is a talented musician, but it's still really just a side project for the rest of us.

The original core of the Johnny Depp Clones was Chris, myself, Peter X., Gender, and Karen Dior. Chris and Peter played the guitar, and the drag queens sang. We went through a long series of drummers and bass players with no one ever sticking. Every time we played live, it seemed like we had somebody different in those positions. But that was okay, because with three drag queens, there were way more than enough stars and egos in the band already.

Gender was eased out after she and I had our final falling-out, and she was replaced with Bradley Picklesimer, a much more stable and dependable partner. Also, at the time of this writing, we seem to be pretty much set on drums and bass for the first time ever. Robert Reemer has joined us on drums, and Jay Lyons on bass, so our lineup now seems pretty much set: Chris, Peter, Karen, Bradley, Robert, Jay, and myself. We get together every now and then to play industry functions at local clubs, although it's still not a real, intense, serious effort at getting good. We all have other jobs, and our busy schedules just don't allow us a lot of time to rehearse. If we had the opportunity to practice, I know we'd get a lot better, but we still manage to have our own little niche as the porn-star/drag-queen band. People come to see us because of who we are, not because we can make music as beautiful as the London Symphony Orchestra's. Frankly, anyone else who played like we do (and sang like Karen, Bradley, and me) would probably be booed right off the stage. But it's nothing that rehearsal and repetition couldn't fix. Recently, in fact, I think I have detected some improvement in us. One of these days our plan is to get into the studio and record a Johnny Depp Clones CD.

Another whim I've indulged is going to France every year. Each May I'm given the chance to fly overseas and perform during (not actually *at* but in the same town at the same time) the Cannes Film Festival. I've done this every year since 1992, and I just love it. I love the French food, I love the French boys, and I love all the culture and adventure. It's one weeklong adrenaline rush with creamy sauces.

On my 1996 trip I got to play Paris for the first time ever. I did a show at the world-famous Palace before one of the largest audiences I've ever been in front of — about 2,000 people. I was backed by French go-go boys who did a choreographed routine, and the crowd just went nuts. A lot of celebrities turned out, and I was able to do interviews with the mainstream media, including television and radio. Since the French are very sex-friendly and at ease about themselves, they're more comfortable with what I do than some Americans.

Honestly, the French are way, *way* less tight-assed than most Americans about sex and nudity. Gay bars in Paris are like sex clubs here; you can go in and have a drink, then retire downstairs to what's called the "lounge" and have casual, uninhibited sex. In fact, the cute young guy who interviewed John Rutherford and me for his radio station there joined us in one of these clubs, and John and I and Jake Andrews got him naked down in this dark, tiny little lounge, all of us groping around for his cock. I also fucked a guy in a bathroom during that trip, and I'm almost *never* a top. I was in drag, in fact, and had to tear a hole in my panty hose to do it.

Jake Andrews and Tom Katt joined me onstage for my big show, which had me stepping out of a pair of giant lips and singing Sharon Kane's "I'm Your Mistress." Jake and Tom then got naked, and Tom crawled down the stage runway on all fours while Jake got down behind him and ate out his ass. Even in France this isn't legal (you can't have sex and alcohol in the same club; you have to choose one or the other), but we didn't get hauled off to the Bastille that night anyway.

I think French people get a bad rap in America. They did not strike me as especially rude, and in fact, the ones I met seemed to be very big on Americans (although I'll admit, I was far from their normal tourist. Maybe they're just nice to big men in dresses). Anyway, I was not lacking for offers of quickies. One boy kept staring at me until he finally came up and said, "Remember me? You blew me in a bathroom last year." Well, truthfully, no, I didn't remember him, but sometimes discretion is the better part of sex, so I just said, "*Oui.* Let's go." I'll remember him next year, promise.

I get more bathroom action in France than almost anywhere else. That's something the division of tourism won't tell you in their brochures, but for me it's a major selling point. For some reason French boys love to do quickies with drag queens, and they don't consider themselves gay for doing it. It is still a heavily Catholic country, so maybe they view sex with men the way guys in the Middle East and Arab countries do: It's just a thing guys do, and it doesn't necessarily mean anything about you. Maybe doing it with a guy in a dress helps them keep a feeling of masculinity.

French boys are kind of aloof, which maybe is interpreted as being rude. They will rarely approach you for sex, but if you approach them, they'll rarely turn you down. There's also very little versatility; they'll top, or they'll bottom — but almost never both.

There is some French porn, but it's hard to find boys there who'll do it. John Rutherford went with me in 1996 to scout for new models, but he wasn't very successful. Most of their porn is imported from the United States, and that includes my films, which are dubbed, subtitled, or just left in English. I don't speak French, which has kind of hampered me during my shows, but by my next trip I plan on learning at least a few phrases I can use onstage. Like "Who here wants to be in a fuck film?"

Straight sexuality in France is equally uninhibited. When Bradley and I walked through the fashion district, it was simply teeming with hookers. We saw women in Versace dresses with parasols and poodles that had been dyed pink. We saw 350-pound behemoths who dwarfed me strutting around in tiny little string bras with lace tassels, flesh pouring out over every edge. Sex was openly for sale just like any other product, and the cops couldn't have cared less. These women weren't bothering anybody; they just strolled up and down the boulevard and waited for guys to come up to them. In fact, I was even mistaken for a whore and picked up. I had great sex with a truck driver in the cab of his rig there on the street at 5 o'clock in the morning.

The French love to kiss, but even that doesn't make them gay. Guys there will suck your face at the drop of a hat. For me, that's *not* good: I devote a lot of time to getting my makeup on just right, and kissing smears it horribly. The first few times I went over, I kissed kind of recklessly and ended up with lipstick around my eyes, which even in France isn't considered high fashion.

Still, they do love their drag queens over there, and I love them for that. Bradley and I were even forced into a little impromptu show on the street in front of Paris's Hard Rock Cafe just to please the dozens of patrons inside who were pressed up against the front windows, whooping and hollering and cheering at us. We developed a spontaneous crowd, and they loved us. It's nice to be appreciated, and I'll continue to go to France as long as they'll have me.

Beyond the glitz and glamour and sex in dark, smelly toilets, with fame comes a visibility and a certain responsibility. These, in turn, can lead to some of the more negative aspects of being a celebrity. I've made a total of three appearances on national network television, and these encompassed both the good and bad.

Roses and Rim Jobs

My appearances on *The Joan Rivers Show* were good. I was on twice, the first time to discuss the porn business and the second to talk generally about fetishes, mine being drag. The original appearance came about when the show's producer called me and asked if I would be interested in participating in a roundtable discussion on pornography. They already had a couple of straight-porn starlets, and they wanted me to represent the gay side. I was kind of surprised to be asked, but if you want an expert, call Chi Chi, I guess. I was happy to do it, though I thought they should include a gay-porn performer as well, and so I talked them into inviting Danny Somers to appear along with me. At first they were a little bit reluctant to do this. A drag queen is one thing, but they weren't certain the audience could handle a gay boy sitting up there and talking about having sex with other men. Middle America is still essentially homophobic, after all. But I persuaded them, and Danny handled it with elegance and class. And I think I came off pretty well too. I was a little nervous at first, but once I got into it, I think I explained and defended our industry pretty articulately, an assessment Joan agreed with in conversations we had during commercial breaks. And let me tell you, Joan Rivers was a class act as well. She was very sweet and very funny, and we got along fabulously. The audience seemed to pick up on the positive vibe, and I think they were solidly on my side by the time we were done. In all, the show was so successful that Joan invited me back for the fetish show just a couple of months later.

As good as the Joan Rivers appearance was, my appearance on *The Marilyn Kagan Show* was just awful. It was a complete setup all along, and they behaved in a hateful, deceitful, classless manner from the very first phone call. I was invited on under false pretenses, ostensibly to discuss my friend who had died, Joey Stefano. What they didn't tell me was that the show was really about drug use in the porn business and how we in the industry supposedly "push" drugs on confused young men and lead them down this road to ruin, where they inevitably die the same kind of tragic, senseless death Joey did.

Working from this bogus premise, I guess they thought it would be a hoot to get this porn director on (he's a drag queen? Even better! More ratings!) and take him by surprise by twisting the facts and calling him names and hitting him in his most vulnerable spot: his dead friend. Sharon Kane, who was also very close to Joey, was on with me, and they deceived her the same way. Let me tell you, these people put the *trash* in trash TV.

Almost from the very second I got onstage, I was under attack from the other guests, a famous porn superstar and a fellow director whom I won't even do the courtesy of naming here. These guys both had bones to pick with me for some reason or another, and I guess they thought they had the perfect forum, a national television audience, to shred my reputation. This porn star even had the gall to call me a drug addict, which was flat-out untrue and as hypocritical as you can get. Talk about the pot calling the kettle black: This guy and I had done drugs together on several occasions, and he had the nerve to call me an addict? I did so many drugs with him, we both got sick, and *I* flushed the remainder of some perfectly good cocaine down the toilet!

Let me clarify the drug point here: I have occasionally used drugs recreationally, but I am not a regular user of anything, and I have never been an addict. Drug use does exist within our industry, like it does in any industry, but I've never allowed it on my sets or encouraged it in anyone. My drug of choice is cocaine, which I may indulge in at parties once or twice a month. I do not use marijuana, amphetamines, or anything else, and anyone who says I do is a bald-faced liar who doesn't have the guts to say it to my face.

My only explanation for this unprovoked assault is just plain old jealousy, which exists like a cancer in the porn business. This vile director had been in the business for years without achieving the kind of notoriety I had, and he couldn't make a movie half as good if he tried, so he had a lot of resentment stored up. As if I were somehow responsible for his mediocrity! Then, as the topper, this guy took copies of the final show (a lot of the most heated exchanges were edited out) and sent them out to everyone: his friends, my friends, performers, writers, studio heads — pretty much everyone who had an interest in the business. I guess he thought he came out better, but that wasn't the consensus I heard. Everyone who saw it told me that despite my surprise at being ganged up on, I managed to come off with more poise and class than these two ranting lunatics.

You may get the sense that I'm still pissed off about this, and I guess I am. Once the slander started, Sharon wanted to walk off the stage then and there, but I talked her out of it. I was afraid that we'd just come off worse if we did that. Sharon and I did call the show's producers the next day and rip them pretty good, and they gave us a half-hearted apology, but they still ran the show. Beyond my own reputation, I think it shone a bad light on the entire industry. Any industry has an underbelly, and we face enough adversity without stabbing each other's backs and airing our dirty laundry in that kind of format. What these people did was harmful to all of us.

I never watched the final cut of that show, and I never will. It was just too horrible. I do recall seeing it promoted on E!'s *Talk Soup,* and I did watch that. Though I was braced for the worst, it really wasn't too bad: They showed just a frivolous little clip of me in this big pink coat, and the host called me the gay Energizer bunny. It wasn't altogether inappropriate; that Kagan show was an ordeal that just kept on going and going and going...

Drug use in the porn industry is a subject that deserves a calmer, more reasoned debate than it got from *The Marilyn Kagan Show.* You're not going to gain any great insights into the problem by treating it in that yellow, sensationalistic, ham-handed way and pandering to the mob mentality that supports that show. To make us in the porn business out to be any worse about drug use than anyone else is unfair and wrong. Sure, Joey Stefano and Christian Fox had drug problems that contributed to their deaths; so did John Belushi and River Phoenix, who as far as I know never did porn. So do thousands of people out there right this very minute who aren't famous and whose deaths you aren't going to hear about.

I do not allow drug use on my sets, and if I catch you doing it, you're history. I've kicked people off sets on several occasions for being fucked-up on something. I don't care if you've flown in from Zimbabwe, that shit's not going to go on with me. Once, after finishing a shoot, I discovered a pair of performers snorting up behind a locked door, and I actually kicked the door in to confront them. One said something about it "enhancing my performance." And I said, "Sorry. No way." That's bull. Neither cocaine nor crystal meth helps your sexual performance.

Individual directors have their own policies on drug use by their stars, and I'm sorry to say that not all of them practice zero tolerance. Here is another instance where being Chi Chi LaRue helps me. I have the luxury of dismissing guys if they behave that way; other directors, who may have smaller budgets and less name recognition, are more likely to be stuck with what they have. Few studios have formal policies about drug use, though most frown on it. The bottom line is that it's a financial matter: They don't want anyone jeopardizing the profitability of a project.

For my money, there seems to be more drug use among the women on the straight side of the business. I can't prove this — it's not an accusation — but it is the perception I've gotten from being around them. After all, women don't have to worry about not being able to get it up.

I'll admit, I'm a bit of a hypocrite. I've done my share of partying in the past, and I still do every once in a while. I've been a casual cocaine user for some time. I'll use it at parties or clubs or in other social settings, never alone or at home or for any other reason than sociability. I use it in a controlled and responsible manner, if it is indeed possible to use cocaine responsibly. I've always managed to stay in control of it, not the other way around.

I like cocaine because it's social, it's good for partying. I usually use it in conjunction with alcohol. Drinking is something else I don't do at home; if I'm given a bottle of something as a gift, it just sits around my house until I give it away. If you came over to visit today, I wouldn't have any booze to offer you. I just don't enjoy being drunk, being sloppy, being out of control. I can handle it — because I'm heavy, I can down ten drinks and still negotiate high heels all night — but I don't seek it out, and I make sure it's rare.

Other drugs have never appealed to me. Pot makes me stupid and sleepy. Special K fucks me up beyond functioning. Crystal is too dangerous and addicts people too easily. Ecstasy makes me sick to my stomach.

I did ecstasy once, and it was fun — until I got violently ill. Then someone told me to do some crystal to get rid of the nausea, and so I did — and didn't sleep for the next two days. I'm not going to put myself at the mercy of those drugs again.

My cocaine use has become less and less frequent as I've aged. It's just not fun anymore. Sure, there are some good times, but more and more often it's just...blah. All anticipation and no payoff.

I think my growing disenchantment with cocaine started with a Christmas trip home I made several years ago. For some reason I had some coke with me at my parents' house. It was Christmas Eve, and they had gone to bed. So I went down to the basement and, quite uncharacteristically, did all this coke. I wasn't in drag, and I didn't have plans or anywhere to go. It was Christmas Eve; what would even be open? But I did the coke anyway. And then I went to bed. And as I was lying there, tossing and turning and unable to sleep, I was overcome with remorse and revulsion and self-loathing. *This*, I remember thinking, *is about the lowest I can go.* I disgusted myself that night.

I guess I'm a very antidrug drug user. And I know that makes me a hypocrite. I just can't help the way I feel about it. When I see crystal freaks in San Francisco tearing the skin off their arms, or when I'm next to a guy on a flight who orders Chivas at 8 o'clock in the morning, I think that's sad. God forbid I ever get like that.

Guys in the porn industry who do use drugs I think are attracted to the glamour. It's almost more about the glamour of scooping it up in the spoon and putting it up your nose than it is about the actual high itself. It makes you part of the scene, you know? I know drug use among everyone is up lately, but for me it's decreasing and likely to continue that way.

What I see as bigger problems than crystal or coke in gay porn are alcohol and compulsive sex. Alcohol is both legal and readily available, and no gay man has ever left West Hollywood wanting for sex. These are much bigger temptations than illicit drugs.

Alcohol flows freely among the porn crowd, and I've had plenty of guys come to town, go out drinking, and then show up hungover on the set the next day. Do you think that helps their performances? That's why some companies are wary of sending their models to L.A. — that over-partying can happen so easily here.

Once I was shooting in a club, and one of the performers reached over the bar, grabbed a bottle, and poured himself a cocktail right there on the set. I took it and poured it out and told him that if he ever did that again, he'd never work for me as long as he lived. If you can't be speeding on crystal on my set, you can't be staggering on vodka.

What's even more common is guys who go out and get sexually spent. They spend the night before the shoot fucking and fucking and fucking, and then they can't perform because their dicks are red and raw and sore or their assholes are painfully overfucked. You have to be a little bit of a sexual compulsive to be a porn star, and a lot of these guys are out having anonymous sex everywhere all the time. Some of them spend hours in bathhouses, then come to the set and have more sex. It's a problem common to porn stars and, I think, a lot of gay men in general. You're all whores. What can be done about that problem, I don't know. You can't criminalize sex, and you can't keep your performers chained up in your bedroom all night. You just have to depend on their professionalism and hope for the best.

———

So that's my assessment of fame and the perks of the biz. Between sex and drugs and disease and vicious backstabbing queens, sometimes I wonder how our industry survives. Yet survive it does, becoming bigger and better with each passing year. For every guy who has a bad experience, two more are ready to step in and take their chances, and an awful lot of them come out better for it. For every movie I make, there's always a bigger and better one to be made around the corner. I don't know what the future holds for any of us, and for me that's incentive enough to keep at it. I can't wait to see what's next.

THE GREAT PRETENDERS
OR
THE ART THAT IS DRAG

DRAG IS COOL. Just look around you: Drag is everywhere. Drag is happening. Drag is now. Face it: As we near the turn of the century, men dressing in women's clothes is the in thing to do. Interpret that how you will, but the facts are undeniable. RuPaul is a star. *The Adventures of Priscilla, Queen of the Desert* and *To Wong Foo, Thanks for Everything, Julie Newmar* were two of the biggest movies of their time. The Lady Bunny's Wigstock, Erasure's *Abba-esque*, the ever-more-popular drag night at your local corner bar — the list goes on and on. It's an amazing trend, considering the limited number of famous drag queens we've had to model ourselves after throughout history. There's Divine and, well...there's Divine. Poor Divine, bless her heart, she was just a little before her time. If she were alive today, she would be as big as Madonna.

Unlike Divine, I was born at just the right time, I think. Society's caught up with her and me and all the other cross-dressing queens who were the objects of scorn and ridicule for so many years. We're laughing now, and we're raking in the dough. Our patience and persistence has finally paid off.

For me, it could never have been any other way. Chi Chi LaRue is the inevitable conclusion of Larry Paciotti's life. As long as I can remember, women's clothes and accessories and other feminine things have held a strange fascination for me. When I was a small child, I was attracted to delicate, frilly things: pretty buttons, lacy doilies, my mother's earrings. I'd try on her jewelry and her dresses when she wasn't around. And I'd play with dolls. Mom had a pincushion doll made to resemble a human female, and I once cut a big hole in the middle of a lace handkerchief to fit it over the doll's head and create a gown for her. Mom was furious, and I was punished (not that that stopped me from doing it again). I'd cut up washcloths, napkins, whatever I could find around the house to make doll gowns out of. I had the best-dressed dolls in town.

As I got a little older, I'd play Barbies with my female friends and my male friends' sisters. I even went so far as to steal a Dawn doll (Dawn was a lesser-known doll of that era) from my younger cousin Roxanne, whom I was baby-sitting. I didn't get away with it; Roxanne missed the doll and told her mom, who told my mom, and my mom confronted me, knowing that I was the only one with both the motive and the opportunity to kidnap Dawn. I denied everything, of course, but the next time I baby-sat Roxanne, I slipped Dawn back into a remote corner of Roxanne's toy box.

As I got old enough to go out trick or treating, I'd dress as my idol, Cher, every Halloween. Of course, being big and a boy, I never looked anything like Cher, but that never stopped me from trying. I'd wear a long black wig and a big serape-type dress, and if anybody challenged me or failed to recognize me, I'd burst into one of her songs. They'd tend to remember me the next time.

Still, it never occurred to me that drag would be the most passionate pursuit of my adult life. Sure, it was fun to play dress-up as a little boy, and if I had thought about it then, I might even have guessed that it would carry over into adulthood. But it just wasn't something I consciously thought about continuing. I had my menial 9-to-5 jobs and settled into a boring rat-race lifestyle and pretty much abandoned my childhood make-believe stabs at feminine glamour.

It wasn't until I got to Minneapolis in my early twenties that the idea of doing drag as a hobby occurred to me. And even then I never suspected I could make a living at it. It started as a lark at First Avenue's lip-synch contest, "The Great Pretenders." And that's when some friends and I formed the Weather Gals. We never expected it to go anywhere, but on our first attempt, our first public drag performance, we won the contest. I guess we were just naturals.

As the Weather Gals' popularity grew, I began to take my drag more seriously. I even shaved my mustache, which I had had since the ninth grade. I loved my mustache, and it wasn't an easy decision, but you simply cannot be a serious drag queen with facial hair. Five o'clock shadow can be covered with makeup, but a big bushy mustache cannot.

For those early Weather Gal gigs, I never wore women's underwear. I'd throw together an outfit out of whatever I could find that would fit, but underneath it all I'd be wearing boxers or briefs — men's underwear. You can tell how real a drag queen is by her underwear: If someone takes his performance art seriously and wants to do it right, he'll go whole hog and do a complete job. And that means the parts you can't see as well as the parts you can. The litmus test to drag queens is lifting their skirts.

Back then I'd wear L'eggs hose, and as time went on, I'd start going to Payless and looking for cheap women's shoes as well. And when I couldn't find dresses off the rack or adapt something someone had given me, I'd have a seamstress friend create things for me. In Minneapolis this was a drag queen named Dee, and once we got to Los Angeles, it was my friend Kevin. The value of a good seamstress to a drag queen cannot be underestimated.

The more drag I did, the more serious about it I became. When I eventually realized that it was going to be a permanent pastime, I started paying close attention to every aspect of my ensembles. Nothing could be skimped on or left to chance; everything needed to be planned and fitted and groomed to perfection and looking as fabulous as it possibly could. After a little time in L.A., I was fretting over my outfits like every night was the Academy Awards.

As I have become more successful, of course, it has become easier to create fabulous outfits. In women's fashion, as in every other walk of life, money talks. By this point in my career, I'm able to have about 80 percent of my clothes custom-made. I've had a number of personal designers and seamstresses who have helped me create some of my most memorable ensembles over the years; you really need the assistance of a talented professional to do a truly bang-up job. A good seamstress can dream up things like, to name just two examples, the black dress with gold Elvis Presleys all over it that I wore to the *Lost in Vegas* premiere party or the shocking red coat made from plastic tablecloth material that I wore to

Paris in 1996. I mean, come on, that sort of inspiration comes only from geniuses and the insane.

———————

The 20 percent of my clothing that's not custom-made I buy off the rack. Now, as any fat man who's ever tried to buy clothes off the rack will tell you, it's not easy to find stuff in our sizes. And that's just with *men's* clothes; trying to find *women's* clothes in my size is next to impossible. I don't know how big gals do it.

So I buy pretty much anything I can find that fits me. I can't be choosy; I have to take what I can get. Whether I'll ever wear it or not is beside the point; I just need to have it. (I'm compulsive this way, and not just in buying clothes. CDs, videos, you name it — I'm a shopping slut.) I'll shop anywhere, from major department store chains like Macy's and Lane Bryant to dingy little side-street thrift stores and middle-class suburban garage sales. Every once in a great while, I'll find a real treasure at somebody's yard sale. You have to keep your eyes open because you just never know where you might find something fabulous.

Also, people give me stuff. I'm picky, and I won't wear just anything, but if something catches my fancy, I'll go to any lengths to get possession of it. I've been known to race around town, going to various locations of the same store to see if they have something in my size. "Put it on hold for me." "Can you order it larger?" "Call them and see if they have one there." Store clerks can come to hate me sometimes, but at least I get them decent commissions.

I'm an impulsive shopper, I can't deny it. Besides dresses and blouses and jackets and wigs, I'll buy any kind of crap that I see and like. I spend way too much money on stuff that's just plain useless, and as a result I have a house full of stuff that's just plain useless. I bought it on an impulse when it tickled my fancy, and most of it I've never used. This goes for drag stuff too; I've been accumulating women's clothes and accessories for years now, so my closets are stuffed full, and I never wear half of what I have. But it's better than not having enough. Sometimes I'll go into a store, not find what I'm looking for, and still spend a couple hundred bucks on other purchases. The credit card companies make a mint off me.

It may occur to you, *Don't you get some negative reactions as a man trying to buy women's clothes in major department stores?* Well, yes, as a matter of fact, I do. But it's not as bad as you might think. No one's ever said anything rude to my face, and no one's ever actually refused to sell me something. But sometimes people react in a bad way. This mostly happens in smaller towns, never in places like Los Angeles or New York (I suppose they're more used to outfitting big drag queens in places like that. "You're the fifth guy today who's tried on those pearls!"). Usually I'll tell whatever clerk happens to wait on me at the beginning that I'm a drag queen and am looking for this or that in this certain size, and that's okay. But when there's no clerk around and I have to fend for myself, that's when the trouble can start. If they see me pawing through their dresses before I can disarm them with my charm, sometimes they clam up. What they'll do is just refuse to acknowledge me. I'll try to catch a clerk's attention through eye contact or by calling out to him or her — or by tearing dresses off the racks and swinging them around over my head — and they'll just ignore me and pretend that they're busy or didn't hear me. That gets frustrating. But in the end, I know I can win them over. I'll share some funny drag queen stories with them, and by the time our little transaction is completed, we'll be chatting like old friends.

I wear a size 24 in women's clothes, so big and tall shops are good for me when regular retail outlets don't cut it. Stuff can be ordered big too. This is an area where my size is a bit of a handicap: I can't wear just anything that looks pretty; it has to flatter my figure as well (or at least not make me look like a stuffed sausage, which tight clothes can sometimes do).

Whenever I go out on the road as Chi Chi, I have a long mental checklist of things to bring along that I run through as I'm packing: Do you have your wigs? Makeup? Earrings? Eyelashes? Bras? Tits? Bodysuits? Nylons? Panties? Shoes? It doesn't pay to forget anything; one missing item can ruin an otherwise terrific ensemble. So in packing drag, unlike in most other things, I'm very organized and oriented toward the details.

There is a basic foundation that never changes, and I start with it for every single outfit I've ever worn: Two pairs of Danskin Too Pretty to Be Support panty hose (one black, one toast); a fishnet bodysuit; a bra or bustier; and panties. That's the core. Beyond that, everything can vary, I have a million options. Item by item, here is how my drag arsenal shapes up:

Wigs: I have about 100 wigs in all. But I am not really a wig person. That's a pretty good number, and it gives me a lot of flexibility with my hair — I can do anything from Crystal Gayle long and straight to a poofy Dolly Parton bouffant ceiling-scraper — but it's not as vast a collection as you might think. Of those 100 about seventy of them are too trashed to wear, and I just haven't gotten around to throwing them out yet. So that leaves me with about thirty to choose from when I'm creating a look. Of those thirty usable wigs, I usually keep about five in heavy rotation.

But I don't really go for the crazy, funny, extravagant wigs. My friend Moist Towelette gets a lot of laughs when she wears her big Afro-puff wig (estimated diameter: three feet), but I prefer to let my personality generate the laughs. Nothing too outrageous for me. When I first moved to Los Angeles, Cher, my idol, was favoring her spiky, colored Rene of Paris (my favorite brand too) two-tone wigs. So I went out and bought a couple of those; I had one that was pink with white spiked ends and one that was black with white spiked ends. The thing is, they just weren't very flattering on me (or, to be perfectly honest, on Cher, but I'd never be the one to tell her). So since then I've tended to use more realistic hair.

Actually, I favor hairpieces over wigs. (The numbers mentioned above include my pieces as well as my wigs.) Pieces hook into your real hair in the front and back, but they're not full wigs per se in that they don't cover your head completely. Their advantage is that they look more natural, and they're not as hot and constricting as full wigs. You don't have those unattractive trickles of sweat dribbling down your face and streaking your makeup.

To put on a piece, you just pull your hair down in the front, hook the piece in, then pull it tight over your scalp and hook it again in the back. It's important to match your true hair color as closely as you can, since your real hair is going to be visible beneath the piece. But if it's done right, people will think it is your real hair. I'm asked that all the time. "Sure it's mine," I'll say. "I bought it myself."

Right now my real hair is brunet (recently dyed), so I try to match my fake hair to that shade. Before being a brunet I was a redhead, before that a blond, and before that a brunet. I like to alter my hair color every now and then because it keeps me fresh. Change is good; a drag queen should never let her look get stagnant.

Makeup: This is a long, painful ritual for me. I have heavy facial hair (a full mustache by the ninth grade and heavy 5 o'clock shadow by noon), so doing a good makeup job on my face is no walk in the park. It takes about forty-five minutes to do my "fast drag" face for normal occasions. For more serious events, like an awards show or a television appearance, it can take more than an hour, and I usually have a professional makeup artist come over and do it to make sure it's done right. At present I'm using two friends, Kevin Hees and Bradley Picklesimer, a fellow DQ. (Bradley, though one of my closest companions, I think has a tendency to overpaint. I think she wants me to be Divine.)

Makeup has never really been my forte, but I have gotten better at it. For this I owe a lot of credit to Gender. When I first met her back in my early days in L.A., when we were performing together at the Four Star, it was Gender who took me under her wing and helped me to become more spectacular. She advised me on my clothes, my songs, my hair, and, most important, my makeup. She did it for me for a long time, and now, even though we're not very close anymore, I still rely on her tips in doing it myself.

When I first started doing drag, I was using a base called Panstick, which I would simply rub all over my face and then blend. But the colors I got with that weren't realistic, and Panstick wasn't true professional makeup in the sense that MAC or Joe Blasco is. It was Gender who told me that Panstick made me look too pink and fake. She also taught me about things like lining my lips with a darker color to emphasize them, contouring my cheeks, and lining my eyes properly (her tip: don't close off the ends). She also taught me to apply fake eyelashes, something I'd always struggled with. I used to get glue in my eyes and would be stumbling around blindly, fake lashes stuck to my fingers, my cheeks, and between my eyebrows, giving me that not-so-attractive unibrow look.

I start my makeup regimen with a good, close shave. I run my face under hot water for a full fifteen minutes to soften up my beard, then get as close as I can using a Gillette Sensor manual razor. I follow by running my face under cold water or using ice cubes to close up my pores. If my chest needs to be shaved (which it does sometimes; it's hellish to be as hairy as I am), I'll do that too. Aveda makes a really good aftershave toner that eases my poor skin, which is invariably raw and nicked.

I start with base, always using MAC's full-coverage C3. I then cover that with powder, usually MAC's N1 loose face powder. The powder sets the base and makes sure that everything is held securely in place.

Then comes the blush, in light orange or soft pink. For the orange I use Prestige warm glow; for the pink, MAC's shy pink. A tip Gender gave me is to add a slightly darker color just underneath the cheekbone for better contours. Since my face is somewhat rounded, this is a good idea for me.

By this point, with all of my pores clogged up with all this crap, I'll need to dab some sweat from my face with a bit of toilet paper. Makeup is really hot and icky, and if straight men ever really knew what women went through to do it, they'd treat 'em a hell of a lot better.

For my eyes I use heavy liner both above and below, but I don't go in for eye shadow. Then, after applying my lashes (Duo Waterproof Clear White glue is the best), I'll go back over the top lid just to touch it up. I'll line my lips in one of two colors, burgundy (MAC vino pencil lip liner) or brown (Aveda agate brown), and if I'm using red lipstick, I'll coat it with Prestige LeBrilliant red gloss.

After that, a little Princess Borghese mascara completes the look, and I take a big powder brush and add some Chanel Eveil Rose No. 5 under my eyes. (Most of the brushes I use are MAC or Sebastian, except for my lip brush, which is Chanel.) Then, since I can't jump in the shower again, I mop up as much sweat as I can with some more toilet paper. It's best to use waterproof makeup for me, because believe me, as a big guy, I could sweat in a Minnesota blizzard.

All of this stuff is easily available at cosmetics or beauty supply stores. I get my lashes at Hollywood Wigs on Hollywood Boulevard, my makeup at the local MAC store, and powder puffs, sponges, etc., at any old beauty supply outlet.

Bras and panties: With my makeup complete, I then slip into my hose. I always use two pair, one black and one toast, and which one goes on top depends on the outfit I'm planning to wear. Putting the toast on underneath breaks up the black a little bit, while putting the black on first gives a nice, dark undertone to the toast. Two pairs of black hose just looks too black, and two pairs of toast creates a strange, unnatural skin color.

After the hose are on, I usually adjust my dick, which always seems to be crimped up painfully in one direction or another. I don't have to worry about tucking, since I'm not as hugely endowed as some lucky drag queens (like Lana Luster and Karen Dior, who have actually done porn roles). If I had a dick like Lana Luster's, I'd really be dangerous!

After the hose I put on a fishnet bodysuit. This is basically a foundation garment that disguises (or at least minimizes) the body's flaws. If there's any scraggly hair growing in on my chest, the bodysuit camouflages it. Ditto for zits and other skin blemishes. Bodysuits are available at any dance store, one size fits all. Unfortunately, for some reason the fishnet bodysuit is the single hottest, most constricting, most uncomfortable thing I wear. People have no idea how uncomfortable it is to be beautiful.

On top of the bodysuit goes my Lane Bryant girdle panties, which hold everything in place, and my Lane Bryant black bra or Princess black bustier. And finally, whatever I wear goes over that.

Tits: What fills that Lane Bryant black bra, you might ask? Well, since big, realistic bosoms are the true determinant of any good drag queen, you can't skimp on the boobies. For a big and bodacious queen like myself, they must be equally big and bodacious. That's why I can't just stuff my bras with any old thing I find lying around. Kleenex isn't "alive" enough; it might work for teenage girls, but it doesn't create the bouncy, pendulous effect real breasts should have. Kleenex is not perky. Ditto for newspapers, which can chafe one's sensitive nipples, and all other paper products. Just forget the paper; that's for amateurs.

Instead I use breast forms, which can be purchased at any major department store or ordered from an actual mastectomy catalog. That's right — those things for women who've lost one to cancer. I don't intend to be flippant about this; breast cancer is not something to joke about, but these are as authentic as you can get. They're made of gauze, foam, and light lycra, and I'll take them in large or extra large, depending on the outfit.

Since I have no desire to become a woman for more than a few hours on a few nights a week, implants are out of the question for me. I may be a woman trapped in a man's body, but it's going to stay a man's body.

Shoes: These are very hard for a big person like me to find. I wear size 11 in men's shoes, which translates to a size 13 in women's, a dimension usually reserved for basketball players and Amazonian princesses.

Right now I'm into the elevated look of platforms and big heels. Actually, this goes all the way back to my childhood fascination with the band KISS (Paul Stanley, yum!), so it's a longtime obsession. Plus, I feel that as a drag queen, you can never be too tall. You *should* be larger than life, a comic-book superhero presence on the stage. You should dwarf people when you meet them so you come across as slightly intimidating. Moist Towelette really grabs people's attention because she's so tall. Moist is better than six feet to begin with, and by the time that girl gets up on those heels with her wig on, she tops out at eight or nine feet tall. Well, six foot six or seven, anyway. You'd better believe that she draws every eye when she walks into a room and stays the center of attention once she's there. None of that will help her if she falls off those heels and breaks an ankle, but as long as she's upright, Moist is truly glamorous.

Moist wears size 16 in women's shoes, so she has a really, really hard time finding footwear. Most of hers, in fact, are custom-made. The same for Jazmine, another friend of mine in the porn biz; she wears a big ol' 15. For me, in my size 13, it's a little easier. I can find nice shoes in regular stores a lot of the time.

As any man who's ever done drag will tell you, learning to walk in heels is the single most complicated thing that women do. Well, maybe childbirth, but the shoes are a close second in both difficulty and painfulness. I salute any woman who can get around in those things. Especially you big gals. When you're heavy, your heels — for that matter, all your shoes — tend to wear out pretty quickly. At 260 pounds, I'm absolute murder on heels. I'm getting my heels retapped all the time, and I'm always breaking them or ripping through the sides or the soles. So I go through an awful lot of shoes. This is expensive and frustrating.

For the 1995 Gay Erotic Video Awards, for instance, I found a gorgeous pair of mesh pumps that were just the right size. They cost eighty bucks, but they were like gloves on my feet, they fit so well, and I was in love with them. By the end of the night, though, my feet had ripped right through the cheap construction, and the shoes were destroyed. They couldn't be fixed, they had to be thrown away. Eighty dollars for one night's wear: Such is the life of a drag queen.

I'll usually pick a pair of shoes and wear them over and over and over again. Right now it's my elastic-strapped mules. I also found these seven-inch platform heels in Paris that I save for especially glamorous occasions.

I'm not really a shoe queen like, say, Bradley, who actually decorates her apartment with the things. I only own about ten pairs. Bradley, on the other hand, owns hundreds. She'll buy anything that catches her eye, while I go for fit and comfort, comfort becoming more and more important as the evening goes on and you're stuck in the damn things for hours on end. Glamorous drag queens do not kick their shoes off.

Other accessories: With makeup, hair, and outfit all complete and in place, it's time to add the perfect finishing touches by way of jewelry and other accessories. Personally, I love earrings, but I'm not so much into bracelets, necklaces, and other things. More often than not, they just get in the way. I own only one necklace, which was a gift from Bradley after I took her to Paris in 1996. It's a big star-shaped thing, absolutely gorgeous but more than a little dangerous. The first time I wore it, one of the points ripped my bodysuit.

I don't wear fake nails, because they just pop off. They make it difficult to drink cocktails and suck dicks anyway, and those are two of the main things I plan on doing when I go out. I'll add a belt if I'm wearing a skirt or a bell-bottomed pantsuit when it would look right and be flattering to my figure, and lately I've been using a lot of headbands, especially when I don't feel like dealing with a wig or a piece. Gloves are good sometimes, but like so much other drag stuff, they tend to get hot, and I always end up taking them off and stuffing them away in my purse, so what's the point?

Earrings, on the other hand, are one of my consuming passions. I own hundreds of pairs, from gaudy $1 closeouts from Walgreen's to $100 rhinestone danglers that you have to glue to your ear because they're too heavy to stay on otherwise. More expensive isn't always better with earrings; some of my favorites are the cheap plastic kind found in little discount shops.

Bradley's also gotten me addicted to fans, the little handheld spreading kind that classy women throughout history have fluttered when swooning with the vapors or watching their plantations burn down. These are a drag queen's savior: They're cheap, they're glamorous, and they're practical, keeping you cool with a minimum of effort. And they fold neatly away for storage in your purse. The downside is that they're also easily lost. I'm always leaving them in bathrooms or in clubs or restaurants. I go through at least one a week.

And speaking of purses, a well-prepared drag queen always carries an emergency pack in hers so that she can repair any damage that might occur to her face during an especially rough evening. For me this includes eyelash glue, whatever shade of lipstick I happen to be wearing, a compact (with MAC pressed powder), and lip liner, because lip liner is easily smeared by sucking dick.

Sucking dick, by the way, becomes more difficult the more complex your drag is. Just forget about your lips; they won't be able to be saved. (You repair what you can, but you'll never look as good as you did when the evening started.) If you sweat from the effort, the rest of your make-up is shot too. And if, God forbid, the lucky object of your blow job comes on your face, you might as well go home right then. Plus, the more necklaces, earrings, and other baubles you're wearing, the greater your chance of (a) losing them or (b) jabbing him with a pointy edge. Even guys who like drag queens tend not to like that.

Clothes: Even by drag queen standards, I am very hard on clothes. I'm very physical and demonstrative during my stage shows; I run around, roll on the stage, sit on people's tables — it's all very theatrical. So my clothes need to be very sturdy. Mothers who have to outfit young boys know what I'm talking about: Buy 'em strong, or you'll be buying 'em over and over and over again.

Many's the time I've shelled out big bucks for some lacy floor-length dress and then, in some drunken late-night fit of lust, gone to my knees on the bathroom floor of some bar to suck some guy's dick. (Not that I don't savor every single second of it, you understand.) And then, the next morning, I'll wake up to find holes in the knees, little rips and tears, unidentified stains that won't come out no matter how much bleach you use. It's one of the hazards of the job.

For the 1995 Gay Erotic Video Awards, I had purchased a long black net skirt, brand-new and to die for. It cost me $200, but I thought it was easily worth it. Well, of course the damn thing started ripping the second I walked in the door of the Hollywood Palladium. After I went up onstage to accept my first award, I went back to the table I was sharing with John Rutherford, and he and I started clearing some of the torn lining out from the inside of the skirt. It quickly became like a scene from a cartoon: The more fabric we pulled, the more unraveled. It just kept tearing and tearing and tearing, my beautiful new skirt getting more and more trashed. Within moments we had material tangled around our feet, our chairs, the table, and several passing waiters. It even migrated over to the next table and tangled up other guests. John got so mummified, he had to cut himself free with a butter knife. And, of course, the skirt was beyond salvation. By the end of the night, I had to tie a knot in the side to disguise some of the damage. It looked okay, I guess, and no one was the wiser, but I was still pretty vexed. When you pay that much for something, you expect it to last more than five minutes.

I have created a general look over the years that I feel is pretty flattering: I go for long coats, open in the front to emphasize length, not width. I don't mind showing my legs, which I think are pretty good, but I want to hide my stomach, which is not. Again, I learned a lot from Gender in those early days when we worked together. She worked with me a lot on my look, telling me what was good for my shape and offering helpful hints and constructive criticism.

Of course, as things turned bad later on, Gender and I stopped getting along. It's kind of a sad story. We'd become good friends performing together at the Four Star, and I knew she was a talented performer and a wonderful makeup artist. The problems arose because we became business associates as well as friends, and the two *do not mix*. It became impossible to stay friends after we started working together on film sets. She couldn't take criticism, and she resented authority. I mean, it's not like I'm some horrible tyrant on the set, and I don't think I'm even overly difficult to work for. Gender just had a problem with my being her boss.

On the other hand, the input she had into my drag and my makeup application gave her some amount of power over me, and she used it to the point of abuse. She never let me forget what she was doing for me and that I couldn't do it for myself, at least back then. She made me insecure to the point where I couldn't function as Chi Chi without her; I'd take her on the road with me to places like Paris, New York, Florida, and New Orleans for fear of embarrassing myself if I tried to do things on my own.

Ultimately, we parted on bad terms, and I learned to fend for myself. I am now fully capable of creating my own glamorous look and doing my own makeup, thank you, and I don't need her or anyone to approve it. Maybe I'm not as skilled at it as she is, but I do all right.

I'm not so much bitter as I am sad at the way things turned out with Gender. She helped me, then turned around and threw it in my face and took credit for everything I accomplished. She even told me that without her, I'd be nothing, and that's bullshit. (If you don't believe it, look at the way our careers have turned out.) I told Gender that if I still had a mustache and was dressed in a torn, dirty muumuu, I would still be Chi Chi LaRue, and I'd still be funny and popular. Gender helped me perfect my look, but Gender did not create me, as she would have you believe.

Unfortunately, a lot of drag queens have that tendency toward bitchy, catty behavior. Including me, as you're about to find out. As I've said before, drag queens are the worst of men and the worst of women all rolled up into a single horrifying package. That's the reason we rarely exchange fashion tips and makeup hints. Drag queens are very jealous and very insecure, always afraid that someone else will look prettier or upstage them. Gender and I were the exception to that rule for a while, but then I guess her true drag queen nature won out, and her insecurities became too great to ignore.

I do try to be an exception to this rule; as far back as my Weather Gal days in Minneapolis, I've always been willing to extend a hand to other DQs. I kind of feel like there's room for everybody, that someone else's success isn't going to threaten me as long as I have my act together. If someone new is coming up and wants some words of wisdom about clothes or accessories or whatever, I'm always glad to help.

Making It Big: Sex Stars, Porn Films, and Me

The last time I went to New York, for the 1996 gay pride festival, I was doing a show at the Limelight when I noticed this young black kid sitting off in a corner by himself. He looked like he was about 15, though he must have been older. It struck me that he had simply a perfect face for doing drag: He was chunky, bordering on fat, and so his face was round and feminine and young-looking. (Fat faces tend to look more feminine because they don't have the crinkles and wrinkles of more slender faces.) He had big, full lips and big, round eyes and a little pug nose — perfect DQ material. So I went over and told him that he should do drag, that he'd be fabulous. I even came up with a name for him on the spot: Ebony Hore. It was fantastic. It couldn't miss.

So the next night I was back at the Limelight, and this young man came running excitedly up to me and told me that his friends were going to kick in so that he could buy the stuff he needed to do drag. Ebony Hore was born, and by the time you read this, she'll probably be in Hollywood directing fuck flicks. It was really gratifying; when this kid told me that, I had this great, swelling feeling of pride. I felt like I had helped this kid in some way, even though I had no idea (and still don't) how it would turn out. I suspect he'll be huge; the quiet ones always blossom the most in drag. All I know is, one night he was this poor little boy in the corner who no one paid attention to, but he could come back the next week as Ebony Hore and be making money and friends at every turn.

It's the same way for me and all other drag queens: When I go out as Larry, no one's going to notice me, talk to me, or take my picture. But when I go out as Chi Chi LaRue, everybody wants a piece of me, and I'm always the life of the party. It gives me a lot more self-confidence, really. I've always been self-conscious as a boy, but as Chi Chi, I revel in the attention.

———————

While I don't want to be evil, I do have certain opinions on some of my peers in this line. Here's my brief assessment of some of the better-known drag queens of yesterday and today:

Karen Dior: Karen, a good friend and an aspiring actress who is crossing over into network television, is as real and as fishy as a drag queen can be. I think she looks like a girl even when she's not in drag. She's blessed with fine, delicate, feminine features and a small, slender, feminine body that looks great in a bikini. In short, she was made to be a drag queen.

Karen also has a really big dick, and she tucks it as well as anybody in the business. It's almost like a retractable penis: She can reel it back in to put on women's clothes and perform, and then she can flip a switch and have it pop out again later that night when it's time for sex. Remarkable.

She's had a lot of work done (plastic surgery), and she'll be the first one to tell you that. But the fact is, it was well worth it; she's beautiful.

As a porn professional, Karen has both starred in and directed films. She's done sexual roles both in and out of drag, and because she can get hard on demand, she's served as a stunt dick on many occasions when other performers couldn't.

Professionally, Karen isn't always totally original, and she can feed off other people's successes in a way that's sometimes kind of derivative. She's very skilled at adapting other people's ideas to her own benefit. We've worked together a lot, so I've seen this. But I still hold her in the highest possible regard. We've had our ups and downs, but we've always remained friends despite it all. We even had sex once, in a group situation. She's beautiful, and she's fabulous. My only regret is that due to our busy schedules, we don't get to see each other very often.

Crystal Crawford: The first time I saw Crystal, I thought she looked like...how I can I put this nicely?...the spawn of Margaret Hamilton and Mr. Ed. Okay, maybe that wasn't so nicely, but I'm just trying to be accurate here. Back then, before she perfected her drag look, Crystal came across as a little witchy. She was much less attractive at that point than she is now. Now, of course, she has a much firmer grip on things and looks a whole lot better. She's learned how to put herself together like a pro. She still needs a nose job, but if she got one, she'd look like Karen Dior, so maybe it's better this way. Her nose is uniquely hers, like Barbra Streisand's.

Personally, Crystal and I aren't exactly the closest of friends. She is very defensive and somewhat paranoid, thinking everyone is out to get her when, if the truth were told, it's more likely the other way around. She's one who, I think, wanted to ride my coattails into this business, both as an entertainer and as a director. If she had to gain 100 pounds to be the next Chi Chi LaRue, she'd do it in a heartbeat. I think she saw my success and thought, *Well, if* she *can do it,* I *can do it,* and she was willing to do just about anything to get what she wanted. And at various times in the past, she's been a vile, malicious, person, but to her credit, she's learned the hard way how cold this business can be, how it can chew you up and spit you out. I've more or less learned to like her for what she is: a scared, insecure person who could be really nice if she ever let herself.

As far as her movies are concerned, I don't think she's made any really great ones. *Manhattan Skyline* was the best, I guess, but it wasn't really hers as much as it was the product of a good cast and crew. Still, if she continues to learn and improve, she could someday be capable of making some good films.

Gender: I've told you about my sad split with Gender, who was at one time one of my closest friends. I guess it was around Christmas of 1995 that we actually split and stopped associating with each other. The situation had just gotten unbearable. She was obsessive, wanting to cosign on a joint bank account and thinking that she should be making as much money as I was from our joint film efforts. Gender wrote some very good scripts, but she was irresponsible too, always late for the set and oversleeping on the road. She'd expect me to wake her up when we'd done the same amount of partying and been up to the same hour the night before. Basically she expected too much for giving no honest, loving return.

Still, I can't minimize the role she's played in my career or the good, good friends we once were. The first time I saw Gender perform, I thought she was the funniest thing I'd ever seen. She did a song called "Teenage Enema Nurse," and she came out onstage in a nurse's outfit smeared all over with shit. She actually sang her own songs, which made her unique among the lip-synching crowd at the Four Star.

We started as acquaintances and became friends over time. I started using her as a makeup artist on my sets, and she became more and more a part of my life. We were inseparable for the longest time, partying together, traveling together, always at my expense. I bought her dinner after dinner, cocktail after cocktail, vacation after vacation — I made sure she was taken care of. Now I think she was just using me for what she could get.

And then she started to get jealous of the popularity I was gaining through my videos, popularity that she, in some bizarre, twisted mental process, felt like she was responsible for. She wasn't, of course; my drag persona as Chi Chi helped to promote my porn videos, and my porn videos helped to promote my drag persona as Chi Chi, so it was basically just timing and marketing and good fortune that led to it all coming together. But Gender didn't see it that way, and she never really appreciated what I did for her.

Today if Gender called me up and wanted to talk (which she would never, ever do; she's too proud and stubborn), I'd jump at the chance. We had way too many fun, scandalous times together for me to hate her forever. But it's not going to happen anytime soon. She and Crystal Crawford share this crazy paranoid delusion that I'm somehow out to get them, that I have all the time in the world and nothing better to do than sit around and plot to destroy their careers. Nothing could be less true. In Gender's case I've even thrown a couple of film projects her way. If those two (or anyone else) think that they play that big a role in my life now, then they need to get their egos back under control.

Jazmine: I love Jazmine, she's a hoot to be around, and we have many, many good times together. We have a lot of common interests. Like me, she goes in for sleazy sex with sleazy tricks, and she'll pick up boys in bars, on street corners, anywhere she can find them. The thing is, Jazmine just tries too hard sometimes, and sometimes she can be a little difficult to be around.

I think Jazmine sees the limelight of the porn business and wants to be a part of it, wants to be known as a drag queen personality on the West Hollywood circuit. And sometimes she goes about achieving that with the grace and subtlety of a bull in a china shop. Everyone likes her up to a point, and then she goes a little over the line, gets a little too much in-your-face. Then I have to take her arm and call a time-out and tell her, "Honey, it's not *The Jazmine Show.*" And she knows then that it's time to rein it in a little. That's even become a running joke between us: "It's not *The Jazmine Show,*" and "It's not *The Chi Chi Show.*" We keep each other in our places.

Jazmine is intent on infiltrating this industry and befriending as many porn stars as she can. She's a world-class schmoozer. One thing that endears her to me and a lot of people is the camera she always carries with her. She never goes anywhere without the thing, and although it gets her a lot of kidding, everyone loves it when she brings the pictures over. I have a lot of wonderful memories captured on film thanks to Jazmine, people and events that would be fading into memory without her. She's probably spent thousands of dollars on film and developing costs, and she gives these prints to her friends without ever asking for anything in return. Whatever her faults, this shows you what kind of heart Jazmine has.

So that's my take on Jazmine: She's the kind of person who would give you the shirt off of her back, then pull it over your head and knock you down to get a picture with a porn star. Jazmine, honey, you have a heart of gold. Just learn to slow down a little.

Bradley Picklesimer: What can I say about Bradley, one of my very best friends in the world? She's very independent, very self-reliant, doesn't need anything from anybody. She's totally clean and sober, so she's great to party with, and if you're fucked-up by the end of the night, she'll take care of getting you home and make sure you arrive there safe and sound. And the fact that she's sober doesn't stop her from putting on seven-inch platform heels and dancing her ass off until closing in any bar we go to.

Bradley is basically a sweet, kind person whom I'm proud to call a friend. I took her to France with me, and I had a wonderful time that wouldn't have been the same without her. We did the whole tourist thing: sightseeing, shopping, eating, partying, cruising for men on the Avenue des Champs Élysées at 7 A.M. Of course, she did say that "fuck" in that glorious old cathedral, so she's probably damned us both to hell, but who could be more fun to burn with?

Moist Towelette: A relative newcomer to the L.A. drag scene, Moist is one of the funkiest, most fabulous, most individual characters to come along in a long time. She's very wild, very New York, and she has a bright, bright future in this business.

I had her perform at my premiere party for *Lost in Vegas* at West Hollywood's Love Lounge, and she stole the show with an enormous black Afro wig and a striptease to Wayne Newton's "Danke Schoen." The girl is creative, you have to give her that.

And she's already breaking into movies; critics loved her as my lover, Muff, in *The Hills Have Bi's*. Watch for this one in the future.

Lady Bunny: Lady Bunny is best known as the brains behind Wigstock, and that's where she and I first crossed paths. When one of the more recent Wigstock festivals was in its planning stages, I asked her if I could be in it, and she told me, "Right now I'd have to say no." So that's become a running joke between us; whenever I see her now, I tell her, "Right now I'd have to say no."

We aren't the best of friends, but we aren't really sworn enemies, although both have seemed to be the case at various times. It's a love-hate relationship, honestly, where we're both nice to each other's faces. She's outstanding onstage, very witty and a fabulous entertainer, so I don't know why she didn't want me in Wigstock. Maybe she didn't want the porn connection, or maybe she was just afraid of being upstaged. But if I were afraid that she didn't like me for some reason, she eased those fears the first time I performed at the Eros Theater in New York. She brought a camera crew down and gave me all kinds of support, taking pictures and being very sweet and enthusiastic. She told me she hoped the gig would be a success, and I believe she genuinely meant it. She's very controlling, and Lady Bunny likes Lady Bunny a lot, but she's not an evil person, and I really have no problem with Lady Bunny.

Lipsynka: This one, on the other hand, I really got off on the wrong foot with. We've met only once, and she definitely rubbed me the wrong way that night.

Our first meeting occurred at Atlas, a club in L.A.'s Wilshire district, during an after-party for a Thierry Mugler fashion show. Lipsynka came strutting up to me wearing

Chanel glasses and a feather coat, lifted her glasses, looked down her nose at me, and said, "Chi Chi LaRue! *I* want to meet Lex Baldwin!" Her first words, honest to God. Not "Pleased to meet you," not "I've seen your work," not even "How's it hangin', toots?" Just this imperial, arrogant, condescending statement that made me dislike her immediately.

I want to emphasize here that Lipsynka is a great entertainer, she was very funny, and I enjoyed her show very much. But she just made a bad first impression. She struck me as conceited, like maybe she'd bought too much into her own publicity. I'm sure she has many good qualities, and I'd love to find out if our paths ever crossed again. Who knows, maybe we could even become friends. But if you want to meet Lex Baldwin, honey, join his fucking fan club.

Daisy Mae: Through no fault of her own, Daisy Mae is a corporate creation, a calculating attempt by Bijou Video to capitalize on the trend of drag queens directing porn. When I got big and Karen Dior and Crystal Crawford and others were making their names, Bijou decided to get in on the game, and Daisy Mae was born. Call her Chi Chi Lite. I met her only once, when I was doing a show with Gender in Chicago, and she was a wonderful person, sweet, sincere, and accommodating, and she was a wonderful hostess in showing me around town and partying with me. Personally we got along fine. But professionally, I fear she's simply a product. I haven't seen her films, but I suspect that she's no more qualified to direct than I am to perform open-heart surgery. She's quite honest about her role and has said in print that Bijou just wanted to create its own Chi Chi, so I will give her credit for shooting straight. I take it as kind of flattering that I've gotten big enough to inspire imitators.

Jackie Beat: Hmm, how to describe Jackie Beat. Try *rude, crude, evil, vile, mean,* and *funny as hell.* Of all the drag queens working today, Jackie comes the closest to approximating my style. She wants to be a legitimate actress and has done some off-Broadway stage work in New York, and she's also had a handful of nonsexual roles in porn flicks where she's simply stolen the show. She's quick and witty and can think on her feet, and on more than one occasion, I've given her scripts and the freedom to rewrite them as she likes.

I recall being at a club called King in New York City and seeing Jackie Beat walk in with her tits pushed up and hanging out of a leopard teddy; she was totally glamorized and looked, I thought, like a 300-pound Anna Nicole Smith. (Another thing I like about Jackie is that she makes me look petite.) One of the best times she and I had was trying to squeeze her into my clothes. She's a big girl, but she's a scream. And I'm glad she's off in New York; I don't need the competition that one would give me.

Lana Luster: Lana is the drag persona of a well-known person who's been around the porn industry for a long time, Vince Harrington. Vince has done movies both as Vince and as Lana, but his claim to fame either way is having that enormous, notorious dick. It's gag-a-horse huge, at least ten inches by my reckoning and eleven by some others'. He loves to show it off at parties and in clubs.

Vince himself is one of the brightest, wittiest, funniest people I know, and that comes across when he's Lana too. I don't know how I like him better, in drag as Lana or in spandex, showing off that huge cock. He's a blast to have around either way.

Holly Woodlawn: One of the more famous drag queens of American pop culture, Holly dates back to Andy Warhol and his crowd, so she's known some of the most brilliant and creative minds of recent history. She's a legend now; Lou Reed wrote "Walk on the Wild Side" about her, and it was an honor to meet her on the set of Madonna's "Deeper and Deeper" video. Her personality is very European, and she's wonderful to talk to, just from knowing and being around so many interesting people. She also has a darn good sense of humor; check her out as the streetwise psychic in BIG Video's *Beverly Hills Hustlers*.

Holly and I got acquainted and hung out during the Madonna video, and I've even loaned her some wigs for various photo shoots. Our busy schedules don't let us see each other much, but we talk on the phone once in a while and try to see each other whenever one is in the other's town.

Jimmy James: Jimmy is originally from Texas but now lives in New York and is probably the most notorious of that whole wonderful lot. She's not as well-known nationally as she should be, and I'm not sure why that is. If it were simply a matter of talent, she'd be bigger than anyone listed here.

I first met Jimmy in L.A. through a stripper named Thom Collins, and we would often hang out together at the house she shared with her friend Bubba. Seeing her perform for the first time absolutely blew me away. She could do impersonations that were so accurate, it was just uncanny. Among the voices she can do are Barbra Streisand, Cher, Patsy Cline, Judy Garland, Marilyn

Monroe — pretty much the whole lineup of gay icons. After seeing her that first night, I went back the next night and the night after that just to see her again; I couldn't get enough of her act.

Jimmy is a sweet person too, though she can be a little bit bitter about her weight sometimes. She's also a tad homophobic every now and then in comments about the various elements of our community, but I guess that happens to a lot of people — being gay ain't easy.

And there may, in fact, be bigger things yet in store for Jimmy James: When crossing through Times Square in 1996, I was stunned to look up and see her sharing a clothing billboard with supermodel Linda Evangelista. Yes, Jimmy is that beautiful.

The rest of New York: Nowhere in the world is the drag scene as fantastic as it is in New York. I don't know why or even exactly what it is, but people are so much more receptive to us there than they are anywhere else. It's the only town that worships drag queens the way they should be worshiped. The vibe is simply wonderful, and the charisma and energy are unequaled. L.A., I think, holds drag queens down a bit. There are some good ones here, but not as many as there are in New York. The girls up there can really tear up a stage.

I can't give each of these wonderful entertainers the individual capsules I'd like to, but I'd like to give them credit nonetheless. If you ever get the chance to see them, any of these girls will give you a show you'll really enjoy: Girlina, Candis Cayne, Sherry Vine, Raven-O, Joey Arias, Miss Understood, Hedda Lettuce, Afrodite, Mona Foot, Miss Guy, Misstress Formika, Sweetie, Faux Pas, Chicklet, Linda Simpson, Cody Ravioli, Perfidia, Kevin Aviance, and

I'm sure many more. If I've left anyone out, please don't hate me. I love you all.

Watching Girlina or Candis lip-synch is a remarkable drag experience; they can really take someone else's song and make it their own. Joey Arias and Raven-O, on the other hand, actually sing live, and if you ask me, they both should have record deals. What all these girls have in common is that they can work nightly because they're so talented and New York is so into what they're doing. And I mean *the whole town,* even those outside of the usual gay and drag circles. New York cab drivers will always let you suck their dick, but not L.A. cabbies. Am I ever envious!

Pussy Tourette: Why Pussy hasn't had a major Top 40 hit yet with one of her wonderful songs is beyond me. She's extremely unique with all her black makeup, and she comes across as a little hard, with a bit of an edge, sort of Julie Newmar meets Marilyn Manson. Pussy has a terrific voice and stage presence, and you haven't lived till you've heard her do "French Bitch." I also happen to know that she has one of the largest penises on the face of the earth.

Lois Commondenominator: Lois is the founder and driving force behind *Dragazine,* the magazine devoted to drag queens and cross-dressers, so she's a great publicist for the DQ community. She's very pro-drag and truly loves the art, and as a person she's sweet and kind and accommodating. A little *too* accommodating at times, I think; sometimes she comes across as downright ass-kissy. But she's also campy and fresh and good for all of us. I wish she'd get out more often.

RuPaul: RuPaul and I go way back, long before "Supermodel" made her a superstar. We have a lot in common and have had some great times together. Once we even went cruising for guys together. I was in drag, Ru was not, and it was after we left a club called Peanuts one Monday night in West Hollywood. We left the bar at closing time and went a short distance down Santa Monica Boulevard to a parking lot by the Yukon Mining Company restaurant, which was known as a drag queen cruise spot. Ru was just shocked that such a place existed, but I knew it well; it's the best place in L.A. for drag queens to get sex. Well, we cruised, and I ended up picking up a guy, getting out of our car, and getting into this guy's car and leaving with him. I waved Ru a hearty good-bye and then called her the next day to tell her how it went. She thought it was great. She's very adventurous and loves fun things like that, so I try to expose her to it whenever I can. I've even taken her to the sleaziest bar in San Francisco, the Motherlode. That night didn't go so well; she was in drag, and her hair kept catching on dangly stuff that was hanging from the ceiling. But we had a good time.

As a person, Ru is sweet and funny. I met her back at the Four Star one night when I was hosting its contest, Drag Search. Ru came in, got up onstage, and did a song called "Star Booty" and won the contest, and I knew then that great things were in store for her. She had that "star" aura that just couldn't be denied.

We didn't become close for a while after that; we'd see each other around and say hi, but we never really talked in depth. Then, one night after "Supermodel" had made her a big deal, Ru was performing at Arena in Hollywood, and I was there in drag. Ru pointed me out from the stage and called me by name, and I loved it: "We have another superstar in the audience, that bitch Chi Chi LaRue!" I was stunned and honored. I had also become more well-known by that time, and since Ru was a big porn fan, she called me up one day not too long after that, and we had a nice conversation and have been friends ever since.

The thing about Ru is, she's busier than one person should ever possibly be. (Maybe you've seen her as the guidance counselor in the *Brady Bunch* movies; she also has a talk show on VH-1 now.) She's a one-person media blitz, so it's kind of hard to get together with her. Still, we chat by phone every so often and hook up whenever she's in L.A. She's come to see me at the Eros in New York, and I took her on the set of a film I was making for Falcon. She's hard to keep up with, but she did make time to come to my birthday party in 1995, and that was one of the best presents I got.

Divine: I saved Divine for last because she's the biggest, grandest, most larger-than-life drag queen ever to grace a pair of pumps. Her work with John Waters in films like *Polyester* and *Pink Flamingos* has made her a legend to generations of gay men, and her reputation has survived and even grown since her death. She pioneered what we're all doing now, and there's not a drag queen working today who doesn't owe some kind of debt to Harris Glen Milstead.

I met her only once, and that was before I was anybody worth mentioning. I was still working at Catalina shortly after coming to L.A., and Leo Ford came into the office for some reason I can't remember now. Leo, a major star of '80s porn, was good friends with Divine, and he told me that Divine was sitting outside in the car waiting for him. Well, of course I rushed right out and introduced myself. She was a he that day, not in drag, so here was basically just a fat bald guy in a pastel pink T-shirt and mint green shorts sitting alone in this car. What struck me was how different his personality was out of drag. He was very quiet and soft-spoken, almost shy, but he was pleasant and very polite, considering he didn't know me from Adam. I was really impressed with how nice he was. Then that night during his show at West Hollywood's Studio One, he pointed me out in a more-typical Divine way, calling me a "big bitch queen." Again, I loved it. Sadly, Divine died soon after that, so I never got the chance to know her better.

The thing about Divine is that even now, years after her death, she still casts a l-o-o-ong shadow. The rest of us are still trying to escape it sometimes. Every once in a while when I'm walking through a club, someone will call out, "Hey! Divine!" just because I'm a big, heavy drag queen. I really, *really* hate that. There's a little bit of Divine in me, sure; she lives on in all of us. But we all want to be treated as the individuals we are. "No," I'll tell them as coldly as I can, "I'm not Divine. I'm Chi Chi LaRue."

And her makeup style lives on as well. As I told Bradley when she was trying to overpaint me in Paris, "You just want me to be *her!*" And Bradley knew exactly who I was talking about. Divine, God rest her soul, has become a reference point for all of us.

So that's the scoop on some of the biggest drag queens working it today. There may be more by the time you read this. As the popularity of drag increases, they seem to be multiplying like flies.

L.A. is a very strange town for drag queens. Professionally, the atmosphere really sucks; clubs aren't receptive to it, and big crowds won't turn out to see it. On the other hand, strangely enough, there is no easier place for a drag queen to get sex. I had no idea of that when I came here. Maybe New York stacks up sexwise, but it's a close call. Actually, in every town I go to, I try to find where the drag queen fuckers (DQFs) congregate, and they are never more plentiful or easier to find than they are in Los Angeles. You may be surprised to know this, but they're everywhere, even in Minneapolis (although the ones there don't seem to get into heavy queens like myself). Wherever you go, you can find men who like men dressed like women. It's an odd phenomenon.

In my early days in L.A., I lived in Hollywood near the corner of Santa Monica and Wilcox, and when I was driving home from the Four Star, I'd be flagged down by guys on the street who just wanted to have sex with me because I was in drag. These were almost always good experiences. Out of all of the guys I ever picked up, I was never beaten up and never got into any serious trouble. There was really only one bad incident, and that involved two young Latino guys. They were both really cute and seemed on the up-and-up; when they got in my car, they had their dicks out and were already hard. Usually, if they take their dicks out, you know you're okay and they're not going to hustle you. But with these two, I had just started to go down on one when they grabbed my purse and jumped from the car and ran. (I presume they stuffed their dicks back in their pants at some point.) Everything I had was in that purse: my driver's license, my car registration, my credit cards. So it was a big pain in the ass to get all that stuff replaced. But really, that's the only bad thing that's happened to me in many, many years of picking guys up for sex.

That restaurant in West Hollywood, the Yukon Mining Company, is known to all of us DQs. Late at night its parking lot is the biggest drag queen cruise spot in the universe. Every town in the world, I think, has one of these spots. From Amsterdam to Paris to London, there are places where the DQFs all go, and most of the time, I've been there. Sometimes they're easier to find than others; in London, especially, I thought I was going to be out of luck. But then we went to this place called the Way Out Wine Bar, and it was jam-packed with what I call "heterovestites," straight guys who dress in drag because it turns them on. Virtually the second we walked in the door, Gender scored a guy, and I ended up blowing this guy in the bathroom. This young man then went with us to another club, where we met the designer Jean-Paul Gaultier. I remember Gaultier saying how much he loved my little see-through fringe dress, and I remember thinking, *I just know I'm going to see this on the runway next season.*

It sounds really trashy to pick up so many guys in parking lots and dirty little clubs, but as long as you play safe, I don't see a lot of problems with it. It's fun, and it gives me a wide-ranging and fascinating sex life that I'd never have as plain ol' Larry Paciotti. The fact of the matter is, a lot of guys who would never have sex with another guy *will* have sex with a drag queen. It's easier to suck a dick if it's sticking out of panty hose, I guess. Whatever the reason, it has proven true all over the world. Maybe it's internalized homophobia; maybe it's just a fetish. All I know is I'm working it to my advantage.

The Four Star was good for straight trade every night of the week. Yeah, there were some weirdos; I once cruised a guy who told me, "I'm looking for a girl who wants to cut my dick off." I was like, "Okay, *freak!*" But those types are the minority, and they're not a big issue.

At Santa Monica and Wilcox I once blew twelve guys in one night. Another time I let this little Asian guy with this tiny little dick pull down my hose and fuck me against the car right there in the parking lot. He was into the dirty talk, so I gave it to him good: "Oh, you're tearing me up with that dick! Oh, you're so big! You're fabulous!" He really wasn't, but you have to give 'em what they want.

You might think that guys turn to drag queens for sex because they can't get other guys, but that's not true. It's not just undesirable guys who have this particular fetish. In New York there's this club called the Vault, and at the end of each month, this big, fabulous drag queen named Sweetie holds this party there called "Third Sex." Well, one time I went home with this straight couple that looked like they were straight out of American Gladiators. They were both big and built and blond and beautiful, and I had sex with them both. I ate her pussy and fucked her with a big black dildo, then ate out his butt and sucked his dick. The guy got turned on watching me with his woman, and the woman got turned on watching me with her man. It was one of the hottest scenes I've ever been a part of.

There's still a lot of bias toward drag queens, even in the gay community. I've been thrown out of the Spike, L.A.'s notorious leather bar, for coming in in drag, and I was once denied entrance to the Probe, another trendy nightspot. I guess that more "respectable" queers feel we present a bad image to the straight community whose acceptance they want so badly. Well, to me that's a form of homophobia every bit as insulting as what comes from gay bashers.

There's nothing more pathetic than a homophobic homosexual, and there are plenty of them out there. Who is any faggot to deny me respect just because I'm wearing a dress?

Doing drag and doing movies have really broadened my horizons, both sexually and as a complete person. I've been exposed to all possible variations on human sexuality, from straight to gay to bi to she-male. (For the record, if you've had breast implants but haven't had your dick cut off, you are a she-male, not a drag queen.) And I've learned to appreciate that different folks like different things. Being a porn director gives me a lot of freedom to explore. I've done she-male videos and lesbian videos, and I even paired a drag queen and a straight woman in a film (Karen Dior and Sharon Kane in *Sharon and Karen*).

Drag has been good to me, and I couldn't be where I am today without it. And you know what? It's still raising people's awareness. In August 1996 I went to see KISS in concert — my childhood heroes had reunited and put on the makeup again for a retrospective tour. It was minutes before we were to leave for the show, and I was dressed pretty butchly in jeans and a T-shirt, when it was suggested to me that I should go to the concert in drag. So I rushed home, scraped my face with a razor, slapped on my makeup in fifteen minutes, and threw on a black vinyl dress, my seven-inch platform heels from Paris, and a top hat.

We had second-row seats, so we were highly visible from the stage, and you'd better believe the band noticed. My heartthrob, Paul Stanley, couldn't keep his eyes off me the whole evening, and he even pointed directly at me at one point with a big grin. I fully expect to run into Paul any night now in the parking lot of the Yukon Mining Company.

Abuse and Flattery
OR
How to Have Them Eating From the Palm of Your Hand

BEYOND BEING A DRAG QUEEN and a director of pornography, I am, at heart, an entertainer. And no chronicle of my life would be complete without a mention of my live act. Since I do probably a hundred or more shows a year, this too is a major aspect of my existence.

Once the drag is finally done and I at last look fabulous, I head for the clubs to dazzle my public. Whether I'm promoting a certain video or just hosting some run-of-the-mill event doesn't matter; I just get a charge out of being up there. It's an adrenaline rush like no other.

But performing live onstage is no piece of cake. I'm sure you all have had occasion to speak to large crowds. Public speaking is one of the hardest things you can do, and for most people, it's their greatest fear. All eyes are on you, and every mistake, every slip of the tongue or slight misstep is visible and magnified and totally humiliating. There's nowhere to hide when you're up there; you are totally alone. And when you're out there dancing and singing, it's even worse. No matter how much of an extrovert you might be, you can't help but feel some anxiety before climbing up on that stage to be the evening's star attraction.

As many times as I've performed live (and there have been probably thousands), I still get nervous before doing shows. Yes, that loud, rude, crass, in-your-face bitch Chi Chi LaRue still has to deal with the sweaty palms and the fluttery stomach before coming to you live. After all these years I just haven't been able to shake those butterflies. It isn't just me, you know. An awful lot of famous entertainers admit to feeling nervous before they go onstage. You're always worried about doing well. That wait backstage can really tie your guts up in knots.

So over the years I've developed a pretty good method of dealing with the preshow jitters: I get drunk. Not really *drunk* drunk, but I do have a cocktail or two to calm me down. There's nothing like a good stiff drink to take the edge off. I mean, it's not like I *can't* perform unless I'm blotto. I'm never actually *soused* when I go onstage, and I could certainly do it sober if I was called on to do so. But as many a public speaker will tell you, a quick gin and tonic beforehand just sort of greases the rails a little bit, lets all of my abundant wit and charm flow a little more freely. Call it lubrication.

The problem for me is that my act isn't always so easy to swallow, especially if you're not familiar with who I am and what I do. I can be loud, vulgar, and completely, utterly obnoxious. That's intentional; that's my shtick. I've honed this persona over the years to where it's really prickly sometimes, yes, but it's all done in good humor. It's not malicious, and it's not meant to be taken personally or seriously. I'm not a mean-spirited person. But I'm Chi Chi LaRue, and this kind of act is what I'm known for.

People expect this kind of rowdiness from me now, people in the industry who know me and people who have gotten to know me in the places I play regularly, like West Hollywood, New York, San Francisco, and Washington,

D.C. Now, after all these years of cultivating this image, I find that it precedes me. People know it's coming, so they're not surprised or offended by what I say. They know I'm a big rude drag queen who loves to shock, and they know I direct porno films, so they expect a show that's pretty raunchy. This creates a different kind of pressure, because then people get disappointed if I'm not outrageous enough. So I always have to be on the lookout for new and creative ways to offend.

That's all well and good for the major cities, the places I perform all the time. It's when I go to a new town and play a place for the first time that I start to sweat it. Since they may not know me, I worry about being understood — or being misunderstood. If I go swaggering out there and tell them, "Hello, you fucking bitches!" they may not know it's just part of the act. They may misinterpret it and think, *Well, who the fuck does this big obnoxious thing think* she *is?* and throw a beer bottle at me or something. (Okay, so that's never actually happened. But people do take offense sometimes and get mad and walk out.) That, more than the possibility of screwing the show up, is what causes me nerves.

Usually the crowd, whether they know me already or are having their first Chi Chi experience, warms up pretty quickly. Most crowds can pick up the vibes — positive vibes, not tense, uncomfortable vibes like you'd get if I really was malicious and trying to insult people. Laughter is the most contagious thing there is, so if I can get a few people to laugh, then it spreads through the crowd, and the others pick up on it and start having a good time.

Still, once in a great while I'll get one of those dreaded bad crowds. This is an entertainer's worst nightmare, and everybody gets them from time to time. Bad crowds are ones that just won't give you anything back no matter how hard you work them. They won't laugh, they won't relax, they just cannot get into what you're doing. It's horribly frustrating. I don't know why it happens or what differentiates a good crowd from a bad one, but let me tell you, for an entertainer, bad crowds are a fate worse than death.

With bad crowds, you laugh, you joke, you talk to them one-on-one, and nothing changes. They're deadpan and stone-faced, and sometimes they're so busy talking to one another that they won't even look at you. That's when I like to tweak them a little bit, to get in their faces. It personalizes things a bit. It's the same thing professional comedians do: You find one particular audience member and single him out, make him a target, and you can bond with the rest of the crowd at his expense. It's not as cold-blooded as it sounds; you don't want to embarrass a person too much, but a little bit is generally okay. Maybe you ask someone where he's from or if he's gay or straight. Anything to create a little back-and-forth, a little give-and-take. If you see someone chatting with a friend, you can put the spotlight on him and ask, "Hey, what are you guys talking about that's so very important that you can't stop to watch the show?" Or maybe you can break down inhibitions with "Oh, that's good, chat him up, girl. He's a cute one, and I'll bet he's got a big dick!"

Sometimes you have to get a little more biting. Like if you're in the South, for instance, you can say, "Do we have anyone here tonight who likes to fuck farm animals?" and then you point to some guy in the front row and say to him, "Why are you blushing, sir?" Maybe you can find some guy with a nice body and pull him up onstage and cajole him into taking his shirt off. That'll normally get people's attention.

In general, abuse and flattery are your greatest weapons. Everyone likes to be singled out for praise, and there's even something pleasing about being singled out for teasing. Really, people don't get too mad very often. Someone may act horrified then, but you can bet he'll go home and proudly tell his friends, "Chi Chi LaRue picked me out for special abuse tonight!"

When even that fails, your only option is to cut your losses and get out. Do your show as fast as you can and get the hell offstage. Make it as brief and painless as the circumstances let you and move on to the next time. There's always the next time.

The Eros Theater in New York is a good place for schizophrenic crowds. Sometimes you'll get a great one that's totally into what you're doing, but sometimes they're just awful. There's no telling what you'll get on any given night. There are nights when you'll get crowds full of these guys who are there on the sly, guys who have told their wives or bosses that they're going out for cigarettes and then secretly slipped down to the Eros to watch the boys beat off. They don't want to be seen because they don't want anyone to find out that they're there, so they won't look at you or talk to you. Well, I have two methods of dealing with guys like that: the spotlight and the microphone. Being noticed is their worst fear, and the look on their faces when you draw attention to them is just priceless. It's very "Oh, my God, you've figured me out!" Serves 'em right. Here's a hint: Don't come to see Chi Chi at the Eros if you want to keep a low profile. I might tell your wife.

People who are fans also get mad sometimes when I can't spend twenty minutes talking to every one of them. I'll be circulating around the bar, for instance, and some guy will come up to me and say, "Chi Chi, I really love you." "Well, thank you," I'll say, "that's very kind," and I'll give him a peck on the cheek and start to move away. Then he'll grab my arm and tell me, "No, I mean, I really, *really* love you." Well, that's very nice, but I have a lot of flesh to press, and I'd like to stay and chat, but I can't. So I make my apologies and try to move on, but he won't let me go: "No, you don't understand, I *really, really* love you." And then I'll tell him, "Look, thanks, I'm sorry, but I need to go," and then he'll get all pissed off, like "Who the fuck do you think you are, bitch?"

It's not a star trip, honestly. When I do these road shows, I just need to circulate and give some of my time, which is very limited, to an awful lot of people. When you see a huge crowd surrounding Madonna after a show, you don't expect her to give every single fan a half hour of personal attention; it just can't be done. I never want to be rude to anybody, but there are a lot of demands on me, so bear with me, people. If you ever meet me out there on the road, by all means stop and say hello, but please don't try to monopolize my time. All I ask is that you treat me the same as you would a lesser superstar. Like Madonna.

———————

Some places are more fun to play than others. A lot of it depends on the region of the country. For instance, while New York City, Washington, D.C., and major cities like that are pretty much anything-goes, even big cities can be really restrictive in conservative areas like the South.

Tennessee, the Carolinas, and some parts of Texas can really just neuter the life right out of my show.

Florida's not bad compared with the rest of the South, and Miami is one of my favorite places to play. And D.C. and New York are great because they allow total nudity. In California, San Francisco is a blast, but Los Angeles is insanely restrictive, a lot more so than you'd think. Laws are very tough in L.A. about how much skin you can show, and the cops there love to run undercover raids in bars, looking for strippers who cross that line. It's not something you would expect of Los Angeles, which has enough real, violent crime to keep its cops busy. But what are a few murders and robberies in South-Central when a boy in Silver Lake is flashing society-threatening pubic hair?

Canada's another very free place where anything goes onstage. Not only do they allow total nudity in Canada, but audience members can come up and do to the stripper anything the stripper allows them to do. I also find that pretty curious, since they're very strict in other ways up there. But a fag can have the time of his gay life in Canada. I've never played there, but I can't wait till I do. I think I'm made for a place like that.

Of course, I have horror stories from certain ignorant redneck parts of the country. I've had promoters cancel shows when they find out I'm coming. I've had dead-eyed trailer-trash crowds in Texas that all look like my family from *The Hills Have Bi's*. (You can't imagine how scary that was. I thought we were just being funny with that film, not realistic.) And like any performer, I've had to deal with hecklers.

In Houston I had to have a guy who kept screaming at me, "Divine did it better!" tossed out of a bar. Maybe she did do it better, but she wasn't doing it there that night. I don't get too much of this, though, because why would somebody pay to get in to see me unless he wanted to enjoy the show? You don't pay good money just to boo. And normally, if I'm being given shit, I just threaten to hurl myself into the crowd and wipe out half of them in a giant tsunami. That always shuts people up.

Texas is weird in that it can really vary from city to city. There's a lot of drunken, macho redneck posturing in Texas, which leads not only to heckling but to bullying by homophobic cops. One time in Austin, I got porn star Marco Rossi arrested because he stuck a beer bottle up his butt during one of our shows. It wasn't really our fault; the bar owner had told us we could get as nasty as we wanted, so I took the guy at his word. We had audience members coming up and licking the butts of Marco and Derek Cruise, and we had Marco and Derek groping all over each other, and we had me sticking microphones in both of their butt cracks, and none of us knew that we were in violation of local law. Well, the cops arrested Marco when he came offstage, and when I protested, they threatened me with arrest too.

At other times I can be pretty intimidating myself. I remember playing Minneapolis and taking Wes Daniels to a party after the show. Well, as we left the party Wes stopped to take a piss in the bushes outside the house. Suddenly, at least twenty cops came swarming out of the bushes, where I guess they'd just been lying in wait for someone at the party to do something illegal. They busted Wes for indecent exposure. I was furious. I went off on the cops, who seemed more scared of me than I was of them. Then I went down to the jail in full drag to bail Wes out, busting into the police station like the Terminator in a red velvet jumpsuit, snarling at everyone and cursing a blue streak. I don't think they had ever seen anything like me before, and I'm fairly sure they never want to see anything like it again.

Other places have other restrictions. In Arizona a bar in Scottsdale had to get a special permit before I (or any other "female impersonator") could perform. And they told me I couldn't say "fuck" onstage. (Of course, it was the first thing I said.) Other places prohibit me from any "simulated masturbatory" actions, which means I can't use the microphone in a dicklike way by putting it between my legs or up my butt or in my mouth. There are even places where I can't give away porn flicks as prizes in the bars; I have to give out certificates that can be redeemed later for the actual movies. You just have to be careful and aware of whatever the laws are wherever you happen to be.

While most drag queens are known for lip-synching their material, I don't normally do that. The only time I lip-synch is at the Dragville club in West Hollywood every Tuesday night. When I go on the road, I actually sing my own stuff. (I've also sung live in film roles that have required it.) I have a short list of songs I work from, and I sing along with taped musical accompaniment. I usually do original stuff, like Chris Green's composition "Rob the Cradle" or "Two Tons of Love," a song written by Mark Stone, the owner of straight porn's Moonlight Entertainment and a musician in his own right with a band called the Stingers. I have an adapted version of Pat Benatar's "Rated X" that I enjoy doing, and I also like Helen Reddy's "I Am Woman" because it's *so* campy and ironic.

When I lip-synch I go for songs like Julie Andrews's "Spoonful of Sugar" from *Mary Poppins* or Tracey Ullman's "Life Is a Rock." I've also been known to dredge up glam-rock stuff from my younger days, stuff like Joan Jett. I always try to avoid the cliché drag queen material like the songs of Whitney Houston and Bette Midler. Nothing against them, but DQs from Alaska to Key West do that stuff, and it's better to be original.

The biggest crowd I've ever played for was in Washington, D.C., at the gay march on Washington back in 1993. It was an outdoor event in the heart of historic Washington, and I played with Pussy Tourette, Lady Bunny, and Gender. I joked with the crowd that I wanted to be taken up in a helicopter and lowered onto the Washington Monument, which has to be the most phallic landmark in the world. There were about 5,000 people there for that show, and their response was so good, it really rattled me. I was so overwhelmed by the outpouring of love and support that I forgot the words to my song and had to make them up as I went along. I almost cried. The crowd was screaming and hollering and carrying on, and there was such a feeling of compassion and brotherhood that it stands out to this day as one of my favorite performances ever.

Other cities where I've had a great time include New Orleans, Cleveland, and Columbus, Ohio. I don't know why Ohio's such a blast. You wouldn't expect it to be, but it is. The only places outside the United States I've played are Paris and Cannes during my trips to France, and those were both sensational. I'd move to Paris in a heartbeat.

Making It Big: Sex Stars, Porn Films, and Me

In all honesty there's nothing quite like performing live. Yes, you have to deal with nerves beforehand, and yes, sometimes you get a bad crowd, but once you get out there onstage and the adrenaline starts pumping, there's no better high in the world. Nothing is quite like it. It's something I'll never stop doing. Even if I never direct another movie, I'm addicted to being up there as the center of attention, making people laugh and have a good time. And since I direct movies, it's a great way of promoting that. People who live in Kansas or Kentucky who may rent my films can get a little taste of real-life porn when I come to town with some hot boys in tow. The films allow me to perform live for audiences, and performing live for audiences helps promote the films. It's one hand washing the other. I just hope there are no places where *that's* against the law.

WORKS IN PROGRESS
OR
WHERE DO WE GO FROM HERE?

WE WERE GOING to a museum opening, and I was complaining about my life to John Waters, the man who brought Divine to the world. I was telling John how often I get compared to Divine and how tired of it I get. Because I'm a big, heavy drag queen, the comparisons are inevitable.

It comes with the territory, I guess. It's a great compliment to Divine that she had such a great impact on drag and on gay culture that all the drag queens who come after her are compared to her. But at the same time, that's frustrating to the rest of us. Especially if we're big and loud and love to be rude and shocking.

Sure, Divine had some influence on what I do. How could she not? I grew up watching her in *Female Trouble* and *Pink Flamingos,* and any guy who's ever put on a dress has probably been influenced some by Divine. But any drag queen worth her weight in cosmetics will want to create an identity of her own, to be known for what she does, not what Divine did ten or twenty years ago. It's easier if you're dark and skinny, not fat and (until recently) blond. Okay, I'll admit that on bad makeup nights, I might even look a little bit like Divine; you just don't turn out glamorous and fabulous every night, you know? But Divine never directed porn, and it's important to me that I be known as Chi Chi LaRue and be remembered for my own work, be it film creations or film appearances or live performances.

But do you know what John Waters said to me that day? He told me, "Larry, you are completely different from Divine. You have your own unique charm, and you are funny on your own."

Well, let me tell you, I will never need any more validation than that. Who better to judge future generations of Divines than the man whose twisted vision brought her to the big screen in the first place? If John Waters says that I can stand on my own merit, then, damn it, that's good enough for me.

I think there's a tendency to marginalize drag queens and the contribution we make to gay culture. People want to pigeonhole us into this little corner, where we can be branded and have our ears tagged and be easily identified and be nonthreatening to the big straight world they want to be a part of so badly.

Jackie Beat is another big drag queen, and she gets the same thing. She'll be walking through a club, and some ignorant person will call out to her, "Hey, Chi Chi!" It's all about comparisons, about looking at us in terms of something else, something people know and have come to grips with, something safe and comfortable that they don't have to worry about.

And you know what? I think that stinks.

Of all the possible groups and communities to be judgmental, the gay community is the last one that has a right. With all the bigotry and scorn we've endured, how can we turn it around and pass it on to others within our community?

But we do. Some fags don't like drag queens. Some fags don't like leather. Some fags don't like porn. And some fags judge other fags who like things those fags think they shouldn't. I've been thrown out of bars for being in drag, like I don't have a place in their community. Bull. We're all in this together, and *we are all family.* You may not like every person in your family all the time, but you stand by them. You can pick your friends, but you can't pick your family. You just have to make the best of what you get. And they should cover your back just like you should cover theirs.

The same goes for porn. Even within the gay community, a lot of people look down on us for satisfying these desires of the flesh. Those people, I guess, are only gay from the waist up.

Despite it all, we somehow manage to survive and even thrive. Each year that passes is bigger and better for gay porn. Profits are up, and more and more people want to make movies and be in them. It's been good, and I see nothing but better things on the horizon for all-male adult video.

The quality of gay porn has never been better. Great directors are directing great stars in hotter and more technologically advanced films. Directors want to top their own previous efforts and better each other's work. Each extravaganza must be bigger and better than the last, so we're always looking for new ways to dazzle porn fans. More money, better special effects, crazier sex — in the end it should all benefit the home viewer.

The core of adult video must remain that hot and crazy sex. All the technical fireworks don't mean a thing if there's not hot sex to back it up. I know that whatever the whistles and bells attached to the final product, I can still provide the hot sex. No film that has that, no matter how little else it boasts, can be all bad.

Porn's enormous profitability has proved to be a double-edged sword. Yes, we can spice films up with better effects than we ever had before, and yes, films today are better than ever. But like any big-money business, it's fostered an ugly competitiveness. If we don't produce bigger and better films, the press says it's a disappointment. Now I have to sit at home and scheme to top *Flesh and Blood* and wonder what Jerry Douglas is going to do next, and Jerry has to sit at home and scheme to top *Lost in Vegas* and wonder what Chi Chi is going to do next. And someone like Johnny Rey, who makes films without the resources Jerry and I have, resents us both for having what he doesn't. Give Johnny a $65,000 budget, and who knows, he could make another *Gone With the Wind*. We must top each other, and we must top ourselves. That cycle never ends.

That's a lot of pressure, and it can wear on you. Sometimes I long for the simpler days, when I could blend in and make a movie and no one would notice me. But those days are gone forever, so we'd all better just get used to it.

If there are no major changes in the business, I could see myself directing for another twenty-five or thirty years. I'm not tired of directing yet, so if the industry doesn't evolve and leave me behind, then I won't abandon it.

Will the business itself change? It well could. I really fear two things for this industry: computer advances eliminating the human element and intrusion by mainstream Hollywood.

We're almost at the point now of being able to tell our computers, "I want a scene where Jordan Young has sex with Rex Chandler." The day will come soon when the computer will be able to give us that, penetration and all, without the actual involvement of either Jordan or Rex. When the human element is gone, I fear what will become of porn. For me, knowing that I'm just watching computer images, not actual people, would ruin it totally. Computers can't re-create the wonderful feeling of a dick in a mouth or up an ass that you know the performers are experiencing. No matter how realistic it gets, it will be sterile and fraudulent.

My other big fear is that megalithic companies like Columbia or Paramount will realize how lucrative porn is and move in on it. Let me tell you, that will mean the end of it for a lot of us. Even Falcon and All Worlds won't be able to compete with the bucks of Hollywood's heavies. They will squeeze us right out the door.

For now, I'm happy and looking to be happier. I want to do some straight films and maybe bring some gay sensibilities to that side of porn. Everyone's looking to Europe now, and I want to direct in France. Hell, I want to move to France and live there for the rest of my days.

Outside of porn, I want to direct a music video, maybe the Johnny Depp Clones if we ever get our act together. I want to be in mainstream films. I'd even take acting classes if someone like John Waters would throw me a role. And I want to see the world, places like Italy and Germany and Spain.

The drag I'm not so sure about. Like the drugs, I fear it may just be getting old, the novelty wearing off. It's seeming like more and more of a chore, and more and more I find myself not wanting to bother. I still like being onstage, but the preparations are too involved. I just want to have Bradley come over and paint my face while I sit back and not worry about it. God forbid I have to take a trip without Bradley or my other main makeup artist, Kevin Hees.

Really, who knows what's going to happen? The political climate could change, and we could all be in prison this time next year. Or society could loosen up, and I'll be hosting *The Chi Chi LaRue Show* Friday nights on Fox. There's no way of telling.

I do know that there's a lot left I want to do, and I will do it. I will continue experiencing life to its fullest and most fantastic. What you've read is an account of the first half or so, and it's not all that there will be to tell. It's a work in progress. There's more to come, so stay tuned. You never know what might happen next.

alyson
books

B-BOY BLUES, by James Earl Hardy. A seriously sexy, fiercely funny, black-on-black love story. A walk on the wild side turns into more than Mitchell Crawford ever expected. "A lusty, freewheeling first novel.... Hardy has the makings of a formidable talent." *–Kirkus Reviews*

2ND TIME AROUND, by James Earl Hardy. The sequel to best-seller *B-Boy Blues.* "An upbeat tale that—while confronting issues of violence, racism, and homophobia—is romantic, absolutely sensual, and downright funny." *–Publishers Weekly*

THE NEW GAY BOOK OF LISTS, by Leigh W. Rutledge. This new edition of the best-selling, compulsively readable gay trivia collection is the perfect gift for all occasions.

MY BIGGEST O, edited by Jack Hart. What was the best sex you ever had? Jack Hart asked that question of hundreds of gay men, and got some fascinating answers. Here are summaries of the most intriguing of them. Together, they provide an engaging picture of the sexual tastes of gay men.

MY FIRST TIME, edited by Jack Hart. Hart has compiled a fascinating collection of true, first-person stories by men from around the country, describing their first same-sex sexual encounter.

THE DAY WE MET, edited by Jack Hart. Hart presents true stories by gay men who provide intriguing looks at the different origins of their long-term relationships. However love first arose, these stories will be sure to delight, inform, and touch you.

THE PRESIDENT'S SON, by Krandall Kraus. President Marshall's son is gay. The president, who is beginning a tough battle for reelection, knows it but can't handle it. *"The President's Son...*is a delicious, oh-so-thinly veiled tale of a political empire gone insane." *–The Washington Blade*

THE LORD WON'T MIND, by Gordon Merrick. In this first volume of the classic trilogy, Charlie and Peter forge a love that will survive World War II and Charlie's marriage to a conniving heiress. Their story is continued in *One for the Gods* and *Forth Into Light.*

These books and other Alyson titles are available at your local bookstore. If you can't find a book listed above or would like more information, please call us directly at 1-800-5-ALYSON.